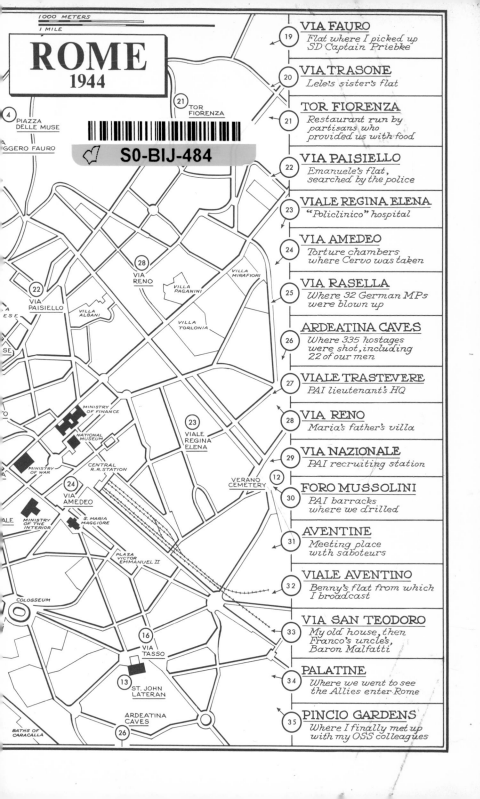

ROME
1944

1000 METERS
1 MILE

S0-BIJ-484

4 PIAZZA DELLE MUSE

GGERO FAURO

21 TOR FIORENZA

22 VIA PAISIELLO

28 VIA RENO

VILLA MIRAFIORI

VILLA PAGANINI

VILLA ALBANI

VILLA TORLONIA

23 VIALE REGINA ELENA

MINISTRY OF FINANCE

NATIONAL MUSEUM

MINISTRY OF WAR

CENTRAL R.R. STATION

VERANO CEMETERY

12

24 VIA AMEDEO

MINISTRY OF THE INTERIOR

S. MARIA MAGGIORE

PLAZA VICTOR EMMANUEL II

COLOSSEUM

16 VIA TASSO

13 ST. JOHN LATERAN

ARDEATINA CAVES

BATHS OF CARACALLA

26

VIA FAURO
19 Flat where I picked up SD Captain Priebke

VIA TRASONE
20 Lele's sister's flat

TOR FIORENZA
21 Restaurant run by partisans who provided us with food

VIA PAISIELLO
22 Emanuele's flat, searched by the police

VIALE REGINA ELENA
23 "Policlinico" hospital

VIA AMEDEO
24 Torture chambers where Cervo was taken

VIA RASELLA
25 Where 32 German MPs were blown up

ARDEATINA CAVES
26 Where 335 hostages were shot, including 22 of our men

VIALE TRASTEVERE
27 PAI lieutenant's HQ

VIA RENO
28 Maria's father's villa

VIA NAZIONALE
29 PAI recruiting station

FORO MUSSOLINI
30 PAI barracks where we drilled

AVENTINE
31 Meeting place with saboteurs

VIALE AVENTINO
32 Benny's flat from which I broadcast

VIA SAN TEODORO
33 My old house, then Franco's uncle's, Baron Malfatti

PALATINE
34 Where we went to see the Allies enter Rome

PINCIO GARDENS
35 Where I finally met up with my OSS colleagues

PETER TOMPKINS

A
SPY
IN
ROME

SIMON AND SCHUSTER · NEW YORK · 1962

FIRST PRINTING

The author and the publishers are grateful for permission to include in this book material from the following sources:

Association of the United States Army for a selection from *From Salerno to the Alps,* A History of the Fifth Army, edited by Lt. Col. Chester G. Starr. Copyright 1948, Infantry Journal Press (now Association of the United States Army). Reprinted by permission of the publisher.

Athenaum-Verlag K. G., Bad Godesberg, Germany, for selections from *Heer in Fesseln* by Sigfried Westphal.

Harper & Brothers for selections from *Calculated Risk* by Mark W. Clark.

Houghton Mifflin Company for selections from *Closing the Ring* by Sir Winston S. Churchill.

The *Sunday Times,* London, England, for extracts from an article by Field-Marshal Earl Alexander.

LIBRARY OF CONGRESS CATALOG CARD NUMBER: 62–7558
MANUFACTURED IN THE UNITED STATES OF AMERICA
BY GEO. MCKIBBIN AND SON INC., NEW YORK, N. Y.

To those in Italy
Of whatever political conviction
Who did as they believed

CONTENTS

PREFACE BY DONALD DOWNES

THIS BOOK is the slightly edited and expanded notes and diary of a spy, written in enemy-held territory in wartime; it violated security in a way mortally dangerous to Peter Tompkins and to his colleagues in Rome and his organization in general. But Peter, at twenty-three, was *confident:* Webster's Dictionary defines *confident* as *well-assured, sure, self-reliant, undaunted, impudent, presumptuous;* and Everyman's Dictionary adds *positive, bold,* and *cocksure.* Not the ideal attributes of a spy! But beyond confidence he had a great deal more: he was courageous despite fear. Any clod who is not afraid can seem brave; to *be* brave, really brave, a man must be also afraid. To sit in Washington and evaluate intelligence or judge the political consequences of certain intelligence missions (like the U-2 flights, or the Cuban fiasco, for instance) may require calm men of deliberate judgment; but to go behind the enemy lines and live for long periods like a hunted beast requires a certain flair, even a little madness, a large measure of Boy Scout loyalty and patriotism, a stout heart, an alert brain, and, I think, a remarkable self-assurance approaching the point of swagger and carelessness—all based on one's belief that one's own keenness, wile, intelligence, wits, and luck are superior to those of the enemy. Knowing Peter well, I think he was justified in this belief.

To land on a hostile coast and go into Rome, with no one prearranged to receive or hide him, required of Peter Tompkins a courage beyond that of charging up San Juan Hill or planting the flag atop Iwo Jima. To live for months on end as a fugitive from justice (or injustice), believing, rightly or wrongly, that your own side was betraying you, to hide in the uniform of the political police who are hunting you, to be in terror of meeting your boyhood friends on the street lest they turn you in, to have your agents caught, tortured and killed—that takes something beyond mere courage; it requires foolhardiness, determination, bravado, and a lusty appetite for adventure and danger, all sharpened by a taste for the cold sensation of fear—for fear can be headier than whisky, once a man has acquired a taste for it.

Peter Tompkins' lack of respect for or confidence in his immediate superiors in OSS was justified by the confusion, inexperience, and incompetence of the top-level OSS officers at Allied Forces Headquarters. Consider the unexplained fact that OSS at AFHQ ceased listening for Peter's radio messages about two months before the fall of Rome and did not even bother to send him spare parts for his communications system. This headquarters was not *exceptionally* bad: excluding David K. E. Bruce in London, Allen Dulles in Switzerland, and Arthur Goldberg everywhere on labor movements, the quality of those directing OSS *in the field* was appallingly low—so low that Bill Donovan, the Director, often found it necessary to use eccentric individualists rather than his more orthodox organization to get important information essential to the Joint Chiefs of Staff. The sending of Peter Tompkins to Rome was such a case.

Donovan was not to blame; he was directed to organize out of whole cloth an espionage organization (the United States had never had one) to compete with secret services that had centuries of experience and tradition. The English were generous with their help; but Donovan's OSS was necessarily amateur, however enthusiastic. And the exigencies of wartime interdepartmental political warfare in Washington forced him to accept many ill-equipped men, especially from the Army, which found OSS a convenient dumping ground for useless career officers (known as the "Bourbon Whisky Colonels"). There were other castoffs from State and Navy, playboys, the stupid sons of rich and politically important families, and so on. Peter sensed all this, and his rage at finding himself offering his life to an organization incompetent to put his sacrifice to full use is understandable. His own departures from reasonable security and rational behavior, looking back to those days, seem inevitable. "Never would I have believed," Peter once wrote me, "it would be made so hard by our own side to try to win the war."

All this, plus the fact that Peter Tompkins is and was a mercurial literary and intellectual roughneck, have combined to give us a book unique in history. I do not pretend to evaluate it on its literary merits. But historically it seems to me to put him in very rare company, among such as Xenophon, Procopius, Marco Polo, Casanova, Benvenuto Cellini, Pepys, Gertrude Bell and T. E. Lawrence.

Like Xenophon, Peter assails his "military betters" with great gusto. Like Procopius in his secret diary, he spares none. Like Marco Polo, he writes about a world essentially unknown to his readers. Like Casa-

10

nova, he is shamelessly honest about himself. Like Cellini, he is supremely confident in his own powers. Like Pepys, he implies much more than he writes. Like Gertrude Bell, he is a spy. He is as colorful as Lawrence, though far less dishonest and histrionic.

For Peter, as for all these tellers of their tales, life was sweet because it was bitter—bitter and dangerous. Like them, he loved and savored every moment, even those when he was most disheartened and disgusted, so great was his appetite for adventure and maneuver. But the stimulus of Peter Tompkins' dedication to a cause should not be overlooked—his devotion to what he believed the United States once stood for and should again.

I dare say there is no record of Peter's mission in the archives of the United States Government. There was none in the autumn of 1944 when I was writing special intelligence reports inside the White House Offices and had Presidential access to all government intelligence files, including those of OSS. Why? Because information unpalatable to the brass had a way of disappearing.

As the years pass, many of Peter's "immature" judgments have been confirmed. Field Marshal Viscount Alexander's estimation of Generals John Lucas and Mark Clark, recently published in his *Memoirs* in the Sunday *Times* (London), is a perfect example: *The whole undertaking . . . had every opportunity of coming off if the operations had been handled with dash and vigour—which, as I have made clear, they were not.* [More Peter and less John and Mark!] *. . . But for some inexplicable reason General Clark's Anglo-American forces never reached their objectives* [Valmontone on the road from Rome to Cassino], *though, according to my information later, there was nothing to prevent their being gained.* [This was when Peter was in Rome.] *. . . I had always assured General Clark in conversation that Rome would be entered by his army; and I can only assume that the immediate lure of Rome for its publicity value persuaded him to switch the direction of his advance.*

Alexander quotes a telegram from Winston Churchill which sounds as if it might have been from Peter Tompkins' diary: *I expected to see a wildcat roaring into the mountains—and what do I find? A whale wallowing on the beaches!*

A classified report of Lieutenant Callanan, intelligence-reports writer for OSS at Caserta, addressed to General Donovan, refers to Peter Tompkins' mission in Rome as the most successful and productive secret-intelligence mission in Central Italy. Further, Peter was the only American known to General Chirieleison, the Italian who commanded the Open City of Rome; he and Eugenio Boggiano-Pico, who negotiated Rome Open City, and Giulio Castelli, who wrote the only comprehensive history of the Open City,* credit our author with having made important decisions (quite without authority, I might add) which allowed them to preserve the city and its public services intact for the Allies—no small contribution to victory.

As far as I know, Peter Tompkins was not given so much as a bit of ribbon or any official thanks for his work—except of course from Bill Donovan, who never forgot "those with guts and initiative," however unorthodox their methods may have been.

To grasp the full implications of this book, the reader should understand something of the events which led Peter Tompkins to undertake his mission.

In November 1942 the Allies landed in French North Africa. In Algiers Peter Tompkins was acting as deputy to the Director of Psychological Warfare. His outfit, helped by a minority of the Office of Strategic Services personnel on the spot, fought an all-out losing battle against the calamitous and shortsighted political policy of Allied Forces Headquarters (anti-De Gaulle, supporting Darlan as Chief of State and flirting with Vichy). This policy, dictated by General Eisenhower and Robert Murphy, survived through misinforming the White House and the Joint Chiefs of Staff on local conditions. By betraying on specious grounds those very elements (Gaullists, Royalists, Communists, Jews, clerics, and just ordinary anti-German Frenchmen) who had made our landings possible, we put every resistance movement in Europe on notice that our promises were soon forgotten and that we were ready to sacrifice our pronounced ideals and war aims to alleged military necessity. Naturally our underground Continental Allies turned to Communism; much of the strength today of the Communist Party in France, Italy, and Greece results from these wartime policies.

Within a few months De Gaulle had to be sent for to take over North Africa, such was the political bog in which the Allies had mired them-

* *Storia Segreta di Roma Città Aperta,* Quattruci, Roma, 1959.

12

selves. The General redressed most of our errors and injustices, but the Allies neither received nor deserved credit for this, and we regained little of our lost prestige. In all this bitter struggle, Peter Tompkins was an active partisan for what he and many of us considered our defense of Americanism, American ideals, F.D.R.'s expressed aims and promises, and our heritage from Jefferson, Jackson, Lincoln, and Wilson. To understand our author's attitude in Rome a year later, it is important to remember how fanatically he felt these things.

In the spring of 1943 the Germans and Italians threw in the sponge in Africa. Early in July the Allies invaded Sicily. On September 8 the surrender of Italy was announced, along with our recognition of the Royal Government of Victor Emmanuel (who had made the advent of Fascism possible), with Fascism's butcher, Marshal Badoglio, the Duke of Addis Ababa, as Prime Minister. Peter Tompkins quite reasonably saw in this a repetition of our tragic North African policy and a confirmation of what the Italian Communists had predicted. The Tompkinses had lived in Italy. Peter had grown up there; Italy was his second country. No doubt this is why he disassociated himself from Psychological Warfare (whose job it was to justify Badoglio and the Royalist conspiracy as it had Darlan and the Vichy conspiracy) and threw in his lot with General Donovan's Office of Strategic Services, where he might serve the United States and also be of help to those elements in Italian anti-Fascism which were also anti- or non-Communist.

At dawn, September 9, 1943, the Anglo-American Fifth Army under General Mark Clark landed on the beaches between Salerno and Agropoli, south of Naples. Peter arrived in Salerno while it was still under German fire. Almost autonomously he set about recruiting and training democratic Italians to do espionage behind the German lines. By the time Naples was captured he had a sizable and enthusiastic, almost personal, espionage service.

Early in January, less than a month before the Allied landings on the Anzio beaches near Rome, General Donovan arrived in Naples, and it is at this point that the daily narrative begins.

One caution to the reader: Unless you do not care to sleep, do not begin this book in bed at night. You may find yourself still reading at dawn, your furniture piled across the door, your windows locked, the shades drawn, and the fire poker or some other lethal weapon handy beside you on your night table.

DONALD DOWNES

ROME, JULY 1961

PART ONE GOING IN

1 IN NAPLES JUST BEFORE ANZIO

THERE IS AN OLD JOKE, retold among veterans of the OSS, about a young subaltern who died in World War II and found himself swimming in a sea of ordure—a sort of *lorda pozza* of the fifth ring of the Inferno. After several attempts to recover his breath he spotted a friendly officer of field grade from a rival branch of the same organization and realized it must be an OSS hell.

"Oh, it's not so bad," spluttered the ranking sleuth, "once you learn to tread water."

There was a pause while he demonstrated the finesse of his own technique to the admiring subaltern, then added with a sigh: "Except, of course, when Donovan comes by on a tour of inspection. Churns up the stuff like mad with his speedboat!"

In that circle of hell, undreamed of even by Dante, that was Naples at the beginning of 1944, the sudden arrival of Major General William J. Donovan meant—and we sometimes wondered why the German secret services didn't use General Donovan's movements as their prime source on impending Allied operations—that something of interest was about to happen in the theater.

This time it was to be "Shingle"—code name for what might have been a daring amphibious operation behind the enemy lines just south of Rome, but which turned out to be the nearly disastrous Anzio-Nettuno landings.

Conceived by Winston Churchill and delivered in a whitewashed villa on the ruins of Carthage on Christmas morning of 1943, Shingle was a brilliant and promising brain child.

Not unlike Hannibal's flanking attack of some centuries earlier, Shingle was to "decide the Battle of Rome" and "achieve the destruction of a substantial part of the enemy army."

That such a "cat claw" thrust behind the enemy lines, as Churchill termed it, had become essential by the beginning of 1944 was clear to the humblest of strategists; a mere eight divisions of Germany's Tenth Army, entrenched behind their strong points of the "Winter Line"

17

based on the apparently impregnable bastion of Cassino and aided by what was officially styled "inclement weather and terrain," were successfully holding up fourteen divisions of the Allied Fifth and Eighth Armies.

The objective of the joint Anglo-American forces assigned to Shingle was to take and hold the key high ground south of Rome known as the Alban Hills, *long enough to cut the enemy's communications* with his Tenth Army facing our Fifth Army on the Winter Line.

In his memoirs Mr. Churchill summed up the scope of the operation by quoting his own cable to the Chiefs of Staff the day after Christmas of 1943:

> The success of Anzio depends on the strength of the initial landing. If this is two full divisions plus parachutists it should be decisive, as it cuts the communications of the whole enemy forces facing the Fifth Army. The enemy must therefore annihilate the landing by withdrawals from the Fifth Army front, or immediately retreat. . . . 'Tis not intended to maintain these divisions for long over the beaches, but rather to bring the battle to a climax in a week or ten days.

D-Day for Shingle was set for as soon after January 20 as possible, with a schedule to be strictly adhered to because of the impending bigger operations in Normandy and the south of France.

Since we had landed at Salerno September 9, I had been developing a peculiar OSS setup in and about Naples, the main purpose of which was to recruit and prepare Italian agents for the suicidal job of being infiltrated short distances through the enemy lines to collect combat intelligence while I waited, impatiently, for official permission to implement my more ambitious plan of parachuting, or landing by submarine, teams of agents well behind the German lines throughout Italy.

Unfortunately, despite the fact that we had been at war over two years, the OSS had been granted little opportunity by field commanders to prove itself an effective weapon of espionage and sabotage behind the enemy lines; most of us were still being frowned on by the brass as a collection of madmen. I had therefore been obliged, by lack of facilities, or even of recognition, to operate more or less clandestinely not only from the Germans, but from our own side as well. To this end I requisitioned a *démodé* four-story palazzo with a dilapidated garden on a back street of Naples belonging to a dispossessed Neapolitan duke, familiarly referred to by my more literate partisan friends as "the Duke of Bilgewater."

In the endless rooms of this weird establishment, where secret radios, high explosives and implements of agents' disguise were incongruously interspersed with the bibelots of the Victorian age, I hid, fed, clothed, protected, and entertained—all as a means of establishing effective resistance operators and recruiting useful agents—Italian politicos and aspirant secret agents of an extraordinary variety, from illiterate saboteurs to that noble successor of Darlan (at least in the affections of high-ranking Allied policy-makers), the Duke of Addis Ababa, better known to the world as Marshal Badoglio.

At my table, where I fed them GI powdered eggs and flour transmuted into delicious *fettuccine* by a terrified Posilipan cook, a collection of heterogeneous anti-Fascist leaders would congregate to plot the future of Italy and the demise of the Nazi-Fascists, invariably embarrassing me with the insoluble problem of how to seat personalities sensitive to their past, present, and future ranks as cabinet ministers or generals of armies in a country which at that time had neither cabinet nor army.

It was in this house, a week before D-Day for Shingle (while agents and politicos were momentarily secreted in the cellars and attics) that General Donovan spent the night on his way back from General Clark's HQ in Caserta and announced, just before going into dinner, that he would like to have an American OSS man in Rome before the landings for the purpose of coordinating intelligence and partisan activities.

Filing into the dining room, where "top secret" shop talk was momentarily taboo, the general took a quick glance at the candle-lit table and frowned his approval. "You are the host," he said, "I shall sit at your right."

This intimacy with individuals of his vast and chaotic organization, was, in my opinion, the most likely of the general's many qualities to assure him the loyalty of a subordinate under the worst conditions of injustice, corruption, ineptness and political back-stabbing which marked the growing pains of the OSS.

Dinner ended, we filed back into what served as my sitting-room-bedroom-operations-room-warehouse, and I wondered, over coffee and Strega, what would happen to my complex organization were I to go into Rome. What would happen to all the teams of agents I had nurtured and equipped to be parachuted into northern Italy? What would happen to the job of organizing Secret Intelligence in Italy which had just been offered me by the Commanding Officer, OSS AFHQ? Would it be there when I returned? Could he be trusted to keep his word when not in his cups? Or would the Italo-American Mafia get him, and then me?*

The following dawn I drove the general to the Naples airfield. As we rolled through the early January mist in my old battered jeep I volunteered for the job in Rome.

Pacing up and down the muddy runway while his plane warmed up, the general outlined what he wanted of the mission; then he shook me by the hand, climbed into the hatch and took off into the chill north wind, leaving me alone on the airstrip with that feeling of dedication which comes when one has been entrusted with a mission by a superior being.

That's all there was to it! No signed military orders, no red tape, no protocol. To prepare for the operation I drove up to the OSS, Fifth Army, headquarters in Caserta and told the boys that the general had said O.K.

The reason it was comparatively easy for me to go on such a mission was that I could speak Italian fluently enough to pass as an Italian. My parents had sailed to Europe in the twenties to see its art, then lingered to absorb it. From school in England I had spent my vacations in Italy, mostly in Rome. Quitting college in 1939 I got a job in the Rome bureau of the New York *Herald Tribune*, and began broadcasting to the States for Mutual. Then, sick of reporting the war from the enemy side, when Mussolini invaded Greece, I went over to the British and the Greeks. I had thus been in the area of the present operations as little as three years earlier, and knew my way around Rome about as well as any *Trasteverino* born in the shadow of St. Peter's.

---

* That I had grounds for fearing such a Mafia was subsequently confirmed when poor Major Hollahan, on a mission for the general into northern Italy, was poisoned, shot and dumped into a supposedly bottomless lake!

Not much was needed to organize the operation other than set the date for an OSS plane to fly me to Corsica, where a torpedo boat could take me close enough to shore to land in a rubber boat behind the German lines. There was no problem of waiting for the proper phase of the moon to approach in darkness; the date for Shingle had been selected in the proper lunar period.

Though still a civilian (too preoccupied with the waging of the war to take time out to become a soldier) I was arbitrarily assigned the rank of major for the duration of the operation, "major" partly because it was the highest rank I could effectively get away with at the age of twenty-four, and partly because our executive officer, John Roller, who assigned it to me, would have seen himself in hell before having his own recently acquired but authentic gold maple leaf outranked by even a spurious silver one of mine.

Incredible as it may seem, there was in those days only the sketchiest equipment with which to prepare an agent for such a mission; not even a false-document service. I was obliged to procure my own false identity papers by having one of my local Italian agents "borrow" the official municipal seal from the civil documents office in the Naples town hall, with which I stamped and filled out a blank card, blotching several attempts and getting myself covered with printer's ink.

As a false identity I had chosen to become the imaginary brother of a real Italian friend of mine, a contemporary at Harvard, who had been killed in the Greek war. I took the name partly because it had a title—the Germans and Fascists still being inclined to respect titles of nobility irrespective of their bearers—and partly because it was essential for me to assume the identity of a friend whose family, servants and properties I could discourse on in reasonable detail were I to be caught by either the German or Italian security police before I managed to get into Rome.

Once in Rome, where such an identity would be as dangerous to me as to my friend's family, I intended to discard it, and make use of a secondary, less distinguished card, which I had sewed into the lining of my coat. Even in peacetime it was a prison offense in Italy to be without one's police identification; to be caught without one in wartime was tantamount to admitting one was a deserter, an enemy agent, or an escaped criminal.

From the Naples Automobile Club I got a driver's license blank to which I attached the requisite number of stamps so as to bring it up to date.

None of these documents was in any way perfect, but I trusted they would get me through a minor jam outside of Rome, and thereafter serve at least till I could make the proper contacts in Rome through which to improve them.

For some months I had assigned my men in Naples to scour the city for secondhand civilian clothes suitable for agents of all sizes, shapes and social conditions. With these I had been outfitting the poor volunteers we infiltrated through the lines. From the pile of shabby mismatched clothing I now selected a discreet blue sharkskin suit, had the pockets cleaned and filled with such routine security props as Italian tobacco shavings (even a shred of Allied tobacco in the lining could be a giveaway). For an overcoat I divested one of my agents of his leather jacket—the sort worn by the Italian Questura police—which I hoped would serve in rough ground, and yet, *de rigueur,* be worn by a nobleman motoring in winter.

My shoes, which had been made for me some months before by a cobbler in Capri, were comfortably broken in, of Italian leather and cut, but sturdy enough to allow me a good deal of walking without blisters—if necessary.

Though I had bought my watch in Rome several years earlier, it was engraved on the back with my name; so I was obliged to exchange it for an inferior Swiss model belonging to John Roller, who was to accompany me as far as the shore.

It was planned that we fly to Bastia in Corsica (where the OSS had a mission) on January 19; from there I was to be put ashore in time to meet a "beach party" of agents bringing out an Italian electronics engineer in whom we were much interested because of his knowledge of guided missiles—a mission on which I had been working for several months. But on the nineteenth the weather was bad, so the operation was postponed till the following morning, making it even more essential that all go well lest I fail to reach Rome before the Allied landings.

Already Operation Webfoot, in which the Allied forces scheduled to land at Anzio had been making amphibious exercises on the beaches

22

south of Salerno, was completed, and the great convoy of LSTs, LSIs, LCTs and Liberty Ships was being loaded.

Once I was ashore, the plan, like most plans in the early days of the OSS, turned out to be sketchy. Some months earlier the OSS had infiltrated a team of four Italian agents into Rome with a radio transmitter whose code name was Vittoria. They had been an ill-assorted group and one of them was later shot trying to escape from an OSS compound where he was being detained on suspicion of being a German double agent.

Not the sort of company I would have chosen for myself, but it was too late for any alternative. This team had made arrangements to use the bailiff's house on a Roman nobleman's estate about a hundred miles north of Rome right on the Aurelian road which runs near the coast between Civitavecchia and Orbetello. It was from this house that they were to meet me on an isolated bit of beach, taking me in as they sent out the electronics engineer. From there I was to make my way into Rome with one of them. Such was the plan as it was radioed to Rome on the nineteenth, but, for reasons which were never satisfactorily explained, the message did not get through.

Nevertheless, on January 20, a bright sunny morning, I walked out of my peculiar and complicated headquarters in Naples, just as if I were going away for the day, climbed into my antiquated Lancia limousine and set off for the airfield with John Roller. As we drove up the hill toward Capodichino overlooking the bay, Vesuvius, which had not yet made its startling eruption, still exuded its familiar wisp of smoke.

We were in a gay mood, excited, pleasantly anticipating the delight we would have if my mission turned out successfully. If all went well we expected to see each other in liberated Rome within a couple of weeks.

Beyond the limousine's separating pane of glass, next to the Italian driver, sat a smiling round-faced Emilian agent of indeterminable age, barely five feet tall, who had twice crossed the lines for me on combat intelligence assignments, and whose capacity for getting out of scrapes astounded me. On one occasion he had avoided being shot by the Germans by releasing a carrier pigeon he had tucked inside the back of his shirt while being carted off on a German tank, and had escaped

23

back to our lines only to spend a month in a British Field Security Service prison because his story seemed too incredible. I was taking him with me into Rome to carry messages and act as bodyguard.

Italian agents were generically known to us in the Fifth Army detachment of the OSS as "bennies," the etymology being partly Algerian and partly attributable to the fact that when we landed at Salerno every Italian who was asked to do something would answer, "*Va bene, va bene.*"

At the airport an OSS B-25 light bomber was waiting for us, and our benny became very excited.

"Does he know where he's going?" John asked.

"Of course not," I laughed. "For all he knows he's going to be dropped through the bomb bay without a chute for some imaginary infraction of nonexistent OSS discipline!"

Crawling into the belly of the plane John and I sat in two small leather-covered seats usually used by the general, the benny in the rear gunner's spot very wide-eyed at the proceedings. From our vantage point we could see one wheel of the plane as it raced across the turf for the take-off. It was a dewy morning and the sparse blades of untrampled grass by the runways were covered with frost.

Circling Naples we saw its bay below us, dotted with a few small sailboats, then suddenly Capri, clear cut in the sunlight.

I wondered what my friends on the island would think of my being overhead in a B-25 about to go on a pretty fantastic mission. I thought of the fire in Eddie Bismarck's study in Mona Williams' pink villa, of the martinis in his sunken bathtub, of how fond of him my parents had been through the years, and if it were true he was then in Rome, working for the Germans.

On the far side of the island Malaparte's house stretched into the sea like a surrealist painting and it revived the pleasure of the lunch I had had with him two weeks earlier. In his workrooms, like the captain's quarters on a ship, he had read me a description of Himmler in the nude from a manuscript of his still unpublished *Kaput;* and after lunch when he had displayed his sunbathing roof with its fan-shaped wall to protect him from voyeurs I had pictured the scene in *Eyeless in Gaza* of a dog falling from an airplane to splatter blood on a couple making love in the strong, strong sunlight.

From the B-25, looking down, I felt the association as even stronger;

24

to dispel it I had to look up the hazy coast to the spot, hidden beyond the Amalfitan peninsula, in the bay of Salerno, where the Shingle expeditionary force was preparing to sail to Anzio.

For the next two hours John and I sat and watched the water and the sunlight, and eventually the coast of Sardinia and then Corsica. My good mood had returned. Having no operational chatter to keep us busy—my assignment was no more specific than to coordinate intelligence and partisan activities with the Allied landings—we joked about the houses and cars and good German gin I would have waiting for the OSS when the Fifth Army got into Rome, about what we would do if a couple of Messerschmitts were suddenly to appear from the blue (we were skirting German-occupied Italy, a lone aircraft without escort, and might easily be spotted and attacked), or about what was going through the mind of the benny who still had no idea where he was going or why.

The pilot wasn't sure he could land a B-25 at Borgo Field near Bastia in Corsica; but he did, and a beautiful landing too.

We barely had time to stretch our legs in the operations shack and admire the best collection of quasi-naked pinup girls in MEDTO, when André Pacatte, a French-American captain in the OSS temporarily attached to the local OSS outfit, came running up to provide us with transport, shaking his great spatulate fingers and patting me on the back with a friendly "Yesus Kleist!"

He was surprised, however, when he learned of my mission, and I could understand why. At that time he was working with a *completely* French Army captain who had recently moved to Corsica from Naples, where he had been operating another OSS outfit similar to mine, and who, for reasons of his own, considered me a rival. Seconded to the OSS, Fifth Army, by that politically malodorous resident general of Morocco under Pétain, General Noguès, this French captain had, since World War I, worked for the Deuxième Bureau; I distrusted him, but for the sake of his reputation I shall simply refer to him as Captain A. Between us a feud had been running because I chose to recruit my agents from members of the anti-Fascist parties of the Committee of National Liberation whereas he preferred to use ex-Fascists, petty professional informers and outright double agents, with results which I foretold were bound to be tragic.

I was then disturbed to discover that it was to his headquarters I was being taken instead of to the regular OSS mission, because Captain A. was planning to infiltrate some Italian agents that night at the same time I was to go ashore. It had been my firm conviction (and the subject of numerous unheeded reports to my superiors) that irrespective of what type of agent the OSS used, or how many types, no agent or team of agents of one political, social or economic coloring should, under any circumstances, be exposed to, or, if possible, become aware of, the existence of other types of OSS agents, lest, once across the lines, they not only risk exposing each other, but start to quarrel. This seemed to me to be such an elementary matter of security that I was amazed at what I considered the criminal lightness with which the brass in the OSS ignored it, and the vicious manner in which Captain A. continued to infringe it, till so many of my agents were being "burnt" that I seriously began to wonder whether Captain A. were not working precisely toward that end.

To land three sets of agents at the same spot on the same night, all on different missions, was a staggering breach of security; but my remonstrances had been in vain.

There was no other craft that could take me ashore that night; I had no alternative but to go as planned or risk not arriving in Rome in time.

The two teams that were going in with me consisted of a pair of saboteurs who were being sent by Captain A. with some plastic explosive to blow bridges at unidentified points (an operation the futility of which is inexplicable to anyone but an expert in such matters), and a woman with a bad leg, accompanied by an elderly male escort, who, after landing, were to make their way north to Milan, an area, incidentally, where Captain A. had no authority at that time to operate. Both missions, in any case, were in no way tied to the immediate D-Day landings and were of no particular urgency.

As we approached Captain A.'s headquarters in a partially bombed-out villa overlooking the port of Bastia, I began to dread what was in store for me.

No sooner had we had lunch—itself an ordeal consisting of a Corsican version of badly prepared GI rations, consumed in a cold, windowless room, amid a motley crowd of uninspiring professional thugs many of whom I knew from before and trusted not at all—than the benny came running up to me very worried to whisper secretly that

26

he had overheard the two saboteurs who were landing that evening say that it would be too bad for me if I couldn't swim. The benny still thought he alone was going on a mission behind the lines; that I was merely going to land him and then come back. I told him not to worry; but I could see from his expression he was unhappy and couldn't understand why he had to be mixed up with such characters.

As there was clearly nothing to be done about it, I spent the afternoon collecting and checking my equipment: a bag with my civilian clothes, my phony papers, 300 gold sovereigns (the only effective international currency in German-occupied Europe), my own secret codes and radio crystals which would produce certain wave lengths, a Beretta 9-mm. automatic, and, foolishly, a small Minox camera. We then piled into several cars and drove down to the port, where two Italian torpedo boats awaited us—the light attack kind known as MAS, from which our own PT boats had originally been developed.

At the docks a movie-hero sort of creature, tall with ravishing gold curls, a classic Greek profile and the authority acquired as a prefect in an English public school, turned out to be the British Navy commander in charge of the two slick craft. As we arrived he was busy giving an Italian two-striper in a weird seagoing battle dress quick and authoritative orders. The presence of an RN officer reassured and cheered me, reminding me of the varied adventures in the Mediterranean I had enjoyed as a correspondent before the U.S. became officially involved in the war, when the British Navy had behaved as if it were all a terrible game, but one to be *played*, preferably with lashings of drinks.

Then came the first of what I feared might be a series of contretemps. The RN commander handed Captain A. a cryptic cipher on the cover of a matchbox; for an awful fifteen minutes we had to wait while Captain A., who had forgotten the decoding device, returned to the villa to fetch it, forcing me to pace the dock, terrified that the trip would have to be postponed, which it couldn't be if I were to get into Rome in time to organize things before the landings.

At last Captain A. came scurrying back in his small captured Axis vehicle and we prepared to embark. The message, he said, was from the radio in the house on shore to say that the electronics engineer would be waiting to be picked up that night at the appointed hour.

John and Pacatte were to go in one boat, Captain A., the ravishing commander and I in the other; so I split my last pint of Scotch with John Roller, bid the local detachment of the OSS farewell, watched the Italian crew cast off just as dusk was beginning to settle.

With one last glance at Allied territory I turned and let the sea breeze blow in my face. We were sailing, one behind the other, toward German-occupied Italy.

2 LANDING BEHIND THE LINES

WHEN WE WERE WELL OUT AT SEA, heading south to round the tip of German-occupied Elba, I went below into the one small cabin of the torpedo boat, removed my uniform, and got into my set of civilian clothes, much to the surprise of everyone—especially the benny, across whose face a broad grin appeared as he realized that I too would be landing with him.

The woman and the old man who were to make their way to Milan looked at me suspiciously, then resumed their chatter. Their mood seemed light for the occasion, and I wondered whether, with its customary lack of security, the OSS had not managed to hire another couple of double agents. If so, I would soon be in trouble.

Just then the woman looked up and exclaimed: "Think of it, if all goes well, in a couple of days I'll see my dog again!"

It was an incongruous remark for the occasion and I could see from the woman's expression that she realized it herself. Yet it reassured me; I got the impression she might merely be doing what many other Italians had done or were still attempting to do—crossing the lines ostensibly to work for German or Allied intelligence, but actually to rejoin their families or businesses from which they had been separated by the Allied landings at Salerno, which had split the country into rival camps. Already Italian wags had labeled the OSS "Opera Sistemazione Spostati"— or "welfare organization for the repatriation of refugees!"

As the small boats traveled through the night, pat-patting the calm sea with their bellies, I half dozed and half reminisced about the war, thinking of the new intelligence organization I was to build up if this mission were successful.

At last I heard the engines being cut; we were about to edge through the water for the last ten miles, almost noiselessly, so as not to attract the attention of enemy patrol craft. Going up on deck I decided to help look for the signal. It was a beautiful night, moonless but filled with stars. Having skirted Elba in a wide circle we had come in toward

29

the Italian coast about fifteen miles north of Tarquinia. Eventually a thin black edge of land appeared in the darkness ahead of us. I kept thinking I saw a light, though I assured myself it could be nothing but a trick of the night. All was quiet except for the swishing of the phosphorescent wake. Checking my watch I saw that it was almost time for the second signal when it flashed, long and green, a mile or so to port. Our boat edged in to where the light had flashed, and the other boat veered too, to follow us, but without communicating. Going below, I warned the others, collected my kit, then came back up. The engines had stopped and the other boat was standing off, slightly astern, guns ready to protect us if we were to run into trouble from an enemy patrol or from some cruising German E-boat. Silence and dispatch were now in order.

The woman, Captain A., the RN commander and I slipped into the first rubber boat, yellow and squishy like the ones I had used so many times in Sicily to practice secret landings, or with the PT squadron I had been attached to moving back and forth along the German-held Sorrentine peninsula during the Salerno landings.

Sitting in the bow I watched the shore while the commander stirred up short paddlefuls of sparkling phosporescence. In a moment we were there, and I could just distinguish a group of figures silhouetted on the sand. Was it a German posse which had captured our agents? The thought was paralyzing!

But no one fired. With a squish we landed safely on Mussolini's untouchable *bagnasciuga* coastline.

Introductions were over in a moment; no names were mentioned, just quick glances and nods. Yet I sensed that something was not as it should be, especially when Captain A. took one of the saboteurs aside for a rapid whispered conversation and I discovered that the entire group on the beach was planning to embark with the electronics expert, leaving no one to take me into Rome. In his nervous staccato voice Captain A. assured me that all would be well, that I'd find someone at the house to do so, that a farmer would take us in his cart as far as the house.

But I was not reassured; in fact I was furious, not so much at the actual danger of the situation, as at the fact that through the lack of vision of a certain OSS colonel, a French Deuxième Bureau officer and an Italian agent should be allowed to endanger not only the life of an American citizen, but a mission of possible consequence to an entire Allied amphibious operation.

The beach, however, was no place to argue; a German patrol might appear at any moment, and those who were about to embark were nervously anxious to do so. I decided to make for the so-called "safe" house as rapidly as possible and work things out from there.

It was a strange sensation to see the rubber boats glide back into the darkness drawn by invisible life lines toward the invisible torpedo boats, my last ties with my own people and my own side of the lines.

Turning and plodding through the sand with the woman and her companion, the two ugly saboteurs, and my benny, I felt the almost physical snap of an umbilical cord and wondered what in heaven had induced me to indulge in such an undertaking.

Icicles shot through my veins as a horse neighed in the darkness. It was the first real sound I had heard on land, and its reverberation over the dunes made me painfully conscious of being ashore. We came upon a pair of horse-and-buggies hidden in the undergrowth and my stomach knotted at the thought that the Germans could have waited for a planted agent of theirs to be safely aboard our craft before putting us under arrest. But the buggies were manned by two farmers from the estate who had driven the outgoing agents to the water.

As one chooses to sit by a pretty girl, my decision was immediate and instinctive: the benny and I would ride in the first buggy, the others could follow.

Sitting by the driver I kept fingering my Beretta, looking into the undergrowth for a German sentinel, wishing now, as the wheels dragged through the boggy sand, that I had none of the horribly incriminating material I was stuck with—no extra identity card, no Minox camera, no 300 sovereigns, no saboteurs with explosives—and especially that I had been allowed to organize the operation entirely on my own.

Now it was too late.

Turning onto a country lane I realized there was no use trying to wish the incriminating material away, that I need not even bother to establish a cover; if caught, I was done for. How stupid could that French captain be? Or was he so stupid?

At first I thought we had only a short way to go, but we kept plod-

plodding through the night making the devil of a noise over each wooden bridge, freezing from cold and misery. Finally we came to a fork in the lane and I watched the other buggy turn along the more protected coastal branch while we moved on toward the main road. I did not like the idea, but the driver leaned sideways and whispered that the car which had brought the others up from Rome was waiting on Via Aurelia. It was the first I'd heard of a car, and I wondered whose it was, what sort of papers it had, and what I could do about it. The farmer, when questioned, seemed to know nothing of the higher echelon plotting, but volunteered that the drivers of the car did not know that a landing had taken place.

A light flashed on the highway straight ahead, making me catch my breath and slip the safety on the Beretta. It was the car, so we pulled up, and I got out with the benny while the farmer asked the drivers to follow his cart to the house. For a moment they whispered together, then one of the drivers came forward and said that the price was not sufficient. I was very frightened by now, and furious at the mismanagement, but behaving as calmly as I could, and talking from protective darkness, told the drivers not to worry about the price, that I would pay them well. Then—almost as if it had been an order —I climbed into the back of the car.

On the main road the cart clop-clopped ahead of us into the night, and I realized with dread that instead of speeding to the safety of the house we would have to creep along behind the cart because the drivers did not know the location of the house. Snuggling in the corner of the back seat, a little warmer, but just as miserable, I thought with a twinge of nostalgia how pleasant it would be to be back in Naples being driven by my own driver, Mario. But the illusion would not persist. Every now and then, especially on hills, the car turned up its headlights and I had the sensation of being floodlighted. And the road went on and on; till at last the car turned off, but not very far, and I could distinguish something concrete sticking up ahead on the road.

Leaning toward me the benny whispered, "It's a roadblock!"

Terrified, I could not answer. However, when nothing happened, I decided it must be the gateway to the estate, which it was. What should have taken us twenty minutes, I now saw by my watch, had taken closer to an hour.

Getting out I found that despite the incredible luck of having gotten that far without running into any Germans, I was still trembling. The scene, as we stood in the glare of the headlights, was like a shot from a gangster movie: leather-coated men with guns, their nostrils fuming in the cold air.

The headlights were dimmed and I was plunged into pleasant darkness. Moving cautiously through the massive gateway onto a colonnade which overlooked the road, we crept up a steep dark stairway till a door opened at the top and a figure appeared with a green lantern motioning us into an immense room where the others, who had got there a little ahead, were sitting on the floor round a fire, drinking coffee. At least that much of Captain A.'s promise had turned out to be correct! But what of the rest?

The bailiff was very nervous and agitated, insisting that on no account could we hang around the house, that the Germans had been there that afternoon and were bound to be back in the morning. There was no sign of any agent with a special pass to take me to Rome, and the only alternative suggested by the bailiff was that we drive to Viterbo and from there take a train. For this idea, I had, understandably, very little sympathy, and would have given anything to send the car away, lie low in the house, and wait for someone from Rome to come fetch me with a reasonably false pass.

This was evidently impossible. Then I realized with a shock that none of the others knew what to do. Even the saboteurs had begun to lose their underworld sang-froid and wanted to be given instructions. They too had been told by the agent we had crossed on the beach that they should go to Viterbo and thence take a train into Rome. But it was obvious to anyone now facing the situation that they could not arrive in the middle of the night in a deserted town with phony papers, two radios and a bag of explosives, to rouse a small provincial hotel. Had I been able to lay hands on Captain A. at that moment I would certainly have strangled him.

The only person who seemed to have any idea of how I could get in touch with our agents in Rome was a youngster called "T." whom we found in the house and whose job had been to act as courier between the estate and Rome; he said he had an address in the city through which he thought one of the agents might be reached. Though as nervous as the others he agreed with me that we might

44019

try to bribe the chauffeurs downstairs to drive us into Rome in their limousine. So I sent him down to offer them a large but not suspiciously large amount of cash to take us into Rome, providing they asked no questions.

I knew that at that time in German-occupied Italy all kinds of black market dealings were being carried on as a matter of survival, and that since Badoglio's desertion, all sorts of disbanded military personnel were moving around the country clandestinely to avoid being conscripted into the Nazi-Fascist forces; I hoped to be mistaken for a member of one or both of these categories—which were generally abetted rather than denounced by all but the police and ultra-Fascist citizens. Were the drivers to suspect that I was an American, or the nature of my mission, our situation would be hopeless, for they would quickly realize that to be caught with me would mean torture and certain death, unless, of course, they turned me in to the Germans first.

T. came back and told me that far from accepting my offer, the drivers were annoyed at having been detained, wanting to know what had happened to the people they had driven up from Rome.

With no place to stay and nowhere to go, and the thought of having to spend the night in the woods to goad me, I decided the time had come to make capital of my phony identity and use some brashness. Not knowing how much the drivers knew, and having no one to tell me, I went down to the car with the hope that instinct would prompt me. Whose car was it, I demanded.

My change in attitude, as I had hoped, brought an instant change in their own, and they named the nobleman to whom the car belonged. Why hadn't they said so to begin with? I made my voice as cutting as possible. He was an old friend to whom I wished to be taken immediately. (Actually he had never been a friend, but I knew enough of him through my family to be able to maintain the bluff.)

Having accepted a suitable sum (20,000 lire) over and above what they had already been paid to drive up to the estate, the drivers agreed to take us to Rome. But my troubles were far from over. The bailiff agreed to hide the lame woman and her companion for a day or so, but refused categorically to harbor the saboteurs; these he insisted should go along with me.

Gritting my teeth I realized there was no way out but to raise the

34

ante and hope the drivers' cupidity would induce them to accept; which it did.

The enforced company of the saboteurs did not improve my mood, but one impasse had been circuited; so, having burnt my extra identity card (it was curious how a plan for cover devised in the safety of one's own headquarters fell to pieces in face of an actual situation), having gotten the farmer to agree to hide the saboteurs' more incriminating material till someone could fetch it at a later and safer date, and having at the last moment shaved off my beard (to fit my new identity and yet leave a false trail in case the lame woman and her companion were arrested and interrogated) we were ready to go.

In the limousine the two drivers sat in the front seat behind their glass partition, the benny, T. and I sat on the back seat, the two saboteurs on the *strapontins*, like a comic scene in a gangster film, and off we went into the night, heading down the Aurelia toward Montalto di Castro and Tarquinia.

The uncertainty of what lay ahead, the knowledge that there could be no possible excuse for seven strange men to be wandering round German-occupied Italy at three o'clock in the morning, and my suspicion that the chauffeurs were quietly planning to turn us in to the first German roadblock, had me pretty well paralyzed. Every mile-post loomed as a German sentry, every crossroad as a roadblock, and I began to think that if only I had some poison soaked into my lapel I would not hesitate to suck it. Even the worst Hamletian nightmare could not be as bad as this gnawing torture of not knowing what was going on in the heads of the drivers, and of having absolutely no story to cover all the occupants of the car. From my earliest schoolboy days I had always coached myself to have a story, any kind of story, before embarking on an escapade; the wildest of excuses, well prepared, might get one off, whereas no story at all was tantamount to an admission of guilt. But nothing I could think of seemed to cover the present emergency.

Finally I became so nervous I decided to stop the car and talk to the drivers bluntly, judging it better to tackle them in open country than near some German sentry. If they were in any way recalcitrant, or threatened us, we could shoot it out and take to the woods. So I told them to stop.

Once out of the car I took the actual driver to one side, fingering the cocked Beretta in my pocket. It was essential, I told him, for reasons of my own, that I get into Rome without being spotted by the Germans, that I would pay them even more at the other end if they succeeded in doing so. There was a pause while he considered my remark, then, before he could answer, I asked if there were no circuitous way of getting into the city without going through a roadblock.

There wasn't he said, especially with such a large car, but as his papers were in order, providing ours were, we should have no difficulty. I did not dare hint that my own might fail the test, lest he become suspicious and be afraid to take us; so I switched the attack by asking what kind of papers he had for the car. It turned out to be a pass from the German Embassy, whereas his assistant had documents from the Department of the Fascist Republican Army. From his explanation I gathered that the nobleman who owned the car must in fact have been working with the Germans irrespective of any facilities he may have appeared to be giving the Allies. I was not at all sure now whether the two drivers were partisans of sorts (with false German papers), which would have been risky in one sense but reassuring in another, or whether they were in fact German agents playing a double game to trap us, or, as I hoped, had merely been running an errand, the true nature of which they were unaware, but which afforded them, thanks to their documents, one of the most richly rewarding forms of black market operations in gasoline- and transport-starved Italy—the conveyance of bodies, anybody's body, from X to Y. As I talked with him, trying to size him up, I got the feeling he was but another typical Roman, basically good-natured, operating an effective racket, and that he might be all right after all.

Just then there was a commotion behind the car between the assistant driver and one of the saboteurs. Well, I thought, this is it! At least we're in the dead of country. But it was not a fight. The noisy exchange resulted from their having recognized each other as classmates in the army—a strong and lifelong fraternity in Italy. The feeling of relief was general.

Getting back in the car we drove off, almost cheerfully, and for a moment I was inclined to forgive Captain A. the type of agent he recruited, though the doubt unaccountably lingered that they might still be planning to turn me in at the first opportune moment. Through

36

my mind the series of false names and strange addresses (trustingly given me by members of the resistance in Naples so that I might find the main leaders of the underground in Rome in case I failed to contact our Vittoria agents) kept leaping ahead of each other, superimposing, and vanishing; to save my neck—quite literally—I could not keep my true and my false identities straight, nor even remember the date of my birth, clearly marked on my false identity card.

Closing my eyes I tried to doze, but that was even more frightening, and the screeching of the brakes made me open them in time to see two German soldiers running out into the road. They were waving red lanterns, shouting and gesticulating, and I knew that we were for it. The driver accelerated, avoided a torn-up patch in the road, took a sharp curve inland, and we disappeared—by some miracle, without being shot at—into the night in the direction of Viterbo. The shock had been considerable, but in the balance of my emotions it was outweighed by relief at the behavior of the driver.

Next came the problem of Viterbo. I wasn't looking forward to driving through a German-garrisoned town, especially that early in the morning, but consoled myself with the thought that it was inevitable, one way or the other—Civitavecchia or Viterbo—and that we would probably look less suspicious approaching Rome from inland than from along the coast.

The landscape was still black, with only the yellow-white swath of road ahead of us distinguishable. But I could tell from the kilometer markers just about where we were, and to relax my nerves thought back to the times I had ridden horseback over this same countryside, of how, as a child, I had gone for day-long rides and picnics on the flat campagna as the guest of a man who then fulfilled the peculiar sinecure of Fascist mayor of Tarquinia.

Then the gray-brown battlements of Viterbo appeared before us. By some bit of luck, which I dared not ponder on, we managed to drive through the sleeping town without being stopped.

Turning onto the Cassia we began to meet isolated German cars, then quite a bit of traffic. There was a slight pallor about the Sabine Hills ahead, indicating the approach of dawn, and it gave me the strangest sensation to be looking at "honest-to-God" German soldiers passing in their vehicles and not have them pounce on me immediately.

No longer being on the coast road improved my sense of security; but not for long. The biggest problem began to preoccupy my whole attention: entering the city of Rome.

The more I thought about it the more it seemed safer for the saboteurs and the benny to get out shortly before the roadblocks, say at La Storta, and go in singly, by bus or on foot, while T. and I tried to pull it off in the car. It would be easier for them to do so with their authentic identity cards, and they would be less conspicuous than in a long shiny limousine which was bound to be stopped and carefully checked at the roadblocks. But the saboteurs pleaded that we stick together.

It seemed risky; but they were tired, and it was cold, and I thought to myself that if something went wrong there was some consolation in numbers.

Just then, to our right, we passed the estate where the Italians, after the "stab in the back," had dragged the members of the French Armistice Commission to make them sign a truce, and I was reminded of the sad scoop I had obtained that day, thanks to a tip from Dino, the second barman at the Excelsior, who had seen the baskets of wine and food prepared for the plenipotentiaries in the hotel's kitchen, an aromatic Adriadne's thread which I then followed to the "secret" meeting. How long ago it all seemed, almost like another life.

Now the dawn was coming up and we were rapidly approaching the outskirts of Rome. Then the engine coughed, spluttered, died. Climbing out into the gray mist I had visions of walking the rest of the way into Rome; but the driver assured us he was merely out of gas and that he had a spare can hidden beneath the back seat.

Standing by the side of the road we clapped our hands against our sides like a bunch of French taxi drivers, our breath condensing in the air, till a German truck came hurtling down on us and pulled up with a screech.

Leaning out the side the German officer seemed to address me in person. But his shouting was merely to extinguish our headlights, which could make a target for an Allied plane; then he whizzed off, leaving me shaking, the raucous order still ringing in my ears.

Back in the car we drove on, discussing the advisability of letting the benny out, right away, before we met a roadblock, so that if any-

38

thing happened to the rest of us he might get away to tell the story, when a figure with a red light loomed out of the mist. It was a German soldier. We were at the roadblock. Stopping the car, the chauffeur got out and showed his papers, while one of the saboteurs, with what seemed to me to be superhuman nonchalance, climbed out saying in a loud decoy voice that if he didn't urinate he'd burst.

In the back, with a different bladder problem of my own, I buried my nose in my collar hoping it would all be over, one way or another, as soon as possible. A helmeted German poked his head through the door and flashed a light in my face, did the same to the benny, requested my papers, glanced at them in a dull and apparently incomprehending fashion, hesitated, then, apparently satisfied, returned them to me.

The others climbed in, and I prayed—as I hope I never have to pray again—the goddamn engine would start. It did, and we were off. Though relieved, we were none of us sure it wasn't a trick, and that at the next roadblock they would be waiting for us with a firing squad. Instead Ponte Milvio, that ancient and lovely bridge across the Tiber, appeared at the end of an empty piazza. There was no roadblock. As we ducked under the archway a trolley loomed into sight from the opposite side. What a time, I thought, to have an accident! But a moment later we were "safely" in Rome.

3 WITH THE GERMANS IN ROME

IT WAS STILL EARLY as we moved along Via Flaminia, and not much traffic was about. I felt excited at being back, and a little as if I had only been away for a weekend, instead of over three years. As we passed the stadium, where I had swum as a boy, I realized how familiar it all was, even to knowing by their numbers where the trolleys were headed.

As we approached the heavy gates of Piazza del Popolo there was a debate about where to stop. I decided that T. and I should be the first to disappear, leaving the benny to guard our rear, lest either the saboteurs or the drivers planned to trail us.

Heading down Via del Babuino I saw two Germans coming out of the Hotel de Russie and instinctively ducked behind my collar. The warm red façade of the building reminded me of Cy Sulzberger in 1939 sitting on an old brass bed with a bottle of Johnny Walker—one of those same Victorian beds I had slept in when first I'd stayed at the hotel in the early twenties and played in the exotic gardens that stretched up to the Pincio. A whole world of afternoon tea and hansom cabs, of military bands and parasoled ladies, was conjured up and vanished.

Reflected in the windows of an antiquarian's shop, outlined against the velvet trays of ancient Roman coins, stood two modern Legionaires, guardians of the "public order," armed with submachine guns, hand grenades and automatics—my first encounter since North Africa with members of Italy's "crack" African Police Force, the PAI; but they were on routine duty and not stopping vehicles.

In Piazza di Spagna, the very heart of Rome, the car pulled up just beyond the entrance to Via Condotti, and T. and I got out; shaking the saboteurs by the hand I realized with amazement that in the last few hours I had become almost attached to them.

The car drove on and we started across the piazza, skirting the sunken fountain, but I was so nervous I had to stop to light a cigarette, joking noisily with T. to pretend we were really busy with a very normal life. Looking up the Spanish Stairs I wished for a moment they were still French extraterritorial property, and that I could run to one of the great granite *fleurs-de-lys* for sanctuary; instead the ghosts of Laval, Pétain, Noguès and Captain A. seemed to mock me while a pair of booted Luftwaffe privates came marching down in unison.

Passing the American Express I wondered what I should do if I were to run into someone I knew. Across the street Mr. Boliger's sign stood above his freighting office and I wondered if he still had our furniture in storage. There was a light in Rampoldi's bar, and the door was open. But I turned away, thinking of the times I had been there for coffee with the boys of the A.P. after playing poker in the cellar of their building across the narrow piazzetta during the fatuous Italian air raid alerts.

It was still too early to approach the address on Via Sistina where we hoped to find the man who could put us in touch with someone of the Vittoria team; the porter would not yet have opened the heavy *portone*. So we wandered around, rubbing elbows with early-rising German officers and soldiers on their way to work.

As the church of the Trinità dei Monti pealed out eight o'clock we headed up the steep hill of Capolecase toward the lower end of Via Sistina. The number turned out to be almost opposite the Hôtel de la Ville; but its massive brass-studded door was still locked and bolted. At first I thought of rousing the porter, but did not wish to cause a commotion by having to explain to him, with one foot in the door, our errand, so I decided to wait a little longer.

Walking up and down on the narrow sidewalk I began to feel conspicuous, especially as the benny had appeared from Trinità dei Monti and was also eyeing the *portone* in a suspicious manner, while Germans kept pouring out of the hotel across the street where they were billeted.

Finally I could stand the ordeal no longer. I felt I was about to break, about to lose such wit as I had left, even collapse on the street, endanger the other two men. Obviously I must find a place to hide till I recovered my nerve.

It was too early to call on any of my "respectable" friends from before the war, and I did not wish to do so, in any case, till after the landings had succeeded. Nor did I wish to get in touch with any member of the resistance till after I had found our own agents and the radio. The only place I could think of was an old palazzo near the Tiber on Via Giulia where I had once lived and where the porter and his wife had been our servants. It was a gamble, but better than breaking under the ordeal of being exposed to too much random danger. So I called the benny and gave him the address, telling him to bring me a message there once T. had made contact with the man who could lead us to our agents. Then I set off across Rome toward the Tiber, heading for the narrow maze of streets beyond the Corso where I hoped I would run less risk of being recognized by a chance acquaintance.

To keep as much of my face hidden as possible as I picked my way along cobbled alleys between moss-covered walls of ancient Travertine, I discovered the trick of pretending to have a cold, continually blowing my nose. For a while I regretted having shaved my beard, which made my features seem all the more naked, but soon concluded I might have attracted even more attention with it than without; in any case I was happy to leave behind me any trace of the *"Commandante Americano colla barba"* who had been running an espionage organization from a back street in Naples.

Ducking along Via Monserrato I came out into the Piazzetta Ricci, exactly as it had always been. The minor Caravaggio frescoes on the palazzo were perhaps a touch more faded than when I had last seen them, and I wondered if Mario Praz were breakfasting in his Empire mausoleum above the flat we used to occupy, or perhaps peeping down at me from behind his damask curtains!

Here too the *portone* was closed. Could Serafino the porter be asleep? He who was always up at five! Had he moved?

If I were to go round by the Via Giulia entrance almost any former neighbor could recognize me; but there was no going back. Slipping along the side passage, glancing up at the shrine of the Madonna, I blew my nose as assiduously as I could, feeling an awful presentiment that the servants were no longer there. Three years was a long time. They might even be dead.

Rounding the corner I caught a whiff of sawdust from a carpenter's nearby shop; but there was no one near the main entrance to the palazzo. I wanted to look back to see if I were being followed but dared not turn because of the distinct sensation that someone from the alley was studying me suspiciously. A few quick steps brought me to the doorway and the familiar darkness of the vaulted palace entry.

At the end of the courtyard the fountain played as usual; where the paving ended I felt the familiar crunch of gravel under my shoes. Everything now depended on the little glass door to the porter's lodge being open. It was; I slipped in unobserved.

The tiny downstairs living room was dark, but exactly as it had always been, even to two discarded flower paintings by my mother, rescued and sentimentally hanging on the wall. One of the servants, at least, must still be around; then I heard a woman's voice upstairs. Without a sound I crept up the narrow wooden staircase to the low-ceilinged bedroom. Dear, good old Virginia was lying on her bed, so I sat down on the quilt by her side, putting a finger to my lips.

"How are you?" she whispered, taking my hand, as nonchalant as if I'd been out to get some groceries. "I have a little fever. God, but these are terrible times! How is the Signora and the Signore?" Then she shook her head. "But you have come too soon. They are still at Cassino!"

"Don't worry," I answered. "It isn't too soon."

"Did you come by parachute?" Her nose wrinkled into that slightly reproachful expression with which she used to greet my youthful escapades.

Then her forehead became furrowed and she ran her hand across it. "You've come too soon. You can't stay in the building. Too many people could recognize you. Are you sure you weren't seen coming in? I must telephone Santino [our former cook] but I haven't seen him for some time. There are strange people in his house [the last one my mother had lived in before the war]. I must get up and phone him right away. I haven't any coffee for you. Serafino will be here in a minute. He's down in the cellar now. You know poor Arcangelo [her son] has been hiding for months. I'm almost desperate about him. He can't go out because they would catch him in the *retate* [roundups of civilians of military age made by the Germans and the Fascist police] and send him off to Germany. He is married, you know."

Then I heard the familiar shuffling footsteps of Serafino coming up the stairs (almost as if he were bringing a tray at cocktail time); when he saw me he smiled and stretched out his warm calloused hand, and cursed the Germans. Then he stopped and the smile grew wan on his lips: "But you haven't won your bet yet. You've come too soon."

After the fall of France I had bet him twelve *fiaschi* of wine that despite the German subjugation of Europe the Allies would win in the end. Now I wondered if either one of us would ever get to enjoy the proceeds of the bet.

I looked at my watch. It was over an hour since I had left T. and the benny, and I felt suddenly terribly tired. Had someone seen me enter the palazzo and gone to advise the police? Would the benny or T. be trailed and lead the police to my hideout? I was almost too tired to care; and though it was a sort of ostrich gesture, I told Serafino that if anyone came and asked for "Don Federico," my phony identity, to tell him to come back in an hour, that I had gone to another hideout. My body was sagging with fatigue, my brain spinning like an outboard motor lifted from the water.

So I lay on the couch, and Virginia put a pillow under my head, treating me like a child, as she had always done, giving me the "*tu*," scolding me for what she called a foolish adventure (for once I was inclined to agree) from which all the romance seemed suddenly to have vanished.

If only the OSS had allowed me to plan a proper organization in Rome when I had suggested and outlined it months earlier, everything would have been in order by now.

What if the benny should fail to make contact? Where could I seek refuge? How could I get in touch with the base?

With Virginia I discussed the possibility of hiding for a day or two at either the Caetanis or the Cesarós; but I was afraid that if I sent Virginia ahead to warn them of my arrival they might become frightened and demur. No. The best method would be to buy a large pot of azaleas from a florist, and deliver it in person, as if I were an employee of the shop, making my entrance first and doing my explaining afterward.

This subterfuge decided upon, it was a relief to lie in the semidark-ened room. But my dozing was marred by an acrostic nightmare of trying to rearrange from memory the penciled notes on the back of my identity card into the proper names and addresses of underground leaders.

Then my muscles tensed at the sound of someone downstairs. The benny was talking to Serafino. They chatted for a while as I strained to catch what they were saying, but all I could hear was Serafino telling him to come back in an hour.

Then Serafino came up with a message that T. had made contact with the person on Via Sistina, that someone would come for me in an hour. He handed me a package of sweets which the benny had brought for Don Federico in case he was getting hungry.

Eating the sweets, which were made of "autarchic" almond paste, and tasted awful, I was wondering when I would ever get another meal when the thought was drowned by the sound of someone's footsteps below.

Serafino poked his head round the top of the stairs and said a man wished to see me. The police? The contact man with our agents? Straightening myself, I tiptoed downstairs with my hand on the cocked Beretta in my pocket, then appeared suddenly from behind the curtain.

In the center of the room stood a small man, well dressed, with olive skin and dark mustache, nodding his head in greeting. My instinct flashed affirmatively. Stretching out my hand I informed him I was the American major they had been told to expect from the base.

From his answer I gathered they had received no message from Caserta to the effect that I was coming. Was this skullduggery, I wondered, or merely security, so as not to give away the imminence of the landing. In either case it left me on my own resources to establish my authority. But the small man seemed readily convinced, and suggested we decamp to a safer address where he could put me in touch with the Vittoria agents. He said he had a Topolino (baby Fiat) parked by the other *portone* in which it would be safe to travel.

I still wasn't sure it might not be a trap, but I bid Virginia, Serafino and the benny—who had suddenly appeared from nowhere—a quick goodbye. Crouched in the back of the diminutive vehicle I hid my head so as to get away from the immediate neighborhood of the palazzo without being recognized and thus endanger Virginia and Serafino.

Once we had reached the Lungotevere by the Ponte Vittorio I sat up and took notice. Driving through the streets of Rome at midday was even stranger than walking through them in the early morning; it was odd to see the Black Shirts strutting about, to look into the faces of all kinds of Germans in assorted vehicles.

The sun had come out in the sharp brilliance of a Roman January;

short gusts of wind made the coats of pedestrians cling to their bodies.

The small man informed me his code name was "Topolino" (also Italian for Mickey Mouse); that he was the man with the requisite papers to drive to the landing area, but had not done so because he had not been warned of my arrival, and because they had been tipped off the Germans were going to set up a command post in the bailiff's house.

I wondered, as we turned away from the Tiber toward Valle Giulia, whether he had been given the code name Topolino because of his car or his diminutive size; in either case it was well chosen, and I was reassured from his knowledge of code names, and the landing area, that he must, in fact, be in league with our agents.

The house he was taking me to was in a brand-new part of Parioli most of which had not existed when I had last been there three years earlier—a large modern block of apartments on the extremity of Rome overlooking the Littorio Airfield and a large loop of the slowly moving Tiber.

In the living room, where a fire was lit to take the chill from the northern exposure, I was introduced to Topolino's wife, his mother, and his young son; then a glass of orange brandy was put into my hand to take the chill from within me. By now my nerves had been taxed to the point where even a sip of alcohol made me wish to curl up and sleep, but I nodded noncommittally as Topolino rattled off a confusing variety of names and pseudonyms till lunch, during which, thanks to the presence of his young boy, conversation was suitably vague and of little consequence.

After "coffee," and a series of double-talk phone calls, Topolino disappeared to fetch the other agents, leaving me to fall asleep in an armchair in the sitting room, only to wake up face to face with a police officer in full uniform, highly polished boots, arm band and revolver.

"Don't jump!" Topolino's wife was quick to reassure me. "It's one of our friends."

As soon as I had introduced myself as the American major from the OSS, the policeman began asking a series of detailed questions, and I realized he was cross-examining me to ascertain my authenticity.

Then, one by one, more men came in, forming an odd and none too reassuring group. Finally an aristocratic young man in a well cut overcoat and an expensive pair of doeskin gloves appeared in the doorway and his debonair smile was reassuring. After a good deal of conversation I managed to get the names or pseudonyms of the four main characters straightened out. The police officer, once I was capable of looking beyond his uniform, I saw to be a pale but sturdy young man in his twenties, called Maurizio Giglio, with the code name of "Cervo" or stag; it was he, I gathered, who had brought the Vittoria radio up from Naples and now took care of moving it about. The young man with the aristocratic manners was Franco Malfatti; he had no OSS code name but appeared to be the gatherer of intelligence for the radio. The man technically in charge of the team I gathered to be the one code-named "Coniglio" or rabbit, a small man with dark piercing eyes more like a ferret's than a rabbit's. Last of the group was a man called Gambareri, a jovial fellow with a paunch who looked quite inoffensive but turned out to be the front man for the Parodi-Delfino industrial combine with a *Cagoulard*-type mind.

Of the lot, the only one I trusted immediately was Franco, and possibly Cervo, the policeman, for he sided openly with Franco.

Despite my misgivings it was time to get down to business; so I informed them there was to be an Allied landing somewhere along the coast, but that for security reasons I could not tell them the exact time or location other than that we would have to act quickly if we were to be of serious assistance to the landing, either through paramilitary operations, sabotage, the saving of installations mined by the Germans, or the gathering of intelligence.

As I questioned them about what was available in the way of personnel, arms and communications in the various underground organizations, and how these were made up, I realized there was some confusion and considerable disagreement between them.

When I insisted that if there was to be any action or coordinated plan in time to be effective, I must know what was really available, Coniglio at last agreed to arrange a meeting for me the following morning with the various military heads of the underground movements in order to coordinate all possible partisan activities.

Here at last was the chance to use several thousand armed men, to attempt seriously to disorganize the German rear in conjunction with the Allied advance. Properly organized, and with good communications, this might be the biggest opportunity in the theater since the one we had muffed at the time of the September 8 armistice by not landing the 82nd Airborne Division round Rome. It would have so bolstered the five Italian divisions which were ready to fight the Germans, that together they could have threatened the German forces in Italy enough to change the entire tactical and strategic picture, avoiding the near disasters of Salerno and the Rapido.

Since that wasted opportunity in 1943 the Italian armed forces had crumbled into civilian life or into the ranks of Mussolini's neo-Fascist army under General Graziani, and little or nothing had been done in the way of serious partisan activities or sabotage behind the German lines.

Having agreed to the essential meeting for the next day I could see from the fading light that my first day in Rome was coming to an end. Topolino offered to put me up, saying he had a room and a pair of pajamas that might fit, but Cervo, the young policeman, interrupted with the suggestion that it would be safer for all concerned if I stayed at his apartment. "Who," he asked with a smile, "would expect to find an American OSS agent in a Fascist policeman's bed!"

I was doubtful about making another move, especially as there were only a few minutes before the six o'clock curfew—when all but Germans and authorized personnel had to be off the blacked-out streets of Rome—and I knew that my papers were inadequate for crashing such a curfew. But I sensed a sort of undercurrent struggle between the agents, and Cervo finally convinced me by saying it would save me an extra trip the following morning when I was to ride to the meeting with the resistance leaders on the back of his policeman's motorcycle.

Leaving Topolino's house we got into another small Fiat (occasionally assigned to Cervo by his police squadron) and headed toward his house across the river in a rather unpleasant part of Rome known as Prati, built up in the worst type of Italian Edwardian architecture on what had once been a bog.

As we drove through the early shadows of evening I wondered if the Allies would really land that night, if Operation Shingle were really under way. It would be a little odd, if not embarrassing, if they did not arrive; and I was glad no one knew the exact D-Day or H-Hour. I almost wished I did not know it myself, for it was no easy burden to carry around the knowledge that even at this late date were I caught infringing the curfew and were tortured by the Germans I might be responsible for the security of thousands of my fellow countrymen as well as the element of surprise in a whole amphibious landing. Could I stand up under torture, or the administration of "truth drugs," or whatever horrors the Sicherheitsdienst had in store for me? Then, for an even more horrid moment, I wondered if the whole venture might not have been a Machiavellian device to send me in, clearly an agent, to be caught, and reveal under torture the date and place of landing— while Shingle, in fact, was destined elsewhere. Or was it another and more colossal of the practical jokes we so often had recourse to in the OSS in an effort to laugh off the endless tragedies, misfortunes and bunglings to which the work continuously subjected us? Had they sent me on a snipe hunt? Were they now sitting round the mess drinking Aurum and Strega and laughing themselves into stitches? Of course not. I had planned the mission myself, and I must either trust the general, or be mad.

Cervo's apartment was at the top of a newish building in the heart of Prati, and his mother, who met us in the hall, gave me a shock when I heard her greet me with a slight German accent. But Cervo's sister, who was in her late teens, was thoroughly Italian, and in any case their welcome was effusive.

A little later Franco Malfatti turned up and joined us at the dining-room table where we sat separated from the rest of the apartment by the usual opaque glazed doors, waiting for the women to fix dinner.

I was anxious to discover from Franco and Cervo not only about themselves and the other agents but about the resistance in general.

Franco said that underground life in Rome had got considerably tougher since the Allies had been held up at Cassino, that the Fascists, with the help of the Germans, were making life extremely uncomfortable.

Dinner, though not up to the standards of Parioli, was none the less welcome, and the good dry wine did much to restore me, both physically and spiritually, and though the atmosphere and furnishings of Prati were what I most despised, I felt more at home there than in the Parioli atmosphere where I had spent the day.

Throughout dinner Franco told amusing anecdotes of underground existence during the last few weeks: of how on Via del Tritone, when an ambulance had been run into by a taxicab, six patients had poured from behind the insignia of mercy to disappear into the crowd before the police could arrive to investigate; of how in Trastevere someone had noticed two monks in animated conversation by a bridge—one of them standing firmly at attention; of how a poor partisan had been arrested in his home for mentioning nineteen pairs of shoes on the telephone (a euphemism for guns) and thus precipitated the police (who regularly wire-tapped from a special center in the Ministry of the Interior) to find out how in hell anyone could own nineteen pairs of shoes in wartime Rome when one could hardly buy a single pair with coupons!

There was something very charming and sympathetic about Franco, and I began to feel, for the first time, that we might get some useful work done, that I had been wise—if only to benefit from his sense of humor—to let myself be shanghaied to this new hideout.

At which point there occurred one of those coincidences which led the original wag to say the world appears so small *parce que ce sont toujours les mêmes types qui s'y balladent!*

As Franco dialed a number on the phone I unconsciously applied the OSS technique of listening for the clicks—only to hear my own number being dialed, the number of the house where I had last lived in Rome. When I could nor forbear an exclamation, Franco explained that the house was now inhabited by his uncle, Counselor of the Knights of Malta to the Holy See. And at that we had a good rich laugh.

While I was being settled into Cervo's sister's small but immaculate bedroom, Franco and Cervo came in to discuss further possibilities for plans and operations. Quite naturally they were as interested in evaluating me as I was in evaluating them; so I filled them in, as best I could, on my own background, yet all the time probing into theirs to form a picture of their capabilities, contacts, experience and basic aims.

To my delight, they gave concrete answers to my detailed questions, and the conversation lasted almost till midnight, further reviving my spirits despite my physical exhaustion.

Being partial to clandestine operators motivated by ideals rather than by the crass prospect of material profit, and preferably by such ideals as might be grouped under the general labels of "individual free-dom" and "political democracy," I was delighted by the sketch of Franco's background as it now took shape—though no doubt my su-periors in the OSS, unacquainted with European resistance, would have considered him a dangerously radical young man.

Brought up partly in Austria and partly in France, where his father had sought refuge as a political exile from Mussolini's *squadristi,* Franco had reacted to Fascism by joining Leon Blum's Socialist party in France, and, at eighteen, worked for the Loyalist cause in Spain. From then on he had been active one way or another in partisan and clandestine anti-Fascist organizations. On a trip to Italy just before the war he had been picked up by the border police, who, in their oc-casional comic-opera style, seeing he was Italian-born, forced him—without much probing into his political past—into military service. After short periods in the French and Albanian campaigns, he had been assigned to the Italian Armistice Commission in France where he had become attached to the Italian Embassy in Paris and had begun to help the French underground against the Nazis.

Back in Italy at the time of Victor Emmanuel's coup in July of 1943, when Mussolini was deposed, Franco had become an intelligence of-ficer on Badoglio's staff in Rome while taking an active part in the clandestine reconstruction of the Italian Socialist Party, whose leaders were then Pietro Nenni and Bruno Buozzi.

When the king, as Commander-in-Chief, and Badoglio, as Minister of War, fled to Southern Italy, leaving Italy's entire land and air forces without orders, to be disbanded by a handful of Germans, Franco, like many another Italian patriot, took part in the popular and heroic in-surrection against the Germans, known as the "Eighth of September" (for which, many years later, he was given a high Italian decoration by that "radical" Prime Minister Alcide de Gasperi). When this in-surrection was in turn betrayed to the Germans by a member of the royal household, Franco shifted to the clandestine organization of a Socialist military underground.

It was then that he came into contact with Cervo, whom he had known on the Italian Armistice Commission in Turin. Learning that Cervo had a secret radio in contact with the Allies, he provided him with whatever intelligence he could collect against the Germans.

Cervo had quite a different background. His father, a career policeman, had risen to the rank of regional inspector in the Fascist Secret Police, or OVRA, but was apparently one of those policemen peculiar to Italian Fascism who considered humanitarian methods best designed for the suppression of seditious anti-Fascism.

Cervo was thus brought up as an ardent young Fascist of the idealist type. Indoctrinated with "popular culture," never having been abroad, and knowing of no alternative, he had believed Fascism to be the only salvation for the country—that is, until he was assigned as a lieutenant to command a company of infantry on the Albanian front, where he was rapidly disillusioned by the extent of the graft and incompetence displayed by Mussolini and his Fascist hierarchy. Returning to Italy badly wounded, and seriously demoralized, he became aware that his father too was beginning to be disappointed, not so much with the Fascist ideal as with the individuals who represented it. The crowning blow to Cervo's crumbling ideals came with the example of the king's defection in the face of danger. Like many another young Italian in his position, in order to regain some sort of respect not only for his country but also for himself, Cervo felt compelled to expiate the evils of monarcho-Fascism by volunteering for the most dangerous assignment he could possibly find on the side of the Allies.

Unfortunately, as there was no organization in Allied-occupied Italy to make use of such Italians who wanted to fight in the front lines, other than the discredited forces scraped together by Badoglio for the king, Cervo was obliged to gravitate to the OSS in Naples, where he had been recruited by none other than Captain A. to form a team with Coniglio and return to Rome to set up radio Vittoria. Having successfully crossed the lines on foot with the small OSS radio concealed in a suitcase and laboriously made his way back to Rome, Cervo had managed, through his father, who was temporarily in Rome from his regular post in Bologna, and who knew nothing of the radio, to obtain a position as lieutenant in the Roman squadron of mounted police of which his father had once been instructor. Searching for reliable sources of information and colleagues with whom to collaborate among the clandestine political organizations in Rome, Cervo had been struck by the efficiency and integrity of Franco, and from him he had then obtained the bulk of the information filed over radio Vittoria up till that time.

It was now almost midnight, but I felt that I would be able to count on some experienced and enthusiastic support during the next few days when there would be plenty of work to be done. To operate clandestinely one must be able to put one's trust in someone, then add further secure elements to that group, in a sort of chain, every link of which must be as thoroughly secure as possible. Suspicion, however slight, cannot be tolerated for effective work. And in the long run, in espionage and partisan operations, there is no more effective criterion for judging the work and reliability of an agent or fellow conspirator than one's own instinct.

That I had succeeded in obtaining their confidence as well as in establishing my identity and authority was evidenced by Cervo's next remarks. From the very beginning radio Vittoria had been his exclusive responsibility, no one knew of its location or the manner in which the messages were brought to and from it other than the two radio operators. In the morning, after my meeting with the resistance leaders, Cervo would take me to it, and thenceforward it would be entirely at my disposal.

This settled, they bid me good night. Almost unbelievably worn out, but considerably heartened, I fell into uneasy sleep, wondering what the morning would bring and if the landings would actually take place.

What I did not know was that at that very moment, concealed beneath a blanket of moonless night, an Allied assault convoy of almost 50,000 men and over 5,000 vehicles had dropped anchor off Anzio. Two hours later, at 0200 of January 22, 1944, the first of the assault craft landed on the beaches and the troops swarmed ashore to find, in the words of the official Fifth Army history:

To their astonishment there was no enemy to greet them. The highly unexpected had happened. We had caught the enemy completely by surprise. Except for a few small coast artillery and anti-aircraft detachments, the only resistance to our push inland from the beaches was from elements of two depleted coast watching battalions.

4 ORGANIZING THE RESISTANCE

IT WAS A GRAY MORNING some six hours later when I was awakened by Cervo's sister with a tray of tea and hot milk. As I shaved and dressed I had no idea whether the Allied landings had in fact taken place; there was no mention of it on the radio, no rumble of artillery, no visible sign as I looked out over the roofs of Rome toward the Alban Hills in the distant grayness.

Our appointment with the military leaders of the resistance was scheduled for nine o'clock in the old part of Rome, not far from the Campidoglio. To reach the meeting place we were to travel on Cervo's motorcycle; but one look at my homemade identity papers convinced both Franco and Cervo that new ones would have to be rapidly procured through underground channels. As an immediate cover it was decided I carry the red-and-yellow arm band of an auxiliary policeman in my pocket and pretend to be just that. To fit into this distasteful role I donned an old gray overcoat of Cervo's, pulled a battered Borsalino hat over my eyes, climbed onto the back of his motorcycle, and—with as surly an expression as I could force—set off across Rome in the pale morning light.

Gripping the rough material of Cervo's military coat, my preoccupation with the politico-military problems that faced me was overcome by the effort to keep my physical and psychic balance in such a starkly unfamiliar position.

For some reason, which he neglected to tell me, Cervo insisted on roaring up the center of the Corso, Rome's crowded and popular shopping center. Naturally my heart was in my mouth, though it amused me to think that the people we passed had no idea an American agent—however frightened—was riding up the main avenue of their capital.

"If anyone stops you," Cervo whispered in my ear, "just say, 'Police!'"

Through my chattering teeth I mumbled "*Sicuro!*" though the only element of security I could feel was the weight of the Beretta automatic in my pocket.

At the end of the Corso we turned into Piazza Venezia and it struck me, as I saw the famous balcony, that for the first time in a generation the great room behind it was no longer the office of the dictator of Italy. Skirting the Palazzo Doria I glanced up at the hospitable windows of Monsignor Hemmick's apartment from which almost four years earlier I had watched a black-gloved Mussolini declare war against Britain and France.

On Via d'Ara Coeli, a narrow street that climbs toward the Capitoline Hill—just then resplendent in a passing ray of sunshine—Cervo pulled up and I saw that we had reached our destination, a small gray house, Number 9. Following Cervo up the dark, dusty stairs, I was ushered into a fourth-floor apartment, unfurnished, even dustier, and quite unheated, where several men stood around in overcoats. No names were exchanged, just a series of formal handshakes, and I realized my position was to be a tricky one, to be handled with what diplomacy I could muster. By the wildest of chances these men might be a collection of phonies waiting to hear what jewels of military information I could bring them before turning me over—along with the information—to the Germans. But this I discounted, again mostly on instinct; yet I felt there was something curious about these men that was far from reassuring.

From the early days of North Africa, Sicily and Southern Italy, I had been meeting clandestinely with Italian partisan leaders of all sorts and denominations, often in disguise, sometimes in situations of considerable risk, and I had become sensitive to the tense, almost psychic conditions of the atmosphere at such meetings, that certain look of power behind the crystal of an unflinching eye, the quick smile and solid handshake of a fellow conspirator, even a well-turned phrase about the condition of the weather or the front. But there was none of this, and it disturbed me.

The purpose of the meeting was for me to inform the underground, as I had already informed our agents, of the imminent Allied landings, explain that their cooperation in hindering the enemy and collecting intelligence was requested by the Allied command. There was, of course, no intimation as yet, other than my presence, of the actual landings; so I wished to be circumspect about giving the actual time and target.

Ad-libbing as best I could, I pointed out the prime requirements in order of priority, paramount among which I stressed channels of communication, that we be in constant contact telephonically (through conventional phrases), and, when the phones were cut, through a service of couriers; a headquarters would be needed for coordinated action, so that, at the proper moment, our operations be in strict conjunction with the Allied forces. Our objective, as I propounded it, was dual: to disrupt German communications and avenues of retreat as much as possible, yet prevent the destruction of bridges, utilities, etc., by the retreating Germans.

It amused me to think that I, a civilian *au fond,* was planning operations and giving instructions like a general; at the same time I realized there was nothing so very mysterious about the art of warfare, that one need but be faced with an actual problem (rather than a textbook one) to see what the solution is likely to be.

However, as I discoursed on the details of mines, roadblocks, and paramilitary operations in general, I began to notice that my remarks appeared to be having very little effect on the group. Could it be, I wondered, that their knowledge of clandestine operations and underground warfare was so superior to mine that they were scornful of my suggestions and queries? Or was it that they simply did not understand what I was talking about. Having no way of knowing, at that time, and no one to turn to for advice, I decided to finish outlining my plans, though in more general terms, and make arrangements for a second meeting after I had done some checking on the underground in general and these characters in particular.

As the meeting broke up, one of the younger members, who had refrained from expressing any opinion, approached and suggested another meeting as soon as possible, that he had been sent to me specially by Franco.

Coming out of the doorway I caught a glimpse of the benny lurking at the end of the street. Wanting him to know as little of the others as they of him, in case anything went wrong and I had to fall back on him in an emergency, I told him to get a room in an inconspicuous hotel where I could contact him independently.

Once more on the back of Cervo's motorcycle we drove off toward Piazza Venezia: straight into a police block. Down the Corso, led by the usually ominous German motorcyclists, came a line of rushing

German trucks bristling with paratroopers armed to the teeth. Unfortunately I was still too new to my role, and too terrified by the sight of these martial creatures to take the elementary step of noting their insignia and totting up their number as they sped away toward Via del Mare: that they were Germany's crack paratroopers was self-evident and disquieting enough.

Clearly the landings had taken place. But we could not linger to investigate; my first prerequisite for action was a passable identity card, for which a photograph was needed.

Sidling down the Corso, we turned into a side street not far from the Foreign Press Club; this proximity to my old haunts had me terrified lest one of my former colleagues on his way to work, say a neutral Swede, or the Swiss resident, pass by and recognize me. But the ordeal was unavoidable as that was where the "safe" photographer had his studio.

I hate being photographed, especially under strong lights and in front of a monstrously antiquated camera, and was happy to be back on Cervo's motorcycle, speeding, I hoped, toward Cervo's home.

But I was obliged to agree—though I had had my fill of seeing Rome for one day—that before going home for lunch I should make contact with the radio operator to establish my presence, my authority, and be familiar with this, our essential channel of communication.

Parking the motorcycle almost opposite the Hotel Plaza we noticed an excited *va-et-vient* of Germans apparently in the process of packing and leaving. Across the street in a horrid Fascist building we climbed by elevator to the top floor, where, in a frigidly modern apartment, the radio operator had installed his radio, its antenna guarded by a parapet outside the window. He had, as we entered, just finished decoding a message from the base in which there was nothing to indicate the landings had occurred and to which I scribbled an answer saying I had arrived, had made preliminary contacts, and awaited orders.

But I was not much taken with the radio operator. Having painfully recruited a number of these extremely hard-to-come-by but key elements of an espionage operation, I had come to the conclusion that there must be only two sorts of Italian "Sparks"; very very nice ones, and very not nice ones.

This one, recruited by Captain A., set up that immediate quiver in my nervous system by which I was wont to make preliminary estimates of people.

Having made a cursory inspection of his equipment and layout I informed the operator that from then on, except in cases of emergency, all incoming and outgoing messages would be routed through me, and that, for security, he would always be able to recognize my messages by a particular coded device.

Back on the street we discovered the rumor was indeed a popular one that there had been an Allied landing on the coast, early that morning, somewhere south of Rome.

It was time for action, but what action? The base had given no intimation. The meeting with the partisans had proven thoroughly unprofitable. Where were the real men of action in the city?

Back at Cervo's house, where Franco joined us, I told them the landing had been scheduled for the night before in the Anzio-Nettuno area. Then the doorbell rang, and the young man who had been at the morning meeting arrived and was introduced as Giuliano (Vassalli), a member of the Socialist underground, saying he had a message for me from the military leaders of the Committee of National Liberation. The morning's meeting, it developed, had been but a cabal of Coniglio's cronies organized to claim that they, and they alone, had aided the Allies at the liberation of Rome. The reason for their silent reception of my paramilitary suggestions was now apparent: they had no following, nor organized supporters, and no greater interest in the defeat of the Germans and the advancement of the Allied cause than their private interests, both political and financial.

The real resistance leaders of the Committee of National Liberation, informed of the arrival of an American agent, now wanted to arrange a meeting with me so as to receive directives from the Allied command in order to coordinate the efforts of all the various resistance groups with Allied operations.

This was indeed a relief, but how could I best discover of what these groups consisted? So far as I had been able to learn during the months since we had first landed in southern Italy, no one (either in or out of the OSS) had any concrete facts and figures on the organized strength of the partisan forces in and around Rome, let alone what their popular following might be. I had been painstakingly (and often clandestinely) putting together a picture of the Italian political scene on both sides of the lines ever since we had landed in North Africa—not because I intended to use what I learned as political intelligence (a game for which I had no stomach after Darlan *and* Badoglio)—but because I maintained that it was only through the underground political movements that we would ever be able to obtain widespread military intelligence and the most effective paramilitary activities.

During the months since Salerno, Italian politicos in Allied-occupied Italy had become divided into two fundamentally different groups: the monarchist-military supporters of the king and Badoglio on one side; and the supporters of the half-dozen anti-Fascist parties grouped into the Committee of National Liberation on the other. With both these groups and their principal exponents I had become intimately acquainted. For months my headquarters in Naples had been a meeting place where the leaders of the CNL could thrash out the new political configuration of Italy; in one of my guest rooms Badoglio had eventually met Benedetto Croce and Carlo Sforza in an attempt to solve the thorny riddle of Victor Emmanuel's abdication. Through Dino Phillipson, Badoglio's under secretary for Foreign Affairs (there were no ministers) and general trouble-shooter with the Allies, whom I had known before the war, and who assiduously frequented the OSS Caserta to influence its commanding officer in favor of the king and Badoglio, I had kept informed of that side of the picture, as well as through some peculiar private sources of my own.

Before leaving Naples I had taken the precaution of secretly obtaining introductions from the leaders of the various parties in the south to their clandestine organizations in Rome so as to have access to them directly if I should need to. Now this seemed unnecessary. Giuliano Vassalli, it developed, had for months been in close contact with the Roman Committee of National Liberation, while Cervo had been in contact with the supporters of the king and Badoglio. From the lot of them I was able to obtain a clearer picture: the situation was basically the same as in the south, but with a different balance of the opposing forces.

On September 9, 1943, the day after the king and his top ministers had fled, leaving the country without a government or military command, it had become clear to the survivors in Rome that resistance to the Nazi-Fascists would have to be organized clandestinely along the lines of the French Maquis. That very day representatives of the six leading anti-Fascist parties—De Gasperi for the Christian Democrats, Casati for the Liberals, Ruini for the Labor Democrats, La Malfa for the Party of Action, Nenni for the Socialists, and Scoccimarro for the Communists—had invited the anti-Fascist and pre-Fascist Prime Minister Ivanoe Bonomi to place himself above party differences and assume the presidency of the CNL. Broadly, the goals of this organization were to serve as a framework around which resistance to the Nazi-Fascist could be organized throughout Italy, eventually to demonstrate that the CNL effectively represented the democratic, anti-Fascist forces in Italy sufficiently to provide the basis for a provisional government by the time Rome was liberated and until a Constituent Assembly could be called.

Though the various parties of the CNL differed among each other on political matters, both in terms of the immediate struggle, and the future political complexion of Italy, they were thoroughly united on one basic point: *uncompromising* resistance to the Germans and the Fascists. Though they agreed to disagree about the issue of the monarchy in general, they all agreed that the king himself, being specifically responsible for Fascism in Italy, and having acted in a manner unbefitting a sovereign and Commander-in-Chief by abandoning his post in face of the enemy, must, sooner or later, abdicate.

However, at the time when the king and Badoglio had scurried southwards they had left in Rome a General Staff officer with the mellifluous name of Colonel Giuseppe Cordero Lanza di Montezemolo to undertake the arduous task of creating a clandestine organization which would be personally loyal to them. Round this really intrepid soldier an organization had grown up known as the "Clandestine Military Front," recruited largely from disbanded members of the armed forces. For the last two months this organziation had been in contact with Badoglio in Brindisi by means of a clandestine transmitter, and its policies naturally reflected those of Badoglio in the south, being as much oriented against the democratic anti-Fascist forces in Italy as against the Nazi-Fascists, determined to defend the king to the bitter end and by any means available. The reason for this intransigence, apart from any question of principle or ideal, was clear enough: as members of the propertied classes, or the bureaucracy of the armed forces, more or less compromised by twenty years of Fascism, the king (being in the same boat) constituted the only obvious guarantee of any economic future (now that the structure of the Fascist state had collapsed) as well as the only bulwark they could see against social and political evolution, let alone revolution.

Of the six parties of the CNL in Rome the three best organized were clearly the Communists, the Socialists and the Party of Action, all of whom could rely on a system of disciplined and more or less well-armed members plus a considerable number of sympathizers and supporters. Though generically misclassed as the forces of the "left," I had long known these three parties, in effect, to be far from homogeneous. The Party of Action, largely supported by intellectuals and university students, was as radically anti-Communist as it was anti-monarchist and anticlerical, though willing to fight side by side with Communist, monarchist or cleric till the liberation; the Socialists, a proletarian movement guided by intellectuals, no matter how apparently fellow-traveling, was basically anti-Stalinist and democratic, unwilling to become extremist unless mortally threatened by extremists of the right as they had been by Mussolini's squads of goons in the 1920s, and as now appeared likely (especially since Darlan) by a right-wing regime arbitrarily and undemocratically forced on them by the armies of the Allies; the Communists, though technically the left wing of the CNL, were inclined to operate exclusively according to their own devious ideas of self or party interest—as was shortly to be proven when, with the arrival of Togliatti in Allied-occupied Italy, they formed a close alliance with Badoglio's ex-Fascist monarchists!

Of the other three parties of the CNL, the Christian Democrats were the most numerous but least well armed or organized for action; they counted as a powerful political force largely by virtue of the support of the Vatican and the number of Catholic Actionists in Italy. The two other parties, the Liberals and the Labor Democrats who formed the right wing of the CNL, were almost insignificant in numbers. What political influence the Liberals had was derived from the historic concept of liberalism in Italy along with the moral support of individual intellectuals (such as Benedetto Croce) and the financial support of individual bankers and industrialists. The Labor Democrats, having nothing to do with labor and little or nothing to do with democracy, had a party with virtually no followers, serving largely as a cover for the political aspirations of a few *démodé* individuals, and as a medium for the undefinable and often changing politics of such independent figures as Orlando and Bencivenga.

As for the forces of Badoglio, their main support came from royalist organizations such as the Carabinieri, which had been disbanded by the Germans, from the ranks of the Grenadiers, and the navy, and such normally monarchist elements of the former armed forces. Elements of the regular police forces, of which there were half a dozen different types in Italy, though employed at the time by the neo-Fascists and Germans, and thus actively disliked by the populace, seemed inclined to be ready to switch their allegiance to Badoglio or anyone who could guarantee them any sort of future.

When I asked if there were now any agreement between these politically rival forces in Rome either as to a common commander or joint operations with the Allies, I was informed that there was not. About a week earlier Montezemolo had had his most recent meeting with Bonomi to inform the latter that a message had arrived by secret radio from Badoglio appointing a General Armellini, then hiding in Rome, chief of *all* the clandestine forces in Rome, and ordering Bonomi to inform the six parties of the CNL not to indulge in any political or partisan activities until the Allies *had* entered Rome. In answer to this, Bonomi, quite naturally, had pointed out that the six parties would under no condition accept such an order from Badoglio, partly because they had received no such word from the Allies, and more especially because they distrusted Armellini as having recently been appointed by Badoglio head of the Black Shirt Militia during the forty-five days after the fall of Mussolini when neither the king nor Badoglio would have anything to do with the various leaders of the democratic, anti-Fascist parties. As an alternative Bonomi had suggested that General Bencivenga, an anti-Fascist of long standing, be placed in charge of the municipality of Rome at the moment of liberation while Armellini could command the forces to maintain public order. This solution Armellini had refused on the grounds that it subordinated him politically to the CNL.

As for the CNL, it had held its most recent plenary meeting three days earlier, on January 18, in an apartment in the heart of Rome not far from Piazza di Spagna, represented by De Gasperi, Ruini, Casati, Nenni, La Malfa and Amendola, under the presidency of Bonomi, with Sergio Fenoaltea acting as secretary. The suggestion that General Bencivenga be in charge of the municipality of Rome was unanimously accepted, but there was a heated discussion about his relation to General Armellini designated by Badoglio as military authority. After three hours it was agreed that the two different organizations would have to remain independent, but "cooperate" where possible.

Thus, with the Allies thirty miles from Rome, two opposing forces stood ready, in clandestinely armed camps, to take advantage of the departure of the Germans to install the provisional authority most compatible with their own interests, and the possibility of the political struggle's developing into an armed conflict between them was very real.

What position should I take?

My own personal sympathies—which in the past had caused me many anxious and unpleasant moments—were with the democratic center-left on the Committee of National Liberation. I recognized, however, the inescapable fact that since North Africa, Allied policy was dictated by a high-level preference for monarcho-Fascist elements. That the formulators of such a policy could get away with it in the politically anachronistic atmosphere of southern Italy had been demonstrated by circumstances, but that they would not succeed after Rome, was, or should have been, clear to anyone purporting to be acquainted with the situation.

To guide me in my predicament in Rome, however, I had a clear mandate from the only person I could reasonably and happily consider my direct superior in the theater. At our early morning conversation on the Naples airstrip General Donovan had told me that on no account did the Allies want an armed insurrection in Rome between elements of the right and the left in the resistance movement. However, as things stood, now that I was in Rome, if the left-wing organizations had decided to engage in open conflict with the right, or, as was much more likely, the right goaded them into it by attempting an armed coup, there was nothing one lone American agent, or anyone else for

63

that matter, could do to stop them—unless it was to succeed in channeling their various efforts as much as possible against the Germans. And this, to the best of my ability, I now intended to attempt.

But the more I studied the problem the more I realized what a terrible decision would have to be made: if the resistance forces were to come out too soon, or piecemeal, they risked being isolated and wiped out, piecemeal, by the German's superior firepower; if they came out too late they would serve no purpose. And I realized also to what Machiavellian purposes this decision could be put if one side were to expose the other, and then refuse to aid it! What was clearly needed at the crucial moment was a catalyzing agent, something to cause an instantaneous flare-up throughout the city, so that each man, instead of having to rely on faulty communications, or having to choose his own moment in cold blood, wondering if the moment were really ripe, could know, instantly, that he must act, and act *now*, or risk not being able to say he had played a part.

And the only catalyst I could think of that would guarantee the mobilization of every last man as well as insure that partisan efforts were directed primarily against the Germans, would be the landing of an Allied detachment of parachutists within the city, equipped if possible by an airdrop of antitank weapons.

That such a drop should be within the city appeared to me to be essential not only for tactical reasons (we could indicate and defend a landing area, have communications, couriers, scouts and interpreters already in action, be in constant contact with the OSS by radio, and, in case of any setback, disappear into the warren of underground Rome) but also for psychological reasons—to raise and cement the morale of the partisans; to depress and disintegrate German morale by the announcement of the fall of Rome!

The most dangerous aspect of the operation appeared to be the daylight exposure of troop-carrying planes to German-manned ack-ack batteries round Rome and between Rome and the sea. But these were fewer than expected, easily spotted, and vulnerable to partisan attack.

So, when Giuliano Vassalli had left to organize a meeting with the real military leaders of the resistance, Cervo, Franco and I began to study the means of putting the air drop into operation. The best

64

location, most easily identifiable, most easy to land on and defend, and one which could be garrisoned in advance without arousing the suspicion of the Germans, was the large open space in the Villa Borghese, Rome's public park, at the head of Via Veneto, within the perimeter of the large oval bridle path, for it was in this area that Cervo's mounted police squadron regularly patrolled and drilled, and its four hundred men could make the nucleus around which the remaining partisan forces could quickly collect.

Next we must establish exactly where the German forces within the city and its periphery were located. To answer this, Cervo brought in a remarkable piece of intelligence. In their thoroughgoing police methods, the Questura of Rome had drawn up a detailed report, by police district, of every hotel, pension or building occupied or used by the German forces in Rome, down to, and including, headquarters, command posts, car parks, food depots, hospitals and psychiatric wards, dated January 19, 1944! Knowing their thoroughness in petty police measures, we could be sure it was eminently reliable.

A close study of the report indicated there could be no more than 1500 Germans in the city at the *utmost*: furthermore, knowing where they were and in what numbers, it would be easier to strike or avoid them at choice.

Clearly the number of Germans in Rome was no great problem. What would be most needed was antitank equipment lest the Germans bring down armored units from the north or try to retreat through the city from the south.

Having made the necessary arrangements with Cervo's squadron to install machine-gun emplacements round its stables in the park, which could then be used as our first command post, I felt sure enough of our position to send off a message to the base outlining the plan and requesting the drop.

If all went well we might play a serious part, not only in the liberation of the first Axis capital, but in upsetting the entire German defense in southern Italy.

5 WE PLAN TO TAKE ROME

PREPARATIONS FOR MY MEETING with the representatives of the CNL were suitably melodramatic. Partisans were posted for blocks round Cervo's house with submachine guns, hand grenades and automatics wrapped in newspaper to look like parcels.

To have seen the actual political leaders such as Bonomi, De Gasperi, Nenni, would have been pointless, both for their sakes and for mine; and in any case I preferred that my identity, other than that of an American "major" from the OSS, Fifth Army, be known to as few people as possible.

To handle military and paramilitary rather than political underground operations the CNL had created a military junta, and it was naturally with the members of this junta, headed by Riccardo Bauer of the Party of Action, that I was to meet.

Those who were to attend the meeting appeared at intervals, unarmed, and with no incriminating documents, but followed at a safe distance by heavily armed bodyguards. As I watched these operations from behind the curtain of the window of my room I knew that I was dealing with reasonably serious organizations.

During the meeting, which lasted close to two hours, as we sat round the dining-room table smoking cheap Italian cigarettes, they informed me of what had already been planned and what they knew of the plans of the Badoglio forces with whom they had now come to certain agreements about safeguarding essential buildings and utilities such as water, gas, light, telephone and radio. I was much interested in safeguarding the Rome radio station and its transmitters, not only because of its material value to the Allies but also because of its psychological value at the moment of the airborne landing for broadcasting bulletins to electrify the people of Rome, and, hopefully, shake the Germans all the way down to Cassino.

One of the next major problems in Rome was the bridges over the Tiber, which were heavily mined and under constant guard; if they were successfully destroyed by the retreating Germans it would not only impede Allied communications but make a horrible mess of Rome.

66

Our problem was to work out the best strategy so as not to act too soon, giving the Germans time to reset the mines, or, needless to say, too late; also, we had to be sure there was no duplication or conflict in the assignments given to partisan groups.

As the spotting of German-laid mines wherever they might be was one of the jobs best suited to the partisans, especially those with widely spread contacts, I requested that every stray report of a mine, however insignificant, be noted, relayed, and, when possible, checked on, so that a comprehensive picture of the situation could be plotted centrally, and action or counteraction be coordinated between the various clandestine groups. There was no way of knowing to what extent the Germans planned to mine Rome and its environs, but in Naples they had not only destroyed the port and most of the utilities, but also hundreds of buildings, many of which continued to blow up long after the Allies had occupied the city, causing considerable damage and casualties as well as an effective psychological depression. I had been obliged to witness this vandalism in impotent despair through a high-powered telescope from the ruins of Tiberius' villa high over Capri, as explosion followed explosion and endless spiraling columns of smoke rose above the devastated city. This time if we acted with acumen and foresight we might impede or considerably dampen their efforts, avoiding the fate of Naples.

When I asked the members of the junta what sort of stocks of dynamite or plastic explosives they had with which to interrupt German communications and road traffic before, during and after the German retreat, and what volunteers there were for such hazardous jobs, they told me they had a surplus of volunteers but a scarcity of detonators. Furthermore, without antitank weapons it would be impossible for the partisans to barricade a road for any length of time against German armored vehicles. Another point in favor of an air drop in Rome of antitank weapons!

I did not want, however, to inform them of any planned parachute drop until I had heard from the base; but I did assure them I would immediately request a drop of detonators and fuse cord.

Another sensitive German spot which was highly adapted to partisan attacks with no greater weapon than a few tossed hand grenades and one which could cause the enemy serious confusion was an attack on his signal corps system of radio and phone communications. So it was agreed to locate and note all possible German signal corps units and, at the psychological moment, attack them with small groups of partisans.*

But above all I begged the members of the junta to concentrate on careful intelligence about the location and movement of German personnel and equipment, to be transmitted to me by courier as often and as rapidly as possible, so that we might inform Allied G-2 of the enemy's whereabouts and movements.

As for the relations between the rival partisan organizations, I made it clear that I was *not* interested in being involved in their individual political problems.

Then Cervo entered with a message for me from the base and I had to do my best to dissimulate my reaction to it. It was a warning not to move on any account, that the liberation of Rome was temporarily postponed, that the proposed landing of parachutists was to be held in abeyance. There followed a top-priority request for information on all German troop movements toward the beachhead.

It was puzzling and depressing news, but for obvious reasons I did not reveal the contents of the message as received. Instead I hinted that there would be a slight delay, requesting that while they perfected their paramilitary preparations, they *please* concentrate on getting information on German movements.

Their reaction was one I had already encountered repeatedly when recruiting Italian partisans to go across the lines. Invariably they were willing to volunteer to fight the Germans, but they considered collecting military information as of secondary importance, if not downright cowardly. At the same time I suspected they were as surprised as I by the order to delay, and may have attributed it to bad faith on my part and a desire to keep them from participating in the liberation of Rome—which most certainly was not the case. However, we managed to part on the best of terms.

When they had gone, Franco and Cervo and I discussed the situa-

* Had the Allies bombed Kesselring's radio station on Monte Cavo when they bombed his HQ, just below it, at Frascati, at the time of the Salerno landings, Kesselring admitted he would have been unable to deploy his southern forces against the Salerno beachhead, and would have had to evacuate to the north of Rome.

tion in its new aspects. As large-scale operations by the partisans were temporarily postponed, would it not be more effective, I asked Franco, in view of the base's urgent request for intelligence, if we could temporarily use the members of his own clandestine party organization to create an effective espionage network rather than have them risk their lives in small attacks on the Germans or petty acts of sabotage which, though heroic, would be of no great military value unless timed to coincide with the Allied advance?

Franco was thoughtful for a moment, then said he would discuss the matter with the other members of his party, principally, of course, Pietro Nenni. Meanwhile both he and Cervo would see to it that all the information collected by the various underground organizations was brought to me at Cervo's house by a continuous system of couriers.

Later in the afternoon, just in time to get away before the curfew, Coniglio came to see me. I did not mention that I was aware of the trick he had tried to pull at the phony conference at Via d'Ara Coeli, for I did not wish to antagonize him any more than I had already done by my mere presence in the capital. Instead I told him of the message from the base and asked him also to concentrate on collecting intelligence on German movements. He was exaggeratedly, almost patronizingly, cordial, which made me wonder what new trick he might be up to, but it was a matter of indifference to me now that I had established my own contacts.

When he too had gone, Cervo set about turning my little room into a makeshift operations headquarters by collecting maps and charts and reference books, so that I could study the road, rail and air communications routes in and around Rome and between it and the beachhead.

We were astonished that the Allies had not already captured their main objective—the Alban Hills. We figured that the Germans must *not* have fallen for the bluff of getting them to pull back from the Cassino front. But why hadn't the Allies *forced* them into it by seizing the hills and cutting their lines of communications? Why hadn't they sent out reconnaissance toward Rome when there appeared to be nothing between the left flank of the beachhead and the city? Were their intentions to fight it out with the main force of Germans between Anzio and Cassino *before* turning toward Rome?

Unfortunately I had made it a point to be as uninformed as possible about the actual size of the Allied forces involved in the landings, let alone the details of their battle order, strategy and tactics, lest, falling into German hands, I have something of value to reveal under torture.

What was actually happening on the beachhead was a tragedy of errors, caustically recorded by Winston Churchill in his *The Second World War*:

But now (after the successful surprise landing) came disaster and the ruin in its prime purpose of the enterprise. General Lucas (commanding the expeditionary force) confined himself to occupying this beachhead and having equipment and vehicles brought ashore. General Penney commanding the British Ist Division was anxious to push inland. His reserve brigade was however held back with the Corps. Minor probing attacks towards Cisterna and Campoleone occupied the 22nd and 23rd. No general attempt to advance was made by the commander of the expedition. By the evening of the 23rd, the whole of the two divisions and their attached troops including two British Commandos, and the United States Rangers and Parachutists had been landed with masses of impedimenta. The defenses of the beachhead were growing, but the opportunity for which the great exertions had been made was gone.

That night, Sunday the twenty-third, as I slipped into the cold, virginal sheets relinquished to me by Cervo's sister and listened to the droning of the planes in the chill Roman night, I was depressed by the turn of events. Had I been able to read what the German Colonel Dollmann, Himmler's secret police representative in Rome, was to write of the situation I might have taken violent action:

At the height of the Battle of Cassino I lived very anxious hours in Kesselring's headquarters when the evacuation of the capital and retreat hung by a thread. The same situation repeated itself in January of 1944 when an energetic thrust of a column of American tanks and a popular uprising within the city would have enabled the enemy to take Rome within 24 hours.

According to Dollmann, Field Marshal Kesselring had no doubt that the heads of the resistance were preparing at last to come out of their hiding places, and that by Saturday night, or the very latest Sunday

70

morning, American tanks would be able to give a hand to the insurgents in the city. "Only a miracle," he quotes Kesselring as saying, "could save us!"

And Kesselring himself in his memoirs says that though "the first hours of 22 January 1944—the day of the invasion at Anzio-Nettuno —were full of anxiety . . . as I traversed the front I had the confident feeling that the Allies had missed a uniquely favorable chance of capturing Rome and of opening the door on the Garigliano front."

The miracle happened. Lack of Allied initiative saved the Germans, not only at Anzio, but on the southern front as well.

As to the causes of this lack of action Winston Churchill outlined them to Field Marshal Smuts in the following bitter terms:

My personal effort did not extend to the conduct of the battle which of course I left altogether to the commanders, once they had landed safely on the right place as they were. In all his talks with me Alexander envisaged that the essence of the battle was the seizure of the Alban Hills with the utmost speed, and to this end I was able to obtain from the United States their 504th Parachute Regiment, although at the time it was under orders to return for "Overlord." But at the last moment General Clark cancelled the use of this regiment and the American General Lucas, a man of 55 who at Salerno had distinguished himself in command of a Corps, seemed to have the idea in his mind that at all costs he must be prepared for a counterattack. As a result, although directly I learned the landing was successful I sent Alexander injunctions that he should peg out claims rather than consolidate bridgeheads, the whole operation became stagnant. . . .

Clearly the use of the 504th Paratroopers was the key to the operation, a fact corroborated by its one-time commander and expert on airborne operations, General James E. Gavin, who maintained that their participation in the landing might well have been "decisive" for Allied success:

Probably the most promising . . . was the plan known as SHINGLE. It called for dropping the 504th Parachute Regiment Combat Team astride the main North-South highway eighteen miles inland from Anzio on the night of the Anzio invasion. The mission was to prevent the movement of enemy troops into the Anzio-Nettuno area. The Combat Team was to be accompanied by 50 CG4A gliders carrying reconnaissance vehicles and anti-tank guns. The commander was directed to conduct active reconnaissance at once upon landing. He planned to push strong motor patrols north beyond Field Marshal Kesselring's command post and into Rome. If the capabilities of the 504th in this situation can be gauged by its performance in combat throughout Italy it would almost certainly have entered Rome. But this is pure speculation for at the last moment the operation was called off and the Combat Team was landed from sea and not from the air.

That our plan to land parachute troops in the Villa Borghese on the second or third day might still have saved the situation is further borne out by General Gavin:

A group of C-47s (36 to 45) flying a tight formation could deliver a battalion of paratroopers in an area 1000 yards long by 500 wide in about two minutes from the time the first chute appeared in the sky. A regiment could be landed in about ten minutes. A well trained parachute battalion could be assembled and moving, with its ground mission well in hand in twenty minutes and at worst it should not take more than an hour. We had also learned that the drop zone should be as close as possible to the unit objectives. Best of all is to land right on the objective.

General Mark W. Clark, in his book so aptly entitled *Calculated Risk*, gives no reason for, and makes no mention of, the use of airborne troops in conjunction with the Anzio landing. It is clear, however, from the rest of the book that he had no particular appreciation of their use as a paralyzing military and psychological force.

In the Fifth Army history one laconic but revealing sentence disposes of the mystery of the 504th:

Up to a few days before the landing it was planned to drop the 504th Parachute Infantry behind the beaches, but this drop was called off [by General Clark], lest it prematurely disclose the area of our main assault; the paratroopers came in by sea as a corps reserve.

And another sentence in the same paragraph gives the key to the failure of the entire beachhead expedition:

The assault plan assumed initial heavy resistance on the beaches and heavy counterattack once the enemy was fully aware of the extent of our landing. Consequently VI Corps held out as a strong reserve the bulk of the 1st Division and placed great emphasis on digging in early on initial objectives to repel armored counter-attacks.

What the devil, one might ask, was the point of landing!

72

6 THE SHIFT TO INTELLIGENCE

THE NEXT MORNING, January 24, Cervo had been out and back before I had breakfast. Soon the first of a series of scraps of paper began to arrive from all sorts of sources: from the various parties, from Coniglio, from such unheard-of splinter organizations as the Catholic Communist Movement, even from a couple of parish priests, all containing scattered bits of information about the Germans. As I studied them I realized the problem of answering the base's priority request about German movements was no nearer solution.

Technically, I should have been delighted by this flood of information. Wasn't that what an intelligence organization lived on? Just file the stuff and let them work it out for themselves at the base. The volume alone would look good, and who was to know, or even care, after the fact, how correct the information had been! Unfortunately I had also been a newspaperman, and some of the stories I had filed in my youthful inexperience still came back to haunt me on stormy nights.

What was I to do? Each piece of paper that arrived contained numbers of vehicles, tanks, German units, etc., that had passed on a certain road. Taken as isolated pieces of information they looked impressive and clearly authentic. Unfortunately, put together, they added up to chaos. One source, observing on one stretch of road from 1500 to 1900, would give a total of twenty-seven trucks, nineteen tanks, twenty-two artillery pieces, while another source, watching from 1700 till midnight from a slightly different spot, would give an entirely different set of figures; nor was there any way I could figure out at what point in time and space they overlapped. It would almost have been better to inform the base, "Traffic heavy southbound," rather than confuse them too with all these figures.

Two alternatives offered themselves: I would need to organize a filing and checking system to eliminate duplication and incongruities, or scrap the lot and set up an entirely independent system of control twenty-four hours a day on all the major arteries in and out of Rome. But how was this to be done?

Calling Cervo, I asked him what other organizations were sending military information by clandestine radio. The only regular source of military information he knew of was provided by Montezemolo's Badogliani, who were in contact via their clandestine radio with the Italian Supreme Command (!) in Brindisi and had instituted a central information bureau known as the Center R.

This, I realized, was a slow medium of communication going to Brindisi, thence to Caserta, thence to the beachhead, having to be translated as well as coded and decoded, possibly more than once, before it could be acted upon, whereas ours would go simultaneously to my OSS colleagues right on the beachhead as well as to headquarters in Caserta, in English, ready to be acted upon instantly. Nevertheless I asked Cervo to obtain copies of this information so that I might check it, avoid duplication, and not send information from the same source which might be mistaken at the base for confirmation.

Then Franco arrived and handed me his first report, page 1 of which was as follows:

Detailed information:
Night 22 to 23 intense southbound traffic through Rome, out Via Appia. All available German units in a radius of 90 kilometers north of Rome have been ordered south. Special units have been formed from various headquarters and offices in Rome. 610 vehicles transited. Noted: 3 battalions of parachutists, elements of 90th Panzer Grenadier Division, five divisional artillery groups. Road followed: Appia Antica, Albano, Via Anziate.

Night 23–24, diminished southbound traffic. "Panther" and "Tiger" tank units, two 88 mm groups, two battalions of motorized infantry. Units of the 29th and 3rd Panzer Grenadier Divisions reported transferred from Garigliano front towards Beachhead. Units Hermann Goering Division moved towards Albano and Beachhead.

Armored units and artillery concentrated at S. Palomba and Lanuvio (astride Albano-Anzio road on perimeter of Beachhead).

Trenches and field defenses being thrown together just south of Rome (Porta S. Paolo on Ostia road). Machine guns and artillery turned *towards* the city. German Headquarters in Corso Italia protected by German and PAI armored cars.

Traffic through Rome out via Appia 270 vehicles, most intense between 1900 and dawn.

General information:

Two armored Divisions are reported ordered towards the Beachhead from Tuscany where they will be replaced by other Divisions from Northern Italy; one already on the move.

The German Command in Rome greatly fears disorders in the city, having sent all available troops to the Beachhead and being left with only the German and Italian police forces. Even lightly wounded personnel have been sent to fight. The Germans are lacking in vehicles and gasoline. German headquarters is afraid of an airborne landing, especially on one of the airfields round Rome; they believe the present landing at Anzio may not be the main one. They are also worried about an Eighth Army flanking attack towards Sulmona.

The instant I read this report I knew I had a grave decision to make. The information was crisp, to the point, and reasonably qualified. But was it true? Were his sources remarkably good, or was it a hoax? And how was I to know?

Far and away the trickiest job in intelligence is *evaluating* the information. There was no possible way for me to go out and check it myself. Yet I must act. Was I to pass up what might turn out to be first-rate intelligence until, with time, I could check and countercheck it? Or should I go out on a limb and risk not only making a fool of myself, but misinform the Allies at what appeared to be a crucial moment in the Italian Campaign?

Once more I was obliged to rely on that most intangible, dangerous, but sometimes sole available weapon both of the journalist and the intelligence officer: instinct. Prose, like poetry, carries certain metaphysical overtones by which one can sense the seriousness or phoniness of a report on the basis of the construction of the sentences, their terseness, the type of word used as qualification. To me, Franco's bulletin had the ring of authenticity.

After working out the situation in detail on the large-scale military maps which Cervo had provided, I decided to take the full risk and drafted my first long cable to the base.

My instinct proved to be right.

We had in fact successfully identified all the basic German units deployed against the beachhead, including elements of the 1st and 4th Parachute Divisions whose presence the Allies did not become aware of for another forty-eight hours.

Later in the afternoon Franco returned with a fresh bulletin of information:

> The situation facing the Beachhead as reported in German Headquarters in Rome is as follows: The Nettuno landings were unopposed because the Germans were taken by surprise. Thereafter the Germans did not attempt to stop the landing operations, waiting for reinforcements, and so as not to expose themselves to fire from Allied naval units. It was first thought that the objective of the landings was a march on Rome, as a result of which German Headquarters in the city were ordered to be ready to leave. It was then noted that disembarking troops were heading south; this the Germans considered fatal to the Allies as they would be trapped between the road and the marshes, an easy target for the 90th Armored Infantry Division already on the spot, and two other forthcoming Divisions (the 29th and 3rd Panzer Grenadiers) being transferred from the southern front to the Beachhead, along with units of the Hermann Goering Panzer Division already heading for the Beachhead and Albano.
>
> German Headquarters in Rome have now settled down again.

How the devil, I wondered, did Franco obtain information from German headquarters in Rome! Should I ask him, at such an early date, to reveal the source of such high-level information? Having pressed him, would I be any surer of its authenticity, or would I still be just as dependent on his word? I could not, after all, go up to German headquarters and look for myself. Was he a German double agent, and I his dupe? Was I being a channel for purposely false information to delude the Allies? After all Franco had admitted having had staff training with the Germans in Austria! Suddenly I saw a whole world of evidence pointing to Franco as a German agent; so much so that it made my head spin like a lover wild with jealous imagination.

Putting down the report I looked him in the eye.

But he smiled back: "You'll have to trust me. It would be dangerous for me to reveal the actual source as yet—and, as you see, it is too good a source to endanger. Also, there are psychological reasons."

Then followed an explanation which I was bound to concede was

76

valid. There were German-speaking comrades from a certain independent country which Hitler had invaded and subjugated, whose young men had been sent off to fight Hitler's wars. But Hitler had forgotten that the fathers of such men, as Socialists, had been murdered by the Nazis, and that that particular country wanted as much as any other occupied land to be liberated from the Germans. It was indeed an Achilles heel in the robust Teutonic armor. But the psychological rub was equally evident: these men disliked betraying their military comrades; in fact, would not even admit to it themselves.

The less said about it, I agreed, the better.

But an almost insurmountable obstacle remained. It was all very well for me to put my faith in Franco. Would the base do likewise with me, and act upon such high-level reports?

Broad indications of enemy tactics or strategy, as well as overall Order of Battle reports, coming from a foreign agent, were inclined to be discounted by the base as being too risky to put faith in, let alone act upon.

There was only one answer. Somehow I must establish the authenticity of Franco's reports to my own entire satisfaction, then, in turn, convince the base to act upon them.

My next problem was a matter of selecting from two more pages of Franco's detailed information what was most likely to be of vital concern to the Allies, what must await confirmation, and what must be, at least for the moment, set aside.

OSS secret communications procedure called for a maximum transmission on a clandestine radio of about five minutes, which meant, at optimum, the equivalent of sixty five-letter words. But this was impossibly little. Yet it was dangerous to send longer messages as it would give the Germans time to triangulate an agent's transmitter and pin down the area or even the actual house from which the signal was coming. By going on the air as many as five times a day, and relying on Cervo's constant moving of the radio, the operator was able to send out as many as three hundred groups. Then, figuring it unlikely that the Germans, under the present stress, with even cooks and stenographers being rushed to the front, could spare the time, equipment or personnel for such operations, I decided to ask the radio operator to ignore procedural precautions and step up his groups.

So the first of a series of increasingly longer messages—as high as six hundred groups in a single transmission!—was tap-tapped out into space to be picked up by the OSS HQ in Caserta, and more directly by the OSS VI Corps on the beachhead, not more than thirty miles away.

7 WHO IS TRYING TO FOOL THE ALLIES?

THE NEXT DAY, Tuesday the twenty-fifth, by payment of a considerable sum, Cervo obtained the first drop-copy of the information bulletin regularly produced by Montezemolo's Badogliani. The price, even for those days, was exorbitant, but judging from the impressive looks of the bulletin, possibly worth the expense.

Typed on tissue-thin rose-colored paper (for reasons which I never discovered), it ran to six closely typed pages, three headed "Military Information" and three "Political Information." Each item was numbered progressively in good Ministry of War protocolary manner, but the first three items, as I avidly read them, left me suddenly perplexed.

"What's the matter?" Cervo asked.

Before answering I glanced over the following pages, but they contained only items such as the fact that the Germans were cutting down trees in the Villa Doria-Pamphili. Returning to the first three items on German movements, I read one of them aloud, scanning it slowly: "001994—From the German Embassy the news comes that eight divisions will transit through Rome the night of the 25th towards the front. The divisions come from Pistoia."

"Eight divisions!" I exclaimed. "Through Rome in one night! Who produces this drivel? Is this really the work of career officers?"

Cervo assured me that it was.

Shortly thereafter Franco arrived with his own new bulletin, and I quickly set to comparing them. Several of the minor items about fortifications round Rome and small German concentrations coincided, virtually identically, indicating that they had either copied one from the other, or obtained them from the same source, but the larger and more important items were strongly in contrast. Who was right? Was I being duped by Franco, or by the others?

Glancing over the section of the Badoglio news bulletin on political affairs, I saw that it mentioned the arrest of two of their generals and of one colonel, by the SS. I thought this pretty surprising, but Cervo assured me their security was so bad that this was a regular occurrence.*

The next bit of news which caught my attention was that the chief of all the armed police forces in Rome, General Presti, was reported to have said he would fight any insurrection by the partisans with all the forces at his disposal. Clearly I had better get as exact a breakdown as possible from Cervo and Franco of the German and Fascist administration of the Open City of Rome, as well as the number, armament, and political reliability of the various police forces, which, in Italy, included such uniformed bodies as the Treasury Police and the firemen.

After lunch they both went out, leaving me to study my maps and reports. For the first time since I had left Naples I felt relaxed enough to be annoyed by the hiatus in operations at the beachhead, and wish for something more exciting to happen. Unfortunately, in espionage, excitement is likely to come from the most unexpected quarters.

When Franco and Cervo came back they told me that Montezemolo had assigned various targets to his officers to be occupied the moment the Germans began to retreat; the news had caused bad blood among the parties of the CNL, because of the highhanded manner in which the Badogliani were acting, as if all partisans other than theirs were but bloodthirsty hoodlums. Bonomi, however, as head of the CNL, had issued explicit instructions to the executive committee and to the military junta of the CNL, appealing to them as good Italians not to become involved in any conflict with the Badoglio forces.

As for the partisans, Franco said that squads of volunteers were all organized and ready to take action against the Germans. Special squads with explosives had been constituted to form attack units. Mobilization centers were functioning in each zone of the city. Targets had been agreed upon and morale was high. More arms were clearly needed, but the partisans, he assured me, were convinced an insurrection against the Germans would be thoroughly successful and they were only waiting for the signal to go into action. As for the police forces, their attitude was still doubtful; many of the lower ranks

---

* At the very moment Cervo and I had been riding down the Corso on the morning of the landings the Germans had flung a cordon of paratroopers round a block near Piazza del Popolo and captured three of the top heads of the Carabinieri underground—a colonel, a major, and a captain—who had been warned in advance *not* to go to the meeting. Brave men, they were all tortured and shot. But what a waste!

appeared now to be favorable toward the partisans, whereas the higher ranking officers still seemed to temporize. To spur them to a decision, the elimination of spies working for the SS, as well as of double agents, had gone into effect. In fact that very day the Germans had made the curfew even more stringent, owing to the increase of isolated attacks on Fascist personnel throughout the city.

However, as we listened on Cervo's small radio to the BBC, it became clear that the situation on the beachhead was such that the chances of a partisan uprising were now almost nil.

The next morning, cold but clear, I could see from my window the white trail of a reconnaissance plane high above the Alban Hills, and hear the deep rumble of artillery from the beachhead.

Another bulletin from the Badogliani, this time all of twelve pages long, contained almost a hundred separate items of military information. But the more I studied it the more I was amazed. On January 19, three days before the landings, there were supposed to have been *four* German divisions resting near Velletri (in the Alban Hills, our main objective, and dominating the beachhead), among them the Hermann Goering. On the twenty-first (the afternoon before the landing), the above-mentioned divisions were supposed to have received urgent orders to take up positions between the Appian road and the town of Littoria, covering the whole right flank of what was to be the beachhead!

Needless to say, if there had been any truth in this report, there would never have been an Allied beachhead at Anzio, but the most terrible carnage. How could they calmly report such nonsense? What was behind it? Whom were they trying to fool? Had such "intelligence" been filed and *believed* by the Allies?

Such information could be more dangerous than no information. Another item ran as follows: "From a German source it is learned that the landing at Fiumicino was thoroughly successful, and the Allies are now about 8 kilometers from Rome on the Via Appia."

Was I dreaming? Or had the base let me down—not even informing me of another Allied landing!

Luckily Franco arrived with his own bulletin, and I was forced, by the logic of its contents, to come to a basic decision about his reliability, and begin seriously to wonder about the Badogliani.

According to Franco, the Germans were *now* concentrating their forces near Frosinone, to serve as a tactical reserve, and especially in the Albano-Velletri area, where forces were being massed for a counterattack against the beachhead. Two hundred armored vehicles of various categories were reported concentrated in this area, as well as five groups of artillery of medium and heavy caliber, two battalions of parachutists, and units of the 90th Panzer Grenadiers. Just south of Rome another concentration had been formed round Tor Carbone between the Appia Antica and the Ardeatina (where I had so often taken visiting compatriots to lunch beneath pergolas of vine and honeysuckle). Here fifty light and medium tanks, plus six Tigers, were reported massed, constituting a reserve to guard Rome. Clearly the Germans were still afraid of a possible airborne landing and of an insurrection by the partisans.

Franco promised a more detailed report would be forthcoming in the afternoon. In the meantime the best news he brought was of a long and detailed discussion with the leaders of his party (principally Nenni) whom he had managed to convince that one of the best ways of serving the Allied cause and doing the Germans the most damage would be to create a first-rate information service. For this he had been granted the use of up to a hundred men to be deflected from their normal partisan activities, entirely at his orders. For obvious security reasons it was not to be known they would be working for an Allied intelligence organization, but merely as an information service for the Socialist party.

This was really good news; it had always been my theory that the best way to gather intelligence in Italy would be with a widespread organization of eyes and ears all over the country. The rest of the OSS —largely for what, to me, were specious political reasons—preferred to work with small groups of professional ex-Fascist Italian army spies. I had little faith in the professionals, not only because of their record in the war against us, but because I suspected, and with good reason, that they would often invent large portions of their intelligence, and that even when they didn't their information was of less value, for one could never be sure of the accuracy of what they passed along.

Apart from the fact that a clandestine political party could cover more ground and have better communications, it alone could offer a basic mechanism of security checking. The mere fact that a member belonged to that particular party meant that he had been investigated or was well known to and trusted by those of his fellows who worked closely with him, whose own skins depended on that man's security. Furthermore the fact that they were being guided by a political ideal rather than monetary recompense made them more stalwart in an emergency, and more easy to direct in operations; being guided by an ideal, they were willing of their own free will to subordinate themselves to the authority of their fellow conspirators. With independent agents there was no such possibility.

To Franco I stressed what I considered the essential prerequisites for a good information service: first, speed of communication; if an important piece of news wasn't transmitted in time, it was useless. Second, no exaggeration; if they didn't know, or weren't sure, then say so. Third, don't pick up items from other clandestine organizations without carefully attributing the source, so that we could create an independent network of *evaluatable* sources.

As for the details of his own organization, these were to be handled by Franco, entirely at his own discretion, and the less I knew of actual names, places and mechanics, the better.

Standing by the window, looking out toward the beachhead, we each raised a small glass of Aurum and drank to the success of our venture.

Then Franco went out to collect and write up the day's second bulletin, which turned out to be extremely interesting, containing not only the regular traffic movement through Rome to and from the beachhead, and several items of general interest, but also a report from Franco's high-level informants from which it was possible to obtain the first reasonably clear picture of the deployment of German forces facing the beachhead.

With the earlier reports, and the bulletin Franco had brought that morning, it was evident the Germans were now massing round the beachhead elements of the 3rd, 26th, 29th, and 90th Panzer Grenadier Divisions, at least two parachute battalions and units of the Hermann Goering Panzer Parachute Division. From German operational overlays it was evident the Germans were planning a false attack from the Genzano-Albano section, whereas the real one was to come with his armored units concentrated in the Pratica di Mare area.

Just as Franco and I were discussing what best to do about this situation, Cervo came in, very flustered, angrily pulling at his gloves, to give us a staggering piece of news. Colonel Montezemolo, head of the Badoglio underground, had been arrested by the SS along with a large part of his clandestine organization. If Montezemolo were to talk, we would all be in imminent danger of arrest.

Both Franco and Cervo insisted I must move. I felt unhappy at the prospect, as I had come to feel reasonably safe and well-installed in the house of a police officer of the Fascist Republican Army, especially with the new identity card Franco had provided me and the real pass Cervo had produced to go with the policeman's arm band to show I was enrolled as an auxiliary agent in Police Chief Caruso's special force. Now all this would have to be abandoned. In my little room I had maps and books and could spend hours checking information, sorting and arranging it. What would happen to all this, and the expanded information service to be built up with Franco?

By the time I went to bed that night it was decided that all incriminating evidence be removed from Cervo's house, and that I go, as early as possible the next day, either to an uncle of Cervo's who had a small villa in an out-of-the-way part of town, or to the apartment of a deaf old lady, till we could learn more of Montezemolo's arrest and his reaction to imprisonment and almost certain torture.

Neither of these alternatives appealed to me, and I cursed the day they had been obliged to deal with the Badoglio forces, let alone inform them of their real identities; yet I could not help feeling sorry for their leader, doing his duty as he saw it, now in the hands of enemy torturers, and the Allies only twenty miles from the city.

8 I FIT MYSELF TO SUIT A TAILOR

THE NEXT MORNING at ten o'clock Cervo returned from a preliminary reconnaissance to inform me that neither of the prospected hideouts had proved satisfactory, that he had found me a hiding place in a tailor's shop.

This sounded even less attractive than the previous alternatives, but he quickly reassured me I would be able to receive and send messages through couriers pretending to be clients.

To add to my disguise Cervo produced a pair of steel-rimmed spectacles whose lenses, though weak enough not to distort my vision permanently, were weird enough to change my appearance quite distastefully.

Decked out in my ridiculous plain-clothes policeman's hat and coat I shook hands with Cervo's mother and sister. It was a tender fare-well, the girl pale, the mother attempting to be cheerful, warning us to be careful, and I felt sincere affection for them, aware that I would miss not only the pleasant security of my workroom but their pleasantly spontaneous hospitality as well.

On the back of Cervo's motorcycle I pulled down the brim of my hat, and we lurched off with an all too conspicuous roar. Passing Germans, I noticed, still made me as uncomfortable as when I had arrived, especially the heavily armed and ominous looking ones that patrolled the bridges over the Tiber.

It was a cool gray day, and as usual Cervo headed into the most populated part of town, right up the Corso, stopping leisurely for red lights while I did my best to hide behind my upturned collar and the back of his army cap.

For a second, as we passed a florist's shop, I was positive I saw the slim elegant figure of Nina Cesaró reflected in the window. But Cervo roared on, and into Via Condotti, the Rue de la Paix of Rome, stopping halfway to Piazza di Spagna, where we dismounted and wheeled the cycle into a baroque *portone* surmounted by a balcony.

The shop was on the first floor up, not a tailor's at all, but an expensive dressmaker's. In the first plush velvet room a rich-looking Roman matron eyed us with suspicion—Cervo's police uniform never being entirely reassuring to anyone, I suppose, but me!

Through a small side door we came into a room full of besmocked midinettes tending a variety of bebosomed mannequins in various stages of dress and undress. Down a narrow corridor I was led to a room just big enough for a sway-backed double bed, bookshelf, chair, diminutive table and tall thin cupboard.

The tailor, a queer little man with pins stuck into his lapel, looked up from under a measuring tape and caressed my hand with delicate fingers, then patted the bed to show it was comfortable, pointing to a row of books along the wall with a smile and a wink to indicate I shouldn't be bored. I noticed a volume of the Marquis de Sade incongruously supported by Pearl Buck's *The Good Earth*!

"I will let you out as soon as it is safe," said the tailor, bowing deferentially—making me wonder what exalted rank Cervo had attributed to me in my new disguise as an Italian officer hiding from the Germans; then he closed the door and locked it. The sound of the turning key gave me a peculiar sensation; for an instant I wasn't sure the whole scene might not change into a wicked, or possibly delightful, assignation—perhaps the rich-looking matron in the outer hall!

After a while when this prospect had dissolved, I took off my coat, put my automatic on the bedside table, peered disconsolately out the window into a desolate *cortile* redolent of lichen and urine, reverberant with the Roman sound of ever-running water, where the sun must never have reached the whole year round.

Drawing the thin white curtains I noticed a telephone extension. At least I was not totally cut off from the world. But whom should I call? The hotel at Anzio! Thinking of the time we had "liberated" Capri and been able, quite casually, to telephone Sorrento, then occupied by the Germans, I was sorry I had not made arrangements with someone at the OSS to phone a certain number in Rome the minute they landed, on the quite possible chance of getting through! God knew now when such a chance would come again.

Gingerly lying on the sway-backed bed I dozed for a couple of hours till I heard the hinges of the door squeak and saw the little tailor appear with a tray laden with *risotto con piselli*, two fried eggs, a kingly portion of bread (for those days of miserable rationing) and an almost full demijohn of luscious amber wine from the Castelli, which, as soon as I had poured a glass, tasted even better than I expected.

Having eaten as much as hospitality required, and sipped glass after glass of heady Marino I began to feel almost content. Outside the door there was a continuous *va-et-vient* of small feet padding up and down the hall, making me wonder, for the first time since I had arrived in Rome (I know not whether from the influence of the wine, the Marquis de Sade, or just plain solitude) if anyone would notice were I to reach out an arm and quell the patter of one small pair of feet for the better part of half an hour.

But the patter eventually died, the tailor came to free me, and for once I was pleased with a curfew that made for early closing.

The main cutting room, with its large flat tables, its diamonds of gray-white chalk, its pincushions, measuring tapes and smell of damp ironed cloth was reminiscent of the twenties except that from behind the heavy velvet curtains on the windows I could see Germans moving up and down on the narrow sidewalk.

After a while a strange young man flitted in, shook my hand as if I were an old friend, then set to pinning black lace on the truncated torso of a stuffed mannequin. Pretty soon another young man with a very fat behind and an appalling Roman accent came in and informed me, as if it were a matter of some importance, that the puppy had wet the carpet.

It was maddening to be out of contact with the outside world and my intelligence operations, but better, I consoled myself, than being tortured in an SD cell.

Seated in the main room overlooking Via Condotti, with eight-foot mirrored cupboards along one wall, heavy velvet curtains, soft-rugged floor and comfortable sofas, I spent the evening looking through old *Vogues* and *Harper's Bazaars*. It was odd to read stories by Moatsie, see pictures of Mona Williams, and endless familiar faces and places. Every now and then one or other of the young men would look over his shoulder from his work and I would have to pretend to be looking at the pictures as if I could not read the text—a task I found not as easy as might be imagined.

Dinner was a peculiar affair cooked jointly by the old man and the fat-bottomed boy, consumed by us all at a table in the kitchen, surrounded by more real wealth than I had dreamed possible. Hanging from the ceiling and stacked against the walls were hams, onions, sausages, vast sacks of flour, rice and *pasta,* bottles of good oil and wine. Obviously Roman society paid for its clothes in goods from its outlying estates, money, short of louis d'or, being worthless.

One large object attracted my attention, for it occupied most of a wall and looked like the sort of trunk circus performers might use to pack the elephant's wardrobe. When I spoke of it, the little tailor rubbed his hands sadly, then giggled. They were the clothes of the famous Petacci sisters (one of whom became Mussolini's favorite mistress and was later hung by the feet, half naked, beside the bullet-ridden body of her lover in Milan's Piazzale Loreto)—most of the clothes, as far as I could gather from the mixed-up descriptions of the tailor and his cutters, were fancy dress costumes the Petaccis had worn in the movies poor Italians were obliged to sit through so the Duce's mistress could disport herself. They had never been paid for.

Other stories followed about furriers and jewelers who had furnished the damsels and their rather frightening mother with a variety of luxuries, none of which had been paid for. The only merchant, according to the tailor, who had managed to get his money back, the sharpest and most successful of the lot, and who presumably needed it least, was an eminent Roman jeweler. Not till later did I discover that he was also a good friend of Colonel Dollmann, Himmler's SS representative in Rome, as well as of that brilliant chief of police, Bocchini, famed for his intimate knowledge not only of people's private lives, but, equally importantly, of their various investments in jewelry.

As bedtime approached I became a little anxious, especially when I discovered that my daily resting place was the *only* bed in the house. But the two sofas in the main room overlooking Via Condotti were prepared with sheets and blankets, one for the thin cutter, the other for me, while the tailor and the fat-bottomed boy disappeared giggling, into the room I occupied during the day.

But I did not sleep much, what with the tramp of military boots on the pavement just below my window, and the rapid ascent of my own blood pressure when a car slowed down to a walk just outside the building—(had Montezemolo talked? Had they extorted a confession under torture from Cervo or Franco?)—only to accelerate again and disappear into the night.

At seven in the morning I was awakened by the tailor with a glass of well-sugared coffee (remarkable luxury for Rome in those days); after which I was quickly spirited back to my room with a warning that I could not get to the bathroom again for a good nine hours.

My great preoccupation was not with the boredom of being restricted but with all the work I had to do now that a climax appeared to be maturing on the beachhead. As there was nothing I could do till Franco or Cervo arrived, I settled down to reading Trilussa's incomparable (at least since Belli's) satiric verse in Roman dialect, wondering about the rumor of his true origin. Occasionally I would alternate this reading with a chapter from the Marquis de Sade, or a bout with *The Good Earth*. Detective stories, under the circumstances, I found to be more nerve-wracking than calming.

At long last the door opened, and Franco appeared, smiling and solicitous as ever. From his report it was clear the Germans were bringing fresh divisions into Italy, though it was not definite whether this was to form a stronger line north of Rome or to build up superior forces round the beachhead. Two armored divisions were reported passing through the Brenner between the twenty-third and the twenty-sixth. The first airborne troops were reported landed on Guidonia airfield on the night of the twenty-sixth. Military traffic on the railroads in northern Italy was extremely intense, the main relay points being Bologna and Verona, and especially the latter. Bombing of the bridges across the Po, especially on the Bologna-Verona line, was imperative. In central Italy the railway centers of Terni and Civitacastellana were extremely active, as were the airfields of Grosseto and Castiglione del Lago. According to Franco, German headquarters were more confident about the beachhead now, but were still afraid of a possible occupation of the Alban Hills which could cut their communications with the Tenth Army in the south.

The big struggle was obviously going to be whether or not the Germans could effectively rush equipment and personnel down the length of the Italian boot under the threat of Allied air attack.

Our job of tracking German movements and conveying correct intelligence of them to the Allies as rapidly as possible was becoming as important as reporting the actual buildup and intentions of the enemy round the beachhead.

Then Cervo arrived with another top-priority request from the base for accurate daily road counts of all German traffic in and out of Rome. At first I was surprised by the urgency of this request, that is, until I realized that not only did all the road and rail lines toward the beachhead bottleneck through Rome, but that here, if properly organized, we could keep a continuous check on them, not only by day but by night (when no air reconnaissance was possible) and that these counts could be quickly and systematically radioed both to Caserta and the beachhead.

For the counts to be effective it was imperative that *all* of the twelve main roads in and out of Rome be watched on a round-the-clock basis. For this a minimum of three men working eight-hour shifts on each road would be necessary, noting everything that passed in both directions. Furthermore couriers would be required to pick up and carry the reports to various regional headquarters and from there to a central one. For such an operation approximately sixty men working full time would be required. Luckily the basic structural setup of the Socialist party underground would suit our purposes admirably, for, as Franco explained, the city and its outlying suburbs were already divided into sectors, each with a secret headquarters to which members of the various cells could report. He could thus choose the spotters and couriers from men within the various sectors.

For the road counts to be effective, everything that passed must be noted on paper, in chronological sequence, with as many details as possible—a risky business, especially at night, after the curfew, when German traffic was usually most intense. Though some of the watching could be done from suitably situated windows, much of it would have to be done on the roads themselves. In view of the apparent importance to the Allies of having this information speedily and correctly, of the fact that most of the spotters would be working men with families to support, and in view of the risks involved, I would have been prepared to pay the men almost any reasonable figure. Franco however pointed out that it was essential for their own security, as well as for ours, that these individual spotters believe themselves to be working strictly for the Socialist party. To collect information for a political organization was still a shade less dangerous than to openly admit to intelligence with the enemy, and clearly, the fewer the people who knew of the actual espionage organization the better for us all. As the Socialist party could not afford, nor did it wish, to pay them much more than a standard daily wage, the sum agreed on was to be the equivalent of one U.S. dollar a day per man. As I totted up the sum I could not help but smile at the memory of the $80,000 reportedly paid by some character in the OSS to the Mafia in Sicily, whose supposed leaders, having pocketed the sum, made that familiar *Mafioso* facial contortion signifying there was nothing they could tell!

This problem settled, in principle at least, we turned to the next most important item. It was beginning to be obvious that one of the main German problems would be the supplying of gasoline and ammunition to their forces, without which, however numerically powerful, they would find themselves paralyzed. If we could locate their main ammunition and gasoline dumps and pinpoint them exactly for the Allied Air Forces we might seriously hamper German movements, perhaps even defeat a counteroffensive against the beachhead. It was an exciting prospect; but to become effective it was imperative that Franco's network function as widely as possible and that the men receive special briefing in noting landmarks so that I could transmit specific coordinates (according to OSS procedure) back to the base.

That brought us to the final point: in my present situation it was difficult if not impossible for me to work—without maps, reference books, typewriter, filing system, etc.—and I begged Franco to do his best to find me a better hideout.

Already, I pointed out to him, it was beginning to be a nuisance having to keep my identity secret from the tailor and his cutters. At supper I could not sit silently eating their food without even a pretense at conversation, and it was incredible how many odd things I would have to pretend *not* to know that had become reflex, as well as the number of things I had to invent, with the straightest of faces, that I hadn't the slightest idea of. Some questions, such as in what church had I been confirmed, and by what bishop, or whether I had found the brothel on Via di Fontanella improved since the war, were within plausible reach of an answer, for, by chance, I had been confirmed by the Bishop of Novara in his Episcopal chapel and spent part of my teens in Rome. But I was at sea in the endless discussion of *faits divers* of local interest which had happened in the last three years of which I was naturally ignorant.

Franco smiled and promised to give the problem priority treatment. As yet there had been no repercussions resulting from the arrest of Montezemolo, but Franco was against my returning to Cervo's house, saying he hoped to find me a completely different type of hideout.

The next day Cervo came to see me and brought not only a new bulletin from Franco, but the Badoglio bulletin of the twenty-seventh, which, despite the disruption of their organization, they were still managing to produce; glancing at it I saw that it contained an item which cleared up my doubts about what the Badogliani had been up to politically in the past few weeks: it admitted textually their deal with the neo-Fascists to forestall a provisional government of the political parties of the CNL.

Why, I wondered, had they let the cat out of the bag? Was it the result of some junior officer's mistake after the capture of Montezemolo, or was it a move by General Armellini, his successor, to establish his supremacy now that Montezemolo had been arrested? In either case it didn't seem to matter; their organization was no longer in a position to do anything but hide, forcing me, ironically, to do the same.

But the more disquieting news brought by Cervo was that Coniglio, out of apparent jealousy of my arrival, had started spreading the rumor in the underground that he was chief of the OSS for all Italy and that I was his subordinate.

I did not need to point out to Cervo that such a situation would be preposterous, that no American, under any circumstances, could be subordinate to any Italian agent, let alone one of Coniglio's caliber, and that to all intents and purposes we were technically still at war with Italy. What worried Cervo, and Franco too, when he arrived a little later, was that it did not look good in the underground to have such rumors spread, making the OSS look as if it didn't know what it was doing. (I trembled at the thought of their realizing how true this could be of the OSS, but managed to laugh it off.)

To my queries it then developed that Coniglio had been passing himself off as General Clark's personal political representative in Italy. That such an assertion might be ludicrous to any American did not affect its value, unfortunately, in underground Europe; rumors had been going around for some time of personal deals between such American generals as Patton and the Vichy General Noguès, and, judging by our own past deeds and propaganda, there was no telling what we were likely to do in the name of expediency.

I discovered also that Coniglio had been waging an anti-CNL fight with one hand while subsidizing their parties with the other. Whoever had given him permission to subsidize political parties as such, with OSS funds, God only knows, though I was beginning to have my suspicions. I also found out that there had been quite a stink among the other parties of the CNL because they had found out he had been giving millions to the Unione Democratica as the only party recognized by Clark, when everyone knew the party consisted of a handful of dubious characters such as Coniglio's co-agent G., with no following, and quite unheard of north of Rome. What I couldn't seem to convey to Franco and Cervo was the impossibility of General Clark's being legally involved in such nonsense, which was, or should clearly have been, beyond his jurisdiction.

In any case I warned them I wanted no part of such shenanigans; that I was in Rome to carry out military espionage and paramilitary operations, and that for this I would make use of whatever political organizations were best qualified, but only on a paramilitary basis, that no one had the power to make political deals in the name of any United States general, least of all an Italian agent. Furthermore I made clear that they could dispose of such OSS funds as they needed, but only in return for information or for the acquisition of arms and explosives for sabotage, for all of which I would require a strict accounting, and that not one cent was to go to any political party as such, no matter if its members were starving.

As a final blow it turned out that the two bits of information I had unwillingly forwarded to the base from Coniglio appeared now to have been incorrect.

Luckily Cervo had always had the radio well in hand and Coniglio didn't even know where it was hidden; so we decided to go calmly about our business, knowing it didn't really matter what rumors he spread, especially as few people seemed to take him seriously. Nevertheless I asked them both to obtain whatever information they could on Coniglio and Cambareri's backgrounds and recent activities in Italy.

93

9 NEW FRIENDS

SUNDAY AT THE TAILOR'S was to be my day of liberty, though not of liberation. As no one came to work I was allowed to wander round the shop at will.

Lunch, cooked for us by the tailor's sister, who visited him regularly on feast days, was an even more spectacular affair than it had been during the week.

Unfortunately the good woman also brought her husband, who, being a traveling salesman, insisted on an interminable series of questions I found almost impossible to answer. Finally when he was let in on the secret—so as not to arouse his suspicions even further—that I was an Italian officer hiding from the Germans, he proceeded to bombard me with detailed questions about the campaigns I had been in. From this ordeal I was able to extricate myself by the happy idea of describing to him in detail the French campaign, the Greek campaign and the various African campaigns I had covered as a war correspondent, but from the opposite side, throwing in an occasional curse directed at some Allied or American commander to prevent his noticing my viewpoint, which was, in effect, his enemy's.

Yet the strain was beginning to tell. Soon I must get away from the claustrophobic shop or blow up, shocking them all with the truth.

When the in-laws finally made their departure to a cacophony of petit bourgeois compliments Cervo arrived with a three-page bulletin from Franco and the good news that Franco had found a better hiding place with "my own kind of people." I wondered who such people might be, but was too pleased to voice anything but delight. Cervo was to pick me up the following day about noon. If all went well, in less than twenty-four hours I would be back at serious work.

Basic to the day's military information, apart from the road counts, was a detailed picture of the German interconnected system of fortifications ringing the beachhead which was of a more solid nature than had at first been noted.

Altogether it was a day for detailed hard news rather than for strategic developments and it took me a good hour to draft a long message covering such disparate items as the condition of the beaches west of Rome from Ostia to Fiumicino complete with location of mine fields, barbed wire entanglements, trenches, concrete pillboxes, gun emplacements, etc., and the location at Terni forty-five miles north of Rome of a large gasoline dump in underground vats in the courtyard of a synthetic rubber factory easily identifiable from the air, but for which heavy-caliber bombs would be required.

At the end I was obliged to omit information for which an agent would normally have been paid large sums of money; the message was far too long. Clearly we needed to be more efficiently organized, but basic to any improvement was an improvement in my own living quarters.

The next morning I was ready and anxious to leave, counting the minutes till Cervo's arrival, when the fat-bottomed boy slipped into my room with a tray of food and warned me that something extraordinary was happening in the neighborhood, that the whole area had been cordoned off by the police.

For me, I wondered? No! Either they would know exactly where I was, or should not know at all. Or were they triangulating the radio, which was about three blocks away?

Whatever it was, the commotion kept up well into the afternoon, keeping me in an agony of suspense, till the door opened and Cervo's sister appeared, pale and distraught. The police, she informed me, were making large-scale roundups in the area, blocking off whole roads, moving up and down them, arresting all men with the exception of the very old or clearly decrepit, taking the men to forced labor. There was no question of my moving that day, and, in any case Cervo was blocked by extra duty with his squadron, which was why she had been obliged to come in his stead.*

The thought of having to spend another twenty-four hours in the little room was infuriating, and I was seriously, or rather wildly, considering going out anyhow, till I realized only Cervo and Franco knew the address of my new hideout.

A sudden and frantic knocking at the door made us hold our

* Though I didn't know it at the time, Hitler had sent his Gauleiter Sauckel to Rome with orders to bring back 300,000 Romans for forced labor. Fortunately only a few thousand were crammed into boxcars before the German embassy intervened with Kesselring and the plan was scotched.

breath; but it was Cervo, flustered and obviously in a hurry. This was no neighborhood for me to be in, he announced, speaking rapidly. They might start searching through the houses. He had taken twenty minutes off from his squadron to see if he could get me to the new hideout before the curfew, which, that day, by happy coincidence, the Germans had decided to postpone an hour, because, as Cervo pointed out in the morning's messaggio:

. . . the greater part of the Roman people are disposed to avoid disturbing the peace, and condemn attacks made on members of the German armed forces by irresponsible persons in the pay of the enemy. . . .

Packing was simple enough: my possessions consisted of my secret files, a toothbrush, razor and a change of linen lent me by Cervo. But the prospect of a motorcycle ride through a police cordon did not attract me.

Luckily Cervo had brought the small Fiat belonging to his squadron, which he had parked in the courtyard, and into which I quickly climbed.

Turning down the Corso we reached Piazza Colonna, only to see the whole area thick with police and German troops, all traffic disbarred. "Don't worry" said Cervo, "they'll think we're part of the raiders."

How rash could one be, I groaned, already aching to be back in the safety of the tailor's little room.

Then a marshal of Public Security, outraged that someone should dare to crash his cordon, stepped before the Topolino, forcing Cervo to draw up with a jerk. Squinting angrily into the interior of the car the marshal caught sight of Cervo's chevrons and the dark purple police patches on his collar, hesitated, frowned, waved us on.

I had not come that close since the roadblock on the Cassia to losing control of my bladder. By the time we reached Piazza Venezia we appeared to be out of the worst of it, only to find ourselves engulfed in a cloud of thick black smoke issuing from the rear of a wood-burning bus which so obfuscated Cervo's view he nearly crashed into an oncoming German staff car. By the time that too had been avoided—by the narrowest of margins, the air thick with Germanic imprecations—I was on the verge of a fit.

Turning to the right we passed the Palazzo Caetani and I was saddened by the thought of all the pleasant hours I had spent there, and of Camillo in the summer of 1940 trying to make up his mind how best to fight a war he loathed without doing dishonor to his name and country.

The *portone* of the Palazzo Antici Mattei was gray and dusty. How frightened I had been, when I had lived there as a child, of the over-life-sized statues in the courtyard.

Much the same fear possessed me now.

Bumping along a cobbled back lane adjacent to the Ghetto, we entered a piazzetta. To my surprise I realized it was to the Palazzo Lovatelli that Cervo was taking me.

Would Filippo and Nena, its owners, be there? Hadn't I heard that Nena had died? How would Filippo receive me, after all his years of Fascist sympathizing? A sudden ludicrous view of him squinting through binoculars at our female house guests bathing naked in the soft waters of Lake Maggiore came to mind and I had to laugh aloud.

Cervo, who was having trouble parking, turned an inquisitive frown to see what the devil I had found to laugh about. But there was no time to explain; indeed I doubt if I could have found words with which to do so.

Darting through the *portone,* which was luckily still open half an hour before the curfew, Cervo led me up the shallow marble stairs to the second story, where he paused to ring a bell six times in three short repeated rings. Was that not Nena's door across the hall? How strangely confused one could be in the most familiar places under the strain of hiding. As we waited, with no sound but our own bated breathing, I wondered what would happen if Filippo were to appear in his doorway. Then our own door opened and a girl in her twenties let us in.

In the tiny windowless hall, crowded with junk and illuminated by a faint yellow bulb, I still had no idea where I was, or who the girl might be, and it wasn't till the door beyond was opened and I came into a vast sitting room with one side leading to a raised terrace that I realized in a flash it was the old apartment of Jim Waring, an English schoolboy friend with whom I had played so often during vacations. Scenes of picnics at Ostia Antica, and of golf with Timothy and Rosemary Peto came tumbling back nostalgically.

But my reverie was interrupted by Cervo, still very nervous and anxious about something, who insisted upon rushing me right through the big sitting room, up the stairs toward the terrace, along a devious corridor which skirted it and into a small bedroom, where, sliding back a bedside table, he revealed the outlines of a secret panel about a foot and a half square. Pushing it open he slid through the aperture on all fours, not without some effort, due to the lavish pleats in Italian officers' coats. Then he beckoned me to follow.

Once through the panel—feeling something like Alice—I found myself in a small bedroom of which all the doors had been walled and papered over, the one window heavily curtained.

Cervo, in a terrible rush to get back to his squadron, from which I gathered he must by now be A.W.O.L., bid me good luck and wormed his way back through the aperture, closing it behind him.

My curious hideout I found rather pleasantly secure, on the whole, but decidedly chilly. The furniture consisted of two beds, a chest of drawers, a chair and a mirrored cupboard.

Ten minutes later there was a tap on the secret panel and the girl's head appeared, bidding me follow her. Across the main sitting room I was led into a smaller room lined with striped pink silk where an electric heater made the atmosphere pleasantly bearable and where she introduced me to two new companions.

One was a startlingly good-looking young man in his middle twenties, dressed in an Italian air force officer's fur-lined flying jacket, with clear-cut features and considerable poise, named Baldo. Beside him stood a tall nervous fellow, a few years older, with red complexion, infectious smile, and a laugh which really made it possible for a moment to forget the Teutonic horror of war with the Germans. His name was Lele.

The girl, now that I had a good look at her, was short and round-faced, but well dressed, with that polish of movement and speech which indicated an aura more of power than of lineage; her name was Maria.

Franco had been right: these were going to be "more my kind of people." We might have something to converse about other than the war, even have a drink as a stimulant to conversation rather than as a knockout for shattered nerves.

Then Franco arrived, immaculate as ever in gray herringbone overcoat and smart chamois gloves, his ubiquitous leather brief case even bulgier than usual. In honor of the occasion he had procured a pinch-bottle fifth of Haig.

What a change from the Castelli wine, and what a change too, to be treated openly as an American instead of an Italian in hiding. Franco, knowing that they had already hidden an occasional escaped British PW in the upstairs secret room till he could be forwarded to an escape route, had hit upon the idea of passing me off as another escaped PW.

After a round of whisky, accompanied by polite conversation suitable to the occasion, Maria disappeared to the kitchen—somewhere, as I vaguely remembered, on another level of the house—to prepare our evening meal during the sole half hour of rationed gas. Lele discreetly offered to assist her, while Baldo, with a quiet wit I was soon to appreciate, made a joke about going to his rooms to "change."

Left alone, Franco rapidly explained my new friends and protectors: Maria was the daughter of an Italian senator and former ambassador with the reputation of a political historian but the none too palatable philosophical ideals of the "*mistica Fascista*"; right then he was on his deathbed at the Grand Hotel. She had rented the flat to hide Lele, the tall aviator, in civilian life a doctor, where he had been joined by his good friend Baldo, in normal life the younger son of a Palatine count. For several weeks the two of them had hidden there to avoid being drafted by the Nazi-Fascists. So that no one would suspect their presence in the building, they had never answered the phone, never gone out, never even looked out the windows onto the piazza side of the building.

Franco then produced his daily bulletin, which, over another glass of whisky, and while the others were still out of the room, we discussed in detail.

The violence of Allied bombardment was beginning to slow up the arrival of German reinforcements, especially from the north. The Verona railyards which we had asked to be bombed three days earlier had been severely hit, causing considerable delay in all military transport to central Italy. Clinking our glasses we drank to this initial success.

Equally important, the bombardments in the Alban Hills and the

Pratica di Mare zone which we had indicated as the base of operations against the vulnerable western flank of the beachhead had hit the Germans so hard they had been obliged to postpone an intended attack. Again we clinked glasses.

Nevertheless the situation was still very delicate. German reinforcements were continuing to move into the front. In both the Termini and Ostiense stations there were trainloads of German vehicles, guns and supplies for the front; admirable targets for sabotage but not so for Allied raids, the area being thick with civilian population. Clearly we would have to organize a parachute drop of special sabotage equipment, the methods contemplated by the partisans being far too primitive for safety.

As we talked, continually looking up to see if the others were returning, it became obvious that if I were going to have to keep the fact secret that I was working, it would be only a *little* easier than it had been at the tailor's. Could I work in a corner of the sitting room without their noticing it or lock myself in the secret room I was to share with Baldo?

Whatever I did was bound to make them suspicious, especially when couriers started arriving. Furthermore, it would hardly be fair to repay them for their hospitality by further endangering their lives with my presence as a spy.

To all of this Franco nodded solemnly, then with a wicked smile admitted he had foreseen the situation; the important step had been to get me installed in the house. Now that this was accomplished, if I were to get along with my new companions, he saw no reason why the next step shouldn't be to warn them of the danger of my presence and see their reaction. He had known them a long time. Though they did not belong to the Socialist party, he believed we might well risk asking them to help us.

I was to study them carefully for the next twenty-four hours, then we would put it to them squarely. If they balked in any way, I would have to move again; if they reacted favorably we would see what use they might be put to.

Dinner took place downstairs in the cold, concrete whitewashed pantry next to a large kitchen and the empty servants' quarters.

The food, I was sorry to see, far from being comparable to the

100

abundant and well-cooked fare at the tailor's, was the divided result of the three miserable ration cards. But the company made up for it so abundantly that for the first time since I had crossed the lines I felt a bit at ease. Baldo's quiet wit was counterpointed by Lele's inclination to florid tales. Maria cast furtive glances with eyes that seemed permanently lustered by drops of belladonna, interspersing an occasional clever remark with a high-strung, nervous laugh. Franco, as I had long since discovered, was admirably endowed with a pleasant sense of humor that ran from the brilliant to the macabre.

After dinner and another good drink of whisky I noticed further assets in my quarters. The owners had left a colossal and thoroughly up-to-date radio-phonograph with which I could pick up virtually any short wave program I wanted in Europe, and could thus follow the Allied broadcasts which interested me, as well as the enemy's.

Franco, who had a pass for the curfew, and had to attend to his new organization, left us to clear the ashtrays, pound the pillows and remove every vestige of a party, in case of a sudden midnight raid by the police—an unpleasant but fairly frequent occurrence.

Baldo and I, who were to sleep in the secret room, crept up to our wing where he showed me how to remove all traces from the bathroom, itself a pleasant affair, not Balkan, like the tailor's, nor bourgeois as at Cervo's, but typically old Roman, with another electric heater and a little sitting room outside which I remembered so well from the days when it had been Jim Waring's playroom.

From inside the secret room Baldo showed me how to slide the bed table in the outer room into position before closing the panel, thus disguising all trace of an opening. The room itself, or "hole," as Baldo called it, was icy, from never being heated, but there were many blankets and coats spread across the beds like layers of pancakes, and after one last cigarette Baldo turned off the light and I crawled into damp but aromatically clean white sheets for the first night's sleep in what was clearly to be a new type of life.

PART TWO # THE REAL WORK

10 HITLER DECIDES TO CRUSH THE BEACHHEAD

THE NEXT MORNING I was awakened by Cervo's bursting into the secret room with an urgent message from Franco to request the base to have the Rome-Florence railway line bombed, especially at the key points of Orte, Chiusi and Civitacastellana.

At first I could not see why there was such urgency in the message. We had pointed out these targets on the main avenues of German transport toward the beachhead, and I was sure the Allies realized the pressing need of bombing them quite as well as we did; however, if Franco sent an urgent message he must have some urgent reason, so I drafted an insistent message to the base. I didn't like doing this without being personally clear as to the reason, but felt that I owed it to Franco to take his word.

Later in the afternoon when Franco arrived he was able to explain the situation and I was relieved that I had done as he asked. Now I only hoped the base would put the same faith in me that I had put in Franco, and act promptly on the request. The German High Command had ordered the Rome-Florence railway line to be fixed *at any cost at no matter what sacrifice*, so that it would be able to function for a period of forty-eight hours, during which they intended to move five special trains from the north loaded with armored vehicles and heavy artillery, as well as two special trains of ammunition and gasoline, the rail line now being the only means by which they could do so within such a short time.

According to a special order from Kesselring, all the reinforcements which had arrived in the last few days and which were scheduled to arrive in the next, were earmarked for the beachhead. None were for the Tenth Army (Cassino) front, which was to remain at its present strength.

Something was about to happen at the beachhead.

Yet there was cheering news in Franco's bulletin. Further Allied bombardments on the Pratica di Mare and Albano and Genzano areas, as requested by us, had obliged the Germans again to desist from their planned flank attack against the beachhead until further reinforcements could be brought up. The German soldiers and commanders were struck by the violence and extraordinary precision of the Allied bombardments and this was having an affect on their morale. In Frascati and the Castelli large concentrations of troops and heavy artillery groups which we had reported on the twenty-sixth had been severely hit by Allied attacks. It was now essential, Franco insisted, that these bombardments be intensified.

A race was clearly on as to whether we could pinpoint targets to the Allies fast enough and get them acted on fast enough to prevent the arrival of German reinforcements, or whether the Germans could succeed in bringing them down fast enough to build up sufficient forces for a major counterattack against the beachhead.

It was infuriating to think that all this would have been unnecessary if they had seized Rome and the Alban Hills the very first days. Not only had we lost our chance; now the tide appeared to be turning against us.

And the situation was having repercussions in the underground. The partisans had been keyed up and ready for action: now they had to sit around waiting, or indulge in isolated acts of sabotage. The Allies having lost the strategic moment for success, the police, at first vacillating, were now being obliged to side more closely with the Germans. New police directors were pouring into Rome from the neo-Fascist north, and it was depressing but inevitable to see the slavish way in which their Roman underlings were making large-scale roundups and arrests on behalf of the Germans. Something, Franco insisted, would have to be done about this situation, especially as larger roundups were being scheduled for the immediate future by Caruso, the new police chief of Rome, a lieutenant general in the Fascist militia, recently arrived from Florence.

The only weapon we could think of with which to counteract the situation would be to get the BBC to broadcast officially that these policemen would be held individually responsible for their behavior when the Allies entered Rome.

I therefore framed a short message to the base, asking them to do just that. I had no great illusions about its actual effectiveness but it would at least enable Franco to show his party colleagues there was some benefit to be derived from collaborating with an Allied intelligence organization; in any case the mere fact of a warning to the police would certainly raise the morale of underground workers in the city.

That done, it was time for us to sound out Baldo and Lele as to whether they would work with us or not. We had decided to tackle them outright, tell them what we were up to, and ask them if they would help me keep my files, check information, plot it on maps, etc. Were they to refuse it would expose us to the risk of finding another hideout; but were they to accept they might prove of considerable value to us, and, what was more essential, free me to work as I pleased without feeling compunctions about subjecting them to the risk of my presence.

But I need have had no qualms; as soon as they heard the proposition their faces lighted up and they chorused that nothing in the world would they like better than to be useful after so many months of enforced idleness. We warned them, of course, that it would mean serious risk to them to be actively involved in espionage and that they would stand little chance of survival if caught. They assured us it was worth almost any risk to get something done instead of sitting around idly.

The problem of Maria, which was more delicate, was handled personally by Franco. Though she would know it was intelligence we were involved in, she need not know the details; I myself would see to it that Lele and Baldo knew only what was necessary for their particular jobs—not because of any lack of trust in them, but because everyone's security depended on each cog knowing as little as possible of the general picture in case any one of us was caught.

We still hoped it would be only a matter of a couple of weeks before the tide turned in our favor at the beachhead, but it was clear that the next days would be critical, and if three of us could concentrate on the information which was flowing in we might be of better service.

This problem settled, we began immediately to organize an expanded system. In the little sitting room with its electric heater, its big radio and silk-striped walls there was a large low coffee table. From the "hole" I brought down the accumulated bulletins and scraps of paper from all the various sources, and we began to sort them out into an intelligent system of filing.

Lele, who had an old battered typewriter, undertook to type out all the scattered handwritten items with several carbon copies, so that information could be filed and cross-filed by subjects as well as chronologically and by geographical areas. Baldo, who had been an aviator in the war, and was well trained as a navigator, became our official cartographer: on even larger military maps provided by Franco he began to work out the coordinates of all localities mentioned in items of intelligence, plotting—in various colored crayons on the maps—artillery positions, antiaircraft, gas and ammunition dumps, enemy battle order, fortifications, and so forth; and the picture of what was happening between Rome and the beachhead became very much clearer to us all.

Next we organized a system of clearing everything out of the place in less than sixty seconds, leaving no trace of our work.

The problem was where to hide this material. Were we to keep it in the "hole" it would still be too incriminating, and I would not have time properly to destroy it. Then Lele found the false bottom in a cupboard where the basic files could neatly be inserted to escape the most astute searcher. Certain key papers I would keep on my person, ready to burn or eat in an emergency.

When we had done as much as we could that evening, and Franco had left to carry on with his outside activities, the three of us sat down by the radio. Maria had retired to her room with a book. As both Baldo and Lele played bridge rather well, I initiated them into a three-handed Yankee version which they took to with alacrity, offering as it did the possibility of gambling and of ganging up on each other—a vast improvement over any twosome. With that, and the soft music from the radio, we were able to while away the time and soothe our nerves late into the night—our solitary damp sheets being no tremendous attraction.

When, however, we finally did go to bed, I had the comforting feeling that at last we were on the verge of a really first-class organization.

The very next day Franco came in early with the first sensational bit of information.

After the failure of the first counterattack against the British left flank of the beachhead from their Pratica di Mare bases, the Germans were now reorganizing for a bigger attack with the use of freshly arrived reserves and better concealment of units. The attack, according to Franco's high-level informants, was scheduled for the next day, February 3, in the same area as the original attack—against the British-held flank; firstly, because the hilly terrain permitted the Germans to approach under cover and thus avoid Allied naval fire; secondly, because the bases near Pratica di Mare permitted the Germans to attack the Allied left flank where, with the occupation of Campoleone, the Allies had overextended their lines; thirdly, because even in case of limited success the German maneuver should enable them to cut off Allied units in the salient and take prisoners.

The arrival of reinforcements and supplies had been hindered by Allied bombardment but not sufficiently interrupted.

The bulletin also contained the first general picture of the German order of battle round the beachhead:

German forces defending the beachhead have now assumed the name of 14th Army. This army is to be composed of two Army Corps with two Divisions in reserve.

At present there are 55,000 men in the actual front lines round the beachhead formed into four divisions: the Hermann Goering, the 90th Armored Grenadier, the 65th Motorized Infantry, and another whose name is not certain but which is presumed to be the 3rd or 15th. Four more divisions are in the course of being transferred to the front, among them the 362nd from Civitacastellana.

Furthermore each Army Corps disposes of non-divisional heavy, long range, and anti-tank artillery groups, which are known to be particularly strong.

We had now identified elements of ten German divisions either at the front, approaching it, or held in reserve: the Hermann Goering, the 1st and 4th Parachute, the 3rd, 15th, 29th and 90th Panzer Grenadiers, the 26th Panzer, the 65th and 362nd Grenadiers, with more as yet unidentified. But from this information there was still no way of establishing the figure of 55,000 men in the actual front lines. How had Franco arrived at this figure?

With his peculiar smile Franco said it had been extrapolated from the daily bread ration ordered from German bakers for front-line troops.

Could the information be authentic? Instinctively I had faith in Franco; rationally I kept asking myself if someone might not be leading *me* on, only to fool us *all* at the crucial moment. But instead of pondering the quandary I sent off a superurgent message to the base warning them to prepare for attack on February 3, underlining the area and bases from which it was to jump off.

Our next worry was the weather, which to us looked bleak and gray. If it were no better round the beachhead the Allies might not be in time to break up the German concentrations by aerial bombardment, unless they had already acted on our information of two days earlier.

However, having sent off the message, I had nothing to do but sit around impatiently and await results.

As it turned out, Franco's information proved to be not only exact, but extremely timely. What actually happened is dramatically recorded by the Fifth Army historian:

> On 2 February General Clark radioed General Lucas to consolidate the beachhead and prepare for defense. . . . All units on the beachhead began immediate preparations of defensive positions in accordance with oral orders of VI Corps issued on 3 February and confirmed on the following day by written plan of corps defense.

That the intelligence was unexpected and caused serious repercussions on a higher level is indicated by General Clark in *Calculated Risk:*

> Alexander brought up the Anzio situation and indicated that he did not agree with my order to Lucas on the previous day rescinding the instructions for VI Corps to continue the attack on Cisterna.* He urged me to be prepared to attack with the 3rd Division again in an all-out effort to get Cisterna and expressed the opinion that the enemy would not counter-attack in force. . . . Later that night, when Alexander's headquarters received additional intelligence reports, he communicated with me at midnight to warn me of the danger of a strong counterattack, and the next day he expressed satisfaction that I had ordered defensive measures.

The attack was launched on schedule.

On the night of 3–4 February the Germans began their Anzio offensive by launching a two-pronged assault from the west and east against the

* In the opposite direction!

110

center of the Allied salient extending up the Albano road from Carroceto to Campoleone. . . . At daybreak on 4 February the attack on the west appeared to be the more threatening. An enemy battalion of the 65th Infantry Division, supported by a few tanks and self-propelled guns, broke through the left flank of the I Irish Guards to reach the Campoleone-Nettuno railroad paralleling the Albano road. . . . Later it became evident that the more serious threat was to the east flank of the salient. . . . As the morning wore on the situation became increasingly difficult for the I Irish Guards and the 6 Gordons. . . . Soon the situation became critical. . . . During the afternoon of 4 February the force of the enemy attacks gradually weakened against the stubborn defense put up by the 24 Guards Brigade and the 6 Gordons. . . . Although the initial German attack had been checked, General Lucas considered that the forward units of the I Division were dangerously exposed, and he ordered them withdrawn to a new and more defensible line. . . . The enemy's objective of wiping out the Campoleone salient had been achieved; his effort to isolate and destroy the 3 Brigade had largely failed. Bad weather had hampered the movement of tanks and other heavy equipment and stubborn Allied resistance had slowed down the enemy infantry attacks. The enemy had suffered heavy casualties—nearly five hundred killed—and during the operation the British took more than three hundred prisoners, most of them captured during the counter-attack launched by the London Scottish and the 46 Royal Regiment. Prisoners complained that the attack had been hurriedly organized without adequate reconnaissance of the ground and that some units had been moved up by forced night marches and thrown directly into the battle.

Thus ended the first German offensive against the beachhead. We had forewarned the Allies of the impending German attack at the correct time and the correct place. From now on I should be able to rely on Franco's information; and the base, judging from their congratulatory messages, should be able to act on mine.

The problem, now, was to really get down to work.

11 TROUBLE

AT THE HEIGHT OF THE GERMAN ATTACK on the Campoleone salient, on February 4, while I sat bundled up in the "hole," wrapped in two overcoats to keep from shivering, poring over Franco's latest bulletin, Cervo burst in white as a corpse and visibly trembling.

"It's all over," he said tensely, "I've been caught!"

Normally such words would have paralyzed me, but I was already half paralyzed.

"A Fascist militiaman in plain clothes caught me taking pictures at the Basilica of San Paolo while the police were making a raid. He's taken my Minox. You must hide me right away!"

As his story unraveled, Cervo's tension began to transfer to me, and I too started to shiver. The police, it seemed, had carried out a raid on the extraterritorial basilica where they had managed to ferret out several Italian officers in hiding, some disguised as monks, one of them an Italian general named Monti.

As Cervo sat on the end of my bed, finishing his story, and wringing his hands, it flashed through my mind that it was his neck that someone should have wrung for such a blatant act of insecurity. But I was now as scared as he, and more preoccupied with how to amend the situation than complain about it.

Then Lele came rushing in to ask why the devil Cervo had driven his Topolino right to the piazzetta outside, where it could easily be followed. So Cervo rushed out and moved it round the corner. When he came back he was just as terrified as before, pounding his forehead with his fist and muttering, "Oh God, what shall I do!"

I did not know myself and was trying desperately to keep calm and show a sense of authority and stability, though I was all a-jitter inside.

Some bold and unexpected move had to be made, and fast; but what? Then, remembering that Cervo had said his father—a high-ranking member of the police in Bologna—had been in Rome for the last few days, I evolved what sounded like a desperate plan. Cervo should go straight to his father, tell him what had happened (so that

112

he might corroborate Cervo's evidence) then rush back to his squadron and start raising hell about having had his camera taken by some idiotic plain-clothes man, that the camera belonged to his father who had got it from an enemy agent in occupied Greece, that he had been taking pictures of the Caruso raid for the hell of it, just to see how the camera worked.

Cervo looked dubious. It appeared too wild a gamble. But I could see no alternative and neither could the others. If Cervo were to disappear from his squadron after such an incident it would be tantamount to admitting his guilt. He would not only be listed as a deserter but strongly suspected of espionage; this way, with luck, he might get away with a reprimand. By a bold attack he would at least have the advantage of a story to work with. Otherwise the search would be on, and our chances of keeping him secreted with us once he was specifically sought would be pretty thin, especially if they arrested and started threatening his family. Furthermore who would handle the radios, and what would happen to his part of the mechanics of our operation?

Poor Cervo was crestfallen. Underneath it all I was furious at his having jeopardized our work by the foolish and totally useless act of taking pictures of no military (and virtually no political) value at a time when the fate of the beachhead lay in the balance. If I hadn't been, perhaps I would not have had the courage even to suggest that he put his head back into what appeared to be a noose.

But Cervo saw what I meant, and agreed to do what I suggested. It was a terrible gamble; he might be walking straight to his death. Nevertheless he went dejectedly out of the flat to see if he could pull it off, arranging to have his family call Franco with a conventional phrase to inform us immediately of the outcome.

Though there was nowhere for us to run, we mechanically packed and hid the most compromising files, in case of a raid, and continued our work.

Franco's bulletin of February 4 contained mostly items in answer to queries from the base and details of traffic movement, ammunition and gasoline dumps. Working on them enabled me to keep my mind off Cervo's (and our own) predicament.

The first of Franco's men were beginning to cover the roads in and out of Rome on a round-the-clock basis, sending in complete breakdowns of all traffic in both directions. However, he still had not succeeded in covering *all* the roads and we were obliged to use approximate estimates on some of these avenues.

The main German strategy for avoiding Allied aircraft was nonetheless clear: moving almost entirely by night and in columns of fifteen to twenty vehicles, each about a kilometer apart, they were managing to bring down reinforcements reasonably unmolested. Allied aircraft were concentrating on bombing towns and villages without apparently realizing that in and around these built-up areas the Germans had constructed or improved (with the use of forced labor) the by-passing roads, and that no matter how seriously a town was damaged there was always some means of getting traffic through it. This same principle applied to freight yards—a favorite target for Allied aircraft—but we warned the base that this was absolutely ineffective in stopping the movement of rail traffic; though trains might be destroyed, there were always sufficient shunting lines available to move more traffic on its way.

What was essential, I emphasized to the base, was to maintain a constant tempo of attacks on bridges, overpasses and other such delicate points, both on rail and road, *outside* the cities, harder to reach and repair, and where, though traffic might be interrupted for only short periods, at least, during those periods, *nothing* could pass. Also this did far less damage to the civilian population—many of the poorer people round the freight yards beginning to complain that for the information passed to the Allies all they got in return was a demolished home!

At the same time we were now convinced that more use would have to be made of partisans—other than for wrecking trains and sowing three-cornered nails on highways—specifically to complement the air force in hampering German communications by blowing up ammunition trains in stations, blowing key bridges and embankments, especially in areas unreached, or unreachable, by Allied aircraft. For this—and it was now the umpteenth time we had struggled with the deficiency—fuse cord, detonators and time pencils were essential for any reasonable margin of success, let alone security; and these could be obtained only from the OSS (or SOE—our British equivalent in such operations).

An air drop would have to be arranged. So I asked Franco to work out the best possible spot on the outskirts of Rome where three fires could be built at a specific time of night, while I convinced the OSS to send in a plane to drop us the required equipment. It would be a risky affair, so close to Rome, both for the pilot, who would have to run the gantlet of flak if spotted as an enemy plane, and for Franco's men, who would have to expose themselves after the curfew in order to light the fires and collect the containers as soon as they reached the ground.

Franco, however, was of the opinion that no risk was too great for such an operation. Not only would it enable the partisans to aid the Allies in a concrete—forgive the pun—manner, but it would also go a long way toward raising the morale of the partisans, which had suffered considerably from enforced inaction owing to the situation at the beachhead, and was inclining them to waste their efforts on petty attacks on German personnel.

When Franco had gone, and the rest of us were sitting around the little living room waiting for developments, the phone rang. Maria answered it, and the sight of her expression made us pale.

"Is it Cervo?" we chorused. "What is it?"

Maria shook her head. "I've got to see my father immediately at the Grand Hotel. Something has happened, but they won't tell me what."

As she was preparing to leave the phone rang again. From Maria's disjointed answers we gathered that some woman was giving her a veiled warning of danger. Was it because of her father, we wondered, or because of Cervo?

The suspense was unbearable.

In either case, if Maria were taken, and though they might have nothing specific against her, our whole hideout would be endangered.

Poor Maria! She was pale and even more nervous than usual, but acting with considerable courage, arranging to phone us as soon as possible to let us know what to do.

That we might be sure it was she who was calling (none of us ever answered the phone lest it become known to whoever might be calling that there were men in the house) we worked out a combination of rings to convey different messages: four rings, then silence, meant it was all right to pick up the receiver the minute the phone rang again.

Two rings, followed, after a definite pause, by two more, meant "Danger! Get out of the house as fast as possible!" Three rings, followed by three, meant "Do not answer, am in danger, cannot talk, but stay where you are."

About an hour after Maria had left, the phone rang, startling us, despite the fact that we were staring at it and waiting for it to do just that: two peals . . . pause . . . two more. Lele tried to make a joke, but it distorted his features into a sort of Grand Guignol.

Just as we were planning to decamp, the phone rang again, four times, and we realized it had been four all along, that Maria, nervous and unused to the new method, had misjudged the rings. Gingerly Lele picked up the receiver and heard that Maria would shortly be home.

When at last she arrived she explained that the Germans were removing all Italian councilors of state from the city and taking them north to be nearer the republican capital of Salo. Her father, being a senator, was to be moved, despite his condition. During the night over a hundred high officials had been arrested, then mysteriously, later in the day, had apparently been released.

So much for that. But we still had nothing about Cervo.

More time passed and it was close to midnight. As we sat around the card table studying military maps and listening to the radio, a truck drove up and parked in the piazzetta outside the front door. Looking at each other we realized the game was up. An ominous clatter of military boots resounded on the cobbles, then someone began to pound on the big *portone*. In a second we had everything hidden. With the suitcase containing the files I stood ready to run for the "hole." Baldo had gone to the farthest window in Maria's room to peer down through the slats of the shutters at what was happening in the square. Suddenly he was back. The Germans, he said, had surrounded the building across the piazzetta and appeared to be removing bundles that looked like bales of cloth. For several minutes we waited in suspense, then came the crashing of a lowered iron store shutter, much stamping and many shouted orders, then the racing of an engine, then nothing but the stillness of the night.

In the morning we discovered the Germans had raided the warehouse of a Jewish cloth merchant across the street.

A little while after the truck had roared off, Franco arrived with news of Cervo and gave us the excuse for a slight celebration. Cervo had been put under technical arrest by his squadron Commander, but everyone seemed to believe his story. Caruso, the new chief of police, into whose hands the camera had fallen, was apparently anxious to have it himself as a souvenir, and was trying to wheedle it out of Cervo. Only one point worried us now: were there any other shots on the film taken previously which might be compromising (there are fifty frames on a Minox film), and had the police chief had it developed?

Until we knew, the suspense would continue.

Changing the subject, Franco told me he had selected and arranged for a spot to receive the drop: a flat piece of marshland in the first sharp bend of the Tiber north of Rome and west of the Milvio bridge, an area scarcely frequented by Germans, yet with nearby workers' houses from which the operation could be organized. So we worked out a plan on the large-scale maps and I prepared a message for the base.

The main purpose of the drop, apart from the possible effectiveness of the sabotage that could be done with the equipment, would be to raise the morale of Franco's men as well as the underground in general, adding inestimably to the prestige of the OSS, myself, Franco, his men and all concerned. I was also anxious to have another radio transmitter dropped in; the two sets we already had were being cannibalized to obtain one that would function properly. With two separate radios in action I would be able not only to double the flow of information but also halve the risk of going off the air completely.

As for the military situation, it was clear from the number of heavy-artillery groups and heavy tanks which were transiting toward the beachhead that the Germans were preparing to build up a preponderant striking force with which to attack once more. On the other hand, according to Franco's high-level sources, the Germans were just then (February 5) preoccupied with the Cassino front, where they were concentrating to halt increasing Allied pressure so as to stabilize the front before turning to an all-out attack against the beachhead—again, according to Franco's informants, against the Allied flank round Carroceto where they had eliminated the salient but behind which large numbers of German reserves had not yet been committed.

On the morning of February 7 Franco's bulletin started off boldly:

The German Command intends to launch the final attack against the beachhead from the Pratica di Mare bases. They expect notable success from a favorable outcome of such action against the beachhead, especially for psychological reasons. The morale of their troops is very high. From these operations the German Command is convinced they will thereafter be able victoriously to counter any further Allied attempts at landing.

However, in the very next paragraph, the bulletin pointed out that for the moment the Germans were using forces relieved by the diminished activity on the beachhead for strong counterattacks in the Cassino area.

Clearly the major attack against the beachhead was some time ahead.

The next day, February 8, Franco's bulletin contained the detailed report of a meeting held by SS Colonel Dollmann in Via Tasso, German police headquarters in Rome, in which he gave the assembled officers news received directly from Berlin to the effect that the Germans intended to make a supreme effort on the Italian front with all units available. In view of the fact that in Russia the present front could not be held and the Germans were being obliged to fall back to "better defensive lines," a success in Italy was indispensable for German prestige.

On February 9 Franco brought me the first really detailed breakdown of German battle order and organization round the beachhead, which he said had been copied from German operation maps in German headquarters, observed as late as that morning.*

* The German Forces facing the beachhead are arranged into two Army Corps, the Ist and the XIVth, each of three divisions with two in reserve, altogether forming the 14th Army. The 1st Army Corps covers the area Littoria to Lanuvio along the line Littoria-Doganella di Ninfa-Torrecchia-Tenuta San Gennaro: among its divisions the *65th Motorized,* the *90th Panzer Grenadiers* with a brigade of *SS Reichsfuehrer,* and the 112th (?).

The XIVth Corps area covers the Pratica di Mare-Albano area with the following probable divisions *26th Armored, Hermann Goering,* and a third whose number is not established.

At the point of juncture between the two sectors is an armored Division in reserve, presumably the 29th, deployed from Ariccia to Genzano to Maschio dell'Artemisio. It depends tactically directly from Army HQ. A second reserve division is in the Rocca di Papa-Artena area for the purpose of rapid movement to face either an Allied breakthrough north-west of Velletri or an

This kind of information, needless to say, I couldn't wait to draft and it was on the air within the hour. But Franco still had no indication of the actual date of the impending main attack so we limited ourselves to filing to the base the order of battle and the intended point of attack, and waited for further information.

There was, however, one more whole page in Franco's bulletin, on an item of counterintelligence which should have been of vital interest to the Allies.

From a down-and-out Italian army cipherer who had been working in close contact with the Germans, we learned—for the price of 10,000 lire (or about $100)—that the Germans were regularly managing to break the code of Allied plane-to-ground communications, and were making great use of these messages, especially for their own defensive measures and to be informed of what Allied reconnaissance was reporting. The laxity which had permitted the Germans to break the codes so easily was apparently due to the fact that Allied pilots, instead of using any varied one of the 31 columns of ciphers available to them, repeatedly used the first. The result was that though the Allied codes, referred to as "Siko-cards," were changed daily, on those days when there was a great deal of movement (convoys, air reconnaissance, fleet movements) the Germans were able to break the code by about 10 or 11 A.M. and from then on till midnight it was as if the Allies were transmitting in clear.

Immediately (February 9) I informed the base of this, and had the base paid speedy attention to this message it might well have enabled the Allies to recapture the Carroceto factory (which they had now lost to the Germans in three days of bitter fighting), an essential key to the forthcoming German offensive.

What happened instead is reported by the Fifth Army historian:

---

eventual attack on Rome, both of which possibilities the German High Command is at present inclined to exclude.

The non-divisional artillery groups, self-propelled and Corps artillery, which are particularly numerous, are mostly in the Solforata-Pavona-Lanuvio-Vigne Vecchie area.

The purpose of the Ist Corps is still to maintain pressure with limited offensive actions around the perimeter of the beachhead, whereas the XIVth Army Motorized Corps is to attack the Allied flank for the actual breakthrough to the sea.

By noon of the 10th [February] the enemy held the Carroceto railroad station as well as the Factory. . . . The VI Corps G–2 estimated that the enemy would need some time to reorganize before renewing the attack. . . . It was important for VI Corps not only to regain the Factory area but also to effect the relief of at least a major part of the I Division. The first step had been taken on the night of 9–10 February when the 180th Infantry under Colonel Dulaney took over the positions of the 2 Brigade just west of Carano. The next night the 179th Infantry under Colonel Kammerer relieved the 168 Brigade south of the Factory and launched a counterattack at 0630, 11 February, to retake the Factory. Aided by the 191st Tank Battalion, men of the 1st Battalion made their way into the Factory in the afternoon, only to be driven out. Though our artillery and tanks converted the buildings into a blazing mass of ruins, the enemy held; *prisoners revealed that an intercepted radio message had given them foreknowledge of the attack.* Another attack before dawn on the 12th likewise failed, and the 45th Division gave up the effort to regain the Factory. [My italics.—P. T.]

As an indication of the all-important intelligence value to the enemy of these intercepted messages, General Westphal wrote:

Aerial reconnaissance could no longer penetrate deeply. Reports of agents were very few. Prisoners were seldom taken. *The only useful information came from the interception and deciphering of enemy radio messages.* The enemy's radio activity was so abundant that these were picked up daily in great numbers, some of them even in "clear." [My italics—P. T.]

It would seem that in espionage it takes as much luck to get one's information acted upon as it does to get the information to begin with!

12 OUR INTELLIGENCE MUSHROOMS

THROUGHOUT MY STAY BEHIND THE GERMAN LINES I kept a sort of running diary, purposely making it as vague as possible, and leaving out all mention of military or espionage data, in case it fall into the hands of the Germans. With this record, however, I was able to catch a little of the atmosphere of day-to-day life. My entry for February 10 runs as follows:

It is midnight. They are playing Moussorgsky's "A Night on Bald Mountain" [on the radio]. Maria had just come in with a tray of tea things [indicative of the peculiar hours we were inclined, or sometimes obliged, to keep]. We've stopped playing gin rummy and are listening to the BBC broadcast the warning to the Rome police we asked for a few days ago. Things are going very badly down on the beachhead. Poor Lele's prostate is giving him hell. The latest bottle of John Haig [another of Franco's many thoughtful provisions] is almost empty. We've had a busy day! I had an awful lot of odd things to do. OSS is dropping equipment to us tomorrow. A British major, an escaped prisoner of war, has sent me a note saying he wants orders! The number of people who want to file through us, or receive directions, is mounting daily. For us things seem to be going all right, but God knows what is going to happen on the bridgehead. Now we are listening to *Deutscher Kurzwellensender Atlantik* [the phony German station actually operated by the British, which put out the best light music late into the night], and strange jazz, in a room draped with pink striped silk, which is a little different job from the one I thought I was coming to do. But, God willing, I will still get a chance to do the other one too. [Help liberate Rome.] The fantastic complications of underground life here, and the incredibly incongruous things that happen are too many for me to put on paper, for obvious reasons, but I hope I can, sometime, because they are utterly incredible. Maria and Lele are now lying on the couch reading *Uncle Tom's Cabin* to each other (in Italian, naturally). The Count [as it amused

121

us to refer to Baldo, because of his constant poise under the most grueling circumstances] is away; otherwise we would be playing cutthroat bridge. He is out getting himself a badly needed night with a blonde!

All this, in the light of time, may need a little explaining.

It had been Franco's opinion for some days, especially since Cervo's incident with the camera, that it would be best to have another hideout prepared in case of emergency. To this end it was agreed that Baldo, who had a small apartment in the Parioli district which he had abandoned when he had gone into hiding, should venture out one afternoon, reestablish his presence with the janitor, give him a good tip, and find out what situation had developed in his absence. As a cover for this operation he was to take one of his numerous and more attractive girl friends to spend the night with him, so that the mission, though hazardous, would not be without compensation.

As for the British escaped POW major who was so anxious to be of assistance to us and who wished to file through us the intelligence he was able to collect, I found myself in a very unhappy position. Bluntly, the chances of his collecting anything which we did not already know or which could be of timely importance were very limited. But this I could not possibly tell him, as it was clearly the only thing which kept up his morale and his sense of being useful; so I undertook to have his messages picked up at regular intervals. To have him with us would have been impossible, as our salvation in case of a raid, or disaster, was to stick to our false identity cards and play them for all they were worth—for which a perfect knowledge of the language was essential. Above all I didn't want him to know the extent of our own espionage network, which was becoming so precise in its mechanics that it would have been folly to endanger its security for any reason other than one essential to our work. We were too big and too well organized to risk endangering our network by the addition of minor sources. With the Badogliani we had already perforce been in contact, so that our existence could not be denied, but even with them I wanted to play down the extent of our ramified operation. Moreover, it seemed to me to be of greater value to the Allies to develop as many *different* and *independent* networks as possible, filing material gathered by their own sources and over their own channels of communication, so as to give the Allies a chance for comparative evaluation.

To this end I let it be known that I would file service messages to facilitate the establishment of such communications, for anyone, in their own private codes, or in clear, or in any manner they chose. We thus helped the Badogliani when they were in trouble, and an Italian naval officer by the code name of Franco who ran a naval intelligence organization known as SIS was eventually able through us to get in contact with the Italian naval base at Taranto and file intelligence, predominantly of a naval character, to Admiral de Courten, Badoglio's Secretary of the Navy. That his code name was "Franco" and that his organization was known as SIS (Secret Intelligence Service) as opposed to *our* Franco's SIS (Socialist Information Service) was the subject of some pleasure and amusement to us; for the Germans were aware of the naval organization, but not of ours, and we were therefore able to handle our comparatively vast network to the confusion of the Germans as well as the other underground movements. In fact this naval officer, who turned out to be Admiral Franco Maugeri, in his book *From the Ashes of Disgrace* refers to himself as head of "Rome Underground," mentioning only that there was a major from the Fifth Army in the city. That virtually nothing was known of the scope and size of our organization, even to those intimately involved in it, is not surprising; it was designed with that intention. Only a few key men were in on the secret, and no one but Franco and I knew the basic mechanics; the lower levels ignoring even for whom their information was destined other than the Socialist party.

As it was, the Socialist party being a mass movement, partly of intellectuals and partly of workers, there were Socialist eyes and ears in practically every office, at every street corner, in the farms and villages between Rome and the beachhead, in the trucks and carts that jogged along the country roads, among the laborers that built the military installations for the Germans, among the fisherfolk in the port and river areas, among the sailors on coastal shipping, everywhere in fact where human beings lived or worked and where the Germans had to pass. But, most important of all, being Socialists, they were organized, and their system of organization, from cell to section to center, meant not only optimum security, but established channels of communication which were as essential in getting information to me as the secret radio was vital in getting it out across the lines to the Allies.

At Socialist zone headquarters in the sections of the city where the farmers brought their wares to the black market they would describe in detail German concentrations in their neighborhood, mine fields, gun emplacements, gasoline dumps, the progress of local fortifications, and, when faced with little sketches of insignia or a type of tank or gun, could shake or nod their heads.

At the main hospitals where the wounded from Allied bombing raids in the Alban Hills were brought, the doctor would nonchalantly gather details from their patients about who was hit and where, and what the targets were around them. When the interns went to help the civilian wounded in the little towns that nestled round the Alban Hills they would bring back detailed accounts of German installations within spitting distance of the beachhead. Children, far back from the front, playing in the fields, within eyeshot of long-range German guns, would tell their parents, who, in turn would tell their neighbors; and so the information would be carried to Rome in the minds of the peasants as they brought their baskets of cheese and vegetables to the market. Once they had been questioned by one of our men, they would gather information more carefully and precisely on the following trip, taking the trouble to count, to note, to specify insignia, type of caliber of gun or tank, or vehicle.

Thus dozens of carefully camouflaged ammunition dumps, gas dumps, gun emplacements, tank concentrations and various military installations would be revealed to us daily through this Socialist grapevine.

From zone headquarters the collected scraps of information, with all the other information both military and political, would be brought to a central headquarters which was changed at frequent intervals. One of Franco's four top men, known only by a pseudonym, would stop here two or three times a day to pick up the total collection of information—which regularly filled a good-sized brief case—and take it to Franco's special information headquarters—unknown as such to any but the top operators of our special information service. Here, for several hours in the morning the information would be sifted, checked, controlled, boiled down and finally typed up in short snappy items on tissue paper to form the daily bulletins which were brought to me. Actually this work took place in the back office of a German publishing house of which Franco was nominally in charge, and behind which he had a small bedroom and bath where he would spend two or three nights a week.

Several secretaries worked in the front office during the day, handling the regular business of the publishing house, unaware that in the back office a complex espionage organization was functioning. Most of the errand boys and some of the customers were actually members of the military underground assigned to guard the place or act as armed escorts for other "customers," and often they carried strange parcels containing grenades, revolvers or submachine guns. Sometimes, Franco told me, their manners with the *real* customers were not as polished as they might have been, but otherwise the operation functioned so smoothly that the regular workers never suspected anything was actually happening other than perhaps a little black marketing.

Once the information was typed up, in order to free Franco from the routine of bringing it down to me, one of the least conspicuous but most trustworthy members of Franco's top organization was selected for this regular job: a short, thin, wiry Neapolitan with dark hair, about thirty years old, named Mario. Every morning, sometime before noon, Mario would appear, punctual as the postman, heralding his presence by the conventional six short rings of the doorbell, bearing the day's information collected overnight and sifted during the early morning at Franco's headquarters.

It may be wondered why, if Franco could provide such good intelligence, he did not file it directly to the base instead of delaying and endangering the intelligence as well as the service by making it pass through an extra step. In cases of emergency or a red-hot item, he would, of course, do exactly that, especially if there was no time to check with me before a scheduled contact with the base. But in practice this extra step was more than essential, resulting not only in better, but actually in faster, intelligence.

To begin with we received far more information than we could possibly file. Someone had to be responsible for exactly what was sent out and when. An over-all record of the whole picture had to be kept so as to know what had already been reported, by us or by others, what had been transmitted to the base or held for confirmation or a more appropriate moment. The bulk of the information at Franco's headquarters had to be destroyed each day to make room for more and not lie around in such an exposed and compromising place. Yet some sort of record and cross-filing had to be kept.

As for speed, we gained many hours' advantage by our system; though I might lose an hour or so editing and preparing a message, I did it with the experience gained from drafting innumerable messages in cablese as a foreign correspondent, cable desk editor, and intelligence officer.

Considering the bulk of information to be filed, and the shortness of the time, messages had to be enormously condensed, yet extremely carefully phrased so as not to lose their meaning. Considering the faintness of our signal, the expertise required for transmitting and receiving it, the inevitable danger of garbling in coding, decoding and transmission, it's a wonder anything ever got through at all without garbling. Even Western Union has to duplicate its figures to avoid confusion.

By receiving messages in English, already qualified, and to a certain extent already evaluated, in terminology and with abbreviations they were accustomed to, the first-rate boys at the receiving end in Caserta and Anzio could rush a piece of vital information to whoever had to act upon it, almost in a matter of minutes.

After Mario had given me all the information and verbal messages from Franco's headquarters he would disappear as inconspicuously as he had come. An hour or so later a young man named Primo would appear. He had a sensitive face with that faraway smile and expression in his eyes that denotes TB. Calm, punctual and, as I was later to learn, intrepid, he had, of course, no idea who I was, believing me to be just another member of the Socialist party, and had no idea of the dynamite contained in the messages he bore, tightly folded and slipped into a ring on his finger so as to be easily swallowed in case of arrest, toward the next link in the chain.

In the neighborhood, at a continuously changing rendezvous, he would meet another young man, who would take the message and transport it across town to the neighborhood of the radio, where it would be picked up by the radio operator or his assistant.

Only these two knew where the radio was located, with the exception, of course, of Cervo, who was in charge of finding suitable locations for it and moving the two sets about town with his motorcycle, conferring with me every now and then about how things were going.

Thus no one along the chain, from the spotter of a piece of information, to the operator who keyed it out, knew anything but what he should, and risks were apportioned according to the danger of the various stages. As one of the most risky parts of the operation was crossing town with the actual message (for at any moment one might be arbitrarily arrested and carted off to forced labor) the couriers were chosen solely for that purpose, so as not to be able to compromise themselves or us, no matter which was caught. Each man fitted into the mosaic, but alone could give no real clue as to the general picture. For such a system to work, each man had to feel that the humblest and most routine job was as vital to the operation as the most brilliant or romantic; and only their ideals could provide such a motivating force.

As a place from which to operate the radio Cervo had made a clever arrangement with the caretaker of one of the many river boats along the Tiber (complex wooden buildings on floating pontoons used during the summer as swimming and boating clubs, but largely unused during the winter except for their locker-room and shower facilities) where the caretaker was only too happy to make a little extra money renting out the cabins and closing an eye to what went on inside—their fame as places of homosexual assignations being well known throughout the city. This particular river boat was almost opposite the Italian Ministry of Marine from which radio signals were bound to be emitted and which I was inclined to believe would add cover rather than draw attention to our own weak signal, in case of triangulation.

On alternate days the operator would set up his radio in one of the dressing rooms, hang his small antenna along the railing and start tapping away to the base. Of this the caretaker was unaware. For his trouble he was paid three dollars monthly. Sometimes the operator would be on the air as long as an hour, wildly dangerous, but essential in view of the bulk of material we had to file.

For the other days Cervo had found a pleasant and willing priest in a small church in the heart of old Rome who was willing to close an eye to messages' being tapped out from the quiet penumbra of his sacristy. There the operator could work with the assurance that even if the enemy were to locate his signal, he would have time to get out the back of the sacristy while the priest delayed the police at the doors of the church.

Thus each day the point of transmission was changed, affording a certain amount of security in case of triangulation by the Germans.

Some two hours after I had sent my message, which usually reached the operator just in time to be encoded before his scheduled contact with the base, I would receive a message from the base in answer to my previous messages, usually in the form of queries for more information, more specific data, along with thanks for effective ones in the past and indications of successful action taken.

Later in the afternoon the whole process would be repeated for a second contact with the base, so that my communications were, on the whole, pretty remarkable, certainly for those days, when no such volume of material had ever been transmitted from a secret radio behind the lines. Yet it was still below the level of what I hoped eventually to achieve.

Though Franco's bulletins contained the bulk of our information (in a six-week period they amounted to ninety-eight single-spaced type-written pages), they were far from the only information provided by him. Another of the regular services was a continuous breakdown of German insignia wherever they were noted. One man, specially qualified in this sort of intelligence, an engineering draftsman, would render them carefully on special thin tracing paper, and forward them to me for transliteration to the base.

Seldom, if ever, did we use anything but our own information, so as not to convey to the Allies that we were independently confirming some other report; also I did not like to use information that was not as close to being first hand or eyewitness as possible. However, as we had access to the information collected by the half-dozen strange organizations that flourished in Rome at the time (but which usually had no way of getting it out, or a much slower channel than ours), we would read it all and file it away for reference. Every little scrap of information that came in was debated carefully before being filed, unless, as was often the case, it was clearly too preposterous for serious consideration. Baldo, our cartographer, would then find the location on his large-scale maps, noting verifiable items when important. Soon we had a suitcase full of typewritten files marked *Battle Order, German Insignia, Ack-Ack, Gun Emplacements, Mine Fields, Gas and Ammo Dumps, Counterespionage, Relations with Partisans, Political Info,* etc.

On Baldo's maps the strong points ringing the beachhead, the individual German command posts, HQs, the concentrations of tanks, artillery, ack-ack batteries, the gas and ammo dumps, the German emergency airfields, all began to stand out clearly. On successive days, after the most urgent items of news, and especially on the slacker days, we would send through to the base comprehensive lists of all ack-ack units noted in the general area round Rome and the beachhead; the strong points round the perimeter; secondary lines of fortification and strong points.

Franco would come in almost daily, and every third or fourth night would stay late for dinner, or spend the night. Then we would have long discussions about the organization, about operations, present and future, and come to the necessary agreements and decisions.

I would explain in detail what was wanted by the Allies and he would explain in detail the methods and difficulties of obtaining it from his end. We worked out our finances, how much was to be paid, to whom, and on what basis, what arms were to be bought or moved, what contacts made or avoided. It was extremely pleasant collaboration and I felt we complemented each other, both in temperament and in our various knowledges, training and special skills. We were the same age, our upbringing had been similarly varied but contemporary, and our reactions to the present mess in Europe and what could be done to ameliorate it, though seen from different viewpoints, extraordinarily compatible. He was a better intelligence officer than I, especially because of his intimate knowledge of German and Italian army equipment, personnel, methods and organization. I, on the other hand, was a better journalist, more preoccupied with speed and accuracy, and, of course, more thoroughly acquainted, as he could not be, with the mechanics of the OSS and the complexities on the Allied side.

129

Not the least of my jobs, however, was the constant effort at keeping high their morale. Though he and his men were anxious to do everything in their power to aid the Allied victory, at enormous personal risk to themselves, they badly needed someone to make use of their efforts, someone from the Allied side to work with who knew what to do with the material they provided, and who at the same time they could trust implicitly not to let them down. This, as time went on, was to become my severest burden.

13 PARTISAN AND PARAMILITARY OPERATIONS

THE MOST PSYCHOLOGICALLY EFFECTIVE SUPPORT one could render the partisans, and the one which gave them the most inspiration to redouble their efforts, was, of course, a parachute drop of equipment. Better than any exhortation over the radio, this was an overt token of comradeship in arms. True, the partisans had a devouring passion for receiving arms, and these arms were inclined to end up in private armories for factional *power*, if not open strife. Yet not arming them would have been worse than sending an infantryman into the line without a weapon: a partisan's weapon constituted a moral as well as a physical necessity: without a weapon he could not truly consider himself a partisan, let alone a combatant.*

Organizing and waiting for a drop was one of the tensest and most exciting part of all our operations. We could never tell till the very last minute if the operation was on or off, as the right weather conditions were a prime prerequisite, and our final indication would come from a conventional phrase broadcast over many channels by the BBC.

Thus, on the night of our first expected drop we sat tensely round the radio listening to the news in Italian, waiting for the announcer slowly to enunciate his special messages: "Catherine is waiting by the well," "The sun will rise at dawn," "Johnny needs sandals," then, like a stab of light, our own special message: "William waits for Mary!" The drop was on, due about midnight.

At first Franco had agreed that I should ride with Cervo on his motorcycle to the spot of the drop and witness the operation; then, after studying the difficulties and dangers, he had, quite rightly, decided against it. There was no point complicating an already complicated operation, and little or nothing I could do to help; nor was there much for me to learn about the mechanics that they could not tell me later.

---

* It had not yet been established that in Italy the partisans were useful as combatants, and it wasn't till May that General Alexander publicly stated they were holding down the equivalent of six full German divisions!

So, while the men waited in the night, ready to ignite their fires as soon as they heard the rumble of an approaching plane, Lele and Baldo and I sat tensely in our darkened sitting room, the window ajar, listening for the drone of an engine. For a long time there was nothing. Minute after minute passed and not a sign or a sound; then, faintly, the rumble of an airplane coming closer and closer, circling in the night. Was it ours? Was it German? Normally I could tell the make by the sound, but now it seemed utterly unintelligible and might have been anything. Almost nightly some lone plane would fly in the darkened sky above the city. Then came three reverberating explosions. By the time they had died away the sound of the plane had also been lost in the night. What the devil, we wondered, could have happened?

Baldo and I had barely got to sleep in the "hole" when we were awakened by Lele bursting in. I always say "bursting" because that is the effect it produced as the trap door unexpectedly opened and a human head popped through.

"There's an emergency," Lele explained, puffing slightly, "but not to do with the drop."

A friend of Maria's wanted her to shelter a British PW for a few days till a permanent hideout could be found for him, or an escape route to the south.

"That's all we needed!" I muttered, annoyed at the thought of further endangering our information service. But we knew, of course, that we would have to help him, if for no other reason than the sake of our own morale.

So Baldo dressed quickly and rushed out sleepy-eyed, without even a cup of that insipid but warming liquid which constituted our normal breakfast, to cross town and pick up the PW.

A couple of hours later he appeared, smiling and unruffled as always, accompanied by a tall, shy, heavy-booted Scots soldier who still wore his British Army Issue boots, and was stuffed into a suit three sizes too small for him.

As Baldo spoke English fairly well he acted as interpreter. I, of course, had to pretend to speak no English; for no matter where he ended up, and especially if he were caught by the German SD, it was essential that our PW know positively nothing of any espionage—for his own sake as well as ours.

132

No sooner had we settled him in the "hole" with a couple of English novels than Mario arrived in a state of great excitement, quite unnatural to his normal calm efficiency. His story was as confused as his behavior.

The boys had heard the plane circling over the city, had lit their fires and waited for the drop; then, inexplicably, there had been a series of explosions.

The best we could make of it was that the pilot, running into flak, had been forced to take evasive action and the packages had fallen astray. In any case all of Rome was talking about the strange plane and the explosions which had followed in its wake.

But that was not the worst of it. The doorbell rang six times, giving us a start, and Franco arrived, shaking his head in a deprecatory manner, to inform us that one of the explosives had fallen—of all places —on the top-floor apartment of one of our own men who was now homeless and destitute, and for whom he requested the authorization of a fifty-dollar sum for emergency relief.

Worst of all, the landing area was now "burnt" and we would have to look elsewhere without having been able to receive a single explosive, detonator, radio, crystal, gold coin, message or anything. Morosely Franco and I patted each other on the back to raise each other's morale, then Franco went off to take care of his varied clandestine affairs.

In the evening, when the maid had gone, and all was clear, we invited our PW to come out of the "hole" and eat and drink with us. He was extremely polite, a very nice boy who said he was a well digger by occupation and that's how we referred to him in our private conversations.

My efforts at broken English, and pantomime gestures, got to be rather ridiculous: "Yesss, noo Bill!" I would say and smile; "Kom Biilll . . ." and made the Italian gesture for eating. But it went off all right.

After supper he described his escape from the Germans, how he'd been living for the last two months in a cave about ten miles out of Rome with a fellow British PW. Once or twice a day a nearby farmer's daughter had taken them food. Otherwise they had sat huddled in the cave with one blanket, day after day, night after night.

Much later when we had successfully headed him toward an escape route we were nearly dangerously exposed by the unwitting farmer's daughter, who attempted to have a message of love forwarded to her well digger. So poignant was the letter that I have always regretted having had to destroy it.

But that night when it came time for bed we fixed him up on the couch in the small sitting room outside our bathroom, with instructions, in case someone rang the doorbell, or he heard anything suspicious, to pick up his bedclothes and run for the "hole."

In he morning the only cheerful news was an announcement by the BBC that in view of the fact that Germans were using Rome as a "stronghold" the Allies intended to bomb it!

Franco's bulletins of February 11 and 12 carried no information about the situation facing the beachhead, and I began to wonder what was happening to the expected German offensive.

There was, however, an item of good news in one of the bulletins: "The BBC's warning to the police has had an extraordinary effect throughout the police forces of Rome, who are now waiting anxiously to see what further steps the Allies may take (such as naming individual culprits, which will put them in a very serious position)."

It was obviously time to send the base our list of top police officers in Rome, especially those most inclined to cooperate with the Germans.

But what of the offensive? Why was there no news?

Then, on February 13, Franco's bulletin arrived with a high-level estimate of the general military situation in Italy:

In German Army circles it is said that Kesselring is in disagreement with the German General Staff. It was his own idea to counter the Allied landings at Anzio with so many units; the German General Staff did not wish to bring further troops and equipment into the Italian "gut." Kesselring nevertheless managed to convince Hitler to listen to him, and now, in view of the success of his initiative, which the German General Staff still considers ephemeral and dangerous to the other fronts, Hitler has been encouraged to support him further. Hence the irritation in the General Staff who see Kesselring's ambition as a grave threat to the general conduct of operations.

On February 14 Franco brought me "hard" news, indicating that the showdown on the beachhead was at hand:

The German High Command has decided to make a supreme effort towards a rapid elimination of the beachhead, not only to have a victory

134

exploitable for internal reasons of prestige, but so as to establish the tactical premise for further operations on the Southern front. It is thus hoped to bring about a change in Italian public opinion and make it possible to implement Hitler's order to maintain the present line at all costs. The German offensive against the beachhead cannot be sustained for long; and the opinion is expressed in German military circles that either the Allies are thrown back into the sea in two or three days or the situation may turn the other way. Lack of gasoline is obliging the Germans to long hauls on foot and to use pack animals to draw artillery. Nevertheless there is still movement of German troops southward.

The Spezia-Rimini line, on which the German units in Northern Italy were based, has been almost completely stripped in order to send men and equipment to the Southern front.

The interruption of the railways has absorbed all German vehicles for logistic necessities; furthermore many German gas dumps have been destroyed by recent air attacks.

On February 15 there was very little news, less than a dozen items of detailed information; then, late in the afternoon, Franco came to see me. He had not had time to inform me and had been obliged to send an urgent message to the base himself, in Italian. The great German attack was scheduled for the next day, February 16, in the area continually indicated by us, the narrow salient round Carroceto.*

Once the area and date of the attack had been indicated there was little more we could do to help the Allies. If, however, the German attack were to end in disaster for the Allies our own position in Rome would be endangered. It was imperative therefore, that we take stock of our own situation, and attempt to improve it. I had come across the lines expecting to stay at most two weeks. Now more than three had passed, and it looked as if I might have to face an even longer siege.

If the Allies were to be thrown back into the sea, our own cover

---

* General Westphal, Kesselring's Chief of Staff, put it thus in his memoirs:

"The assault could be made from either of two directions: from Cisterna towards the south-west, or through Aprillia (Carroceto) to Anzio. Hitler's headquarters ordered the latter, that is to say, the shortest and most direct route to the sea. Not content with this however, they also laid down the breadth of front, namely a narrow strip only six kilometers wide. For years we had been so weak on all fronts that it had never been possible to form more than a "line"; now it was intended to act with weight and "depth," so that every condition for an overwhelming victory was satisfied. For Hitler set great store by the success of this attack."

would need drastic tightening and our capacity for mobility would need to be greatly increased.

Luckily Franco had not been idle. For some weeks he had been in close contact with a young man from the Alto Adige (the former Austrian regions of northern Italy) by the name of Ottorino Borin, a lieutenant in the Italian Command of the Open City of Rome, who, owing to the fact that he spoke fluent German, was acting as liaison officer between the Italian commanding general, with the extraordinary Greek name of Chirieleison, and the German commander of the Open City, General Maeltzer. From Ottorino Borin, needless to say, we had received some of our prime intelligence. Now Franco was to bring him wholeheartedly into our organization, and through him obtain phony papers for us, accrediting Franco and me as officers in the Command of the Open City of Rome. Crucial to the success of this plan was to obtain the agreement of Borin's immediate chief, a colonel named Bonzani, who would have to vouchsafe for our documents, at least over the phone, if we were stopped and interrogated by the regular or the military police. Though Borin had successfully convinced him we were merely Italian officers who needed the documents so as not to be transported north by the Germans, Bonzani was still loath to take such an obvious risk.

What he didn't know was that Franco was already carrying papers provided for him by Borin which identified him as a captain in the Command of the Open City of Rome, printed in German and Italian, permitting him to circulate freely at all times, including the curfew, in civilian clothes and carrying a pistol.

So far the mere flashing of the document had got Franco past routine patrols at night, but he was continuously in danger of the most elementary checkup with the actual Command of the Open City, which would immediately reveal the fraud.

With Borin, however, whose papers were similar but authentic, they had been able to circulate on more dangerous assignments.

Now that the situation was getting desperate at the beachhead, and though the colonel was still temporizing, Borin and Franco decided to go ahead and issue me a similar pass accrediting me as a Captain attached to the headquarters of the Open City, under the false name of Luigi Desideri, for which I had the requisite identity card, etc.

136

The result of all this plotting was that Franco was to bring Borin to me so that we could meet personally. Thereafter, armed with my new paper, I was to start regaining my weather legs by circulating in the city in my new disguise, going with Franco on a tour of inspection in an Open City police car, then visiting his private headquarters to settle several outstanding problems of the organization.

It was just two weeks now since I had been out on the streets at all, and, during that period, a curious psychological change had taken place within me, making me frightened of coming out of the "hole," let alone going out into the city. In the days when I had been at the tailor's I had been terrified, whether indoors or on the streets, but with a fear conditioned by the hope that it would only be for a few days, that if I could just hold out, keep up my nerve, get on with the job, the Allies would soon arrive to relieve me. Now, with the picture so radically changed, instead of my nervousness growing less with habit, it seemed to increase.

The time had come to break the vice.

My diary for February 16 read:

Franco came to fetch me about 6 P.M. I was ready, still wearing the ghastly gray hat and coat I had worn as an auxiliary policeman. We slipped downstairs and into the street without being seen by the *portiere*. There was a grayish light in the cobbled piazzetta, and a few people hurrying to get home before the curfew. Round the corner, by the side entrance to the Palazzo Antici Mattei, a small gray, four-door Fiat sedan was drawn up against the wall. As we approached, two men in uniform got out. A soldier sat in the front by the driver's seat, with a submachine gun between his knees. I felt like asking him not to wave it so ostentatiously in the faces of the startled passersby, then I noticed the Italian Republican General Staff tag on the windshield, and got in saying how-do-you-do politely to the occupants.

A moment later we were speeding through Piazza Venezia, up the Corso, up the Tritone toward Via Veneto. It was just gray enough to make it very difficult for anyone to recognize me at a glance. So I had great fun watching the people on the sidewalk, noting the various German vehicles, wondering what it would be like when I could walk down those streets freely and enjoy all the things I like about the city.

In front of the Excelsior Hotel (which was General Maeltzer's head-quarters) there was a roadblock of frieze-horses and barbed wire, and SS men scrutinized the documents of all the cars that passed. But they let us through without a hitch. Parking a little further up, and across the street, we got out and leisurely walked toward the door of the building in which Franco had his headquarters; then I saw the placard *Domus* which was the name of the publishing house in which it operated.

The others left us, driving off into the penumbra, and Franco showed me up the stairs to the first floor, opening the door with his latchkey. As it was after working hours there was no one in, and we could have the place to ourselves. Three main rooms gave off the hall facing Via Veneto and onto the side street, Via Romagna. They were decked out with office furniture, gay posters on the walls, typewriters, reference books, calendars, etc. In the back Franco had a tiny, immaculate and very modern private room and bath where he spent the night when not out in the various sections of his underground organization.

Through the shuttered windows I could see across the street to the German sentries round the Excelsior.

In his polite, efficient, businesslike manner, Franco showed me the mechanics of how it all worked, explaining in detail how the information came in and was collected and collated before being drawn up and sent down to me.

Then Cervo arrived and we discussed at length the problem of the radios and where best to place them. Again it was clear that if we could only get another radio, rent a top-floor apartment and set it up permanently we could use it for the overflow of intelligence as well as in case of emergency. Furthermore, to perfect our security, there should be certain places that *each* of us knew, but none that *all* of us knew, so that, depending on who was caught, the survivors might have a safe refuge and means of communication with the Allies. Of this we had a hard time convincing Cervo, who could not seem to understand that there were things it was better he know nothing about, for his own peace of mind as well as for ours. I suppose Franco, with his political background, and I with the burnings I had received in North Africa and southern Italy, owing to poor security among the Allies, were instinctively inclined to overprecise security, whereas

138

Cervo, though courageous and loyal, seemed childishly brash in such matters, seeming to think that if there was something we did not tell him it was an indication we did not trust him. He could not understand, though I tried desperately to convince him, that there were things I told Franco that I did not tell Cervo, and things I told him I did not tell Franco; that for there to be security each man should do his own job and try to know as little as possible about everyone else, or how they operated, because what you didn't know you couldn't tell.

Also among the items Franco and I had to go over were the expense accounts for all the men he was employing in the network, which I insisted be kept to the last lira. Records were kept with coded names, if for no other reason than this: horrible as it may seem but true, I suspected that certain characters in the OSS would try to do anything to discredit our work because it was done with Socialist party members —therefore "radicals"—and I wanted to be sure every penny I spent was accountable for, and likewise every penny spent by Franco.

Among the recurrent items in one of Franco's accounts were the words "Cognac per Fruehling," meaning, literally translated, "brandy for springtime." When I asked what the devil it meant, he explained, with his usual smile, that, just before I had arrived, he had been arrested and taken to Via Tasso under the phony accusation of being a "Badoglio parachutist." There he had been befriended by SS NCO, Untersturmfuehrer Fruehling who, once Franco's innocence of the charges had been satisfactorily proved, became friendly with him, meeting him regularly during his off-duty hours. As most Germans were partial to, but could seldom find, or afford, good *Schnaps,* Franco would regularly provide him with a bottle (at OSS expense), sometimes acquiring it at the same time he acquired the welcome bottle of whisky or gin he would bring to me.

To demonstrate his point, Franco picked up the telephone and called SD headquarters at Via Tasso, and, in impeccable German, asked to speak to Untersturmfuehrer Fruehling. After chatting amiably for a while, Franco made a date for the following afternoon, then hung up with a nonchalant "Heil Hitler."

Not to be outdone, Cervo picked up the phone and put a call through to Italian Police headquarters, chatting in the proper staccato tone of a Fascist police officer.

A couple of hours later, when we had finished discussing everything that was then to be settled, Cervo and I bid Franco good night, tiptoed downstairs, climbed once more onto his motorcycle and set off into the dark damp streets of Rome.

Though I was now provided with a facsimile of a curfew pass, there seemed to be no purpose in pointedly courting trouble; so we put-putted slowly through all the most intricate and unheard-of little streets to avoid the roadblocks. At one point I had a nasty shock when we just missed a police car moving slowly across our path from a side street, its small blue blackout lights giving no warning. Then, just as we came out into Piazza Venezia from the narrow lane that skirts the church of Santa Maria di Loreto, we found ourselves in the middle of a slowly moving column of PAI policemen, and it was only by some special grace that we did not run into one or more of them, thus putting an end, if not to theirs, certainly to our existence.

At last, my heart beating unbearably, my gloveless hands freezing in the cold night air, we arrived at the small piazzetta where Cervo quickly deposited me and drove away so as not to attract attention by stopping and restarting the motor.

For the first time since the morning I had arrived I found myself alone on the streets of Rome, three hours after the curfew. To add to the horror, when I inserted the key into the lock, I found the *portone* had been barred from within. Half terrified, half infuriated that Lele or Baldo had forgotten to come down at the appointed time and unbar it, I panicked at the thought of how I would manage to get in. Cervo had disappeared into the night. Owing to the curfew there was no public place from which I could phone. I did not dare shout under our second-story windows for fear of giving away the whole secret of our presence in the building. Yet something had to be done; police-men from the local police station, only half a block away, might be out on their rounds any minute.

Then I heard footsteps on the cobbles in the nearby lane, sending waves of paralyzing fear to my brain—much like the first night with the two strange chauffeurs. There was only one thing to do: pound on the door till I could rouse the *portiere*. He would be surprised, never having seen me before, especially arriving three hours after the cur-few, but it was clearly the lesser of several unpleasant risks, and so I started ringing and pounding.

In the alley the footsteps approached. Inside, no sound of the porter. At last, when I'd almost given up hope, I heard the big steel bar being slid in its grooves and the door opened a crack. Without standing on any ceremony or making the slightest explanation, I pushed my way in, muttered a "Thank you," and rushed for the stairs. Though I did not know it at the time, the porter was, in fact, a very good fellow at heart, and made no remonstrance, assuming, as was natural, that I was some Italian who had come to stay with friends in the building and obviously did not want to be caught outside after the curfew.

But my pounding had aroused an old and rather nondescript female who lived on the ground floor, and who began bombarding me with questions about who I was and where I was going. A little frigidly I answered that it was none of her damned business, then ran up the stairs as fast as I could, hoping Baldo or Lele would answer my insistent six-peal ring. Luckily they arrived promptly and I didn't even have time to reprimand them for not unbolting the door (which in fact they had done, but which someone had thereafter rebarred) before they were mockingly shaking their heads at me. "We know where you've been," they said in chorus, wagging their fingers. "We know all about it. You've mobilized half the police force of the city, had motorcycles and automobiles stolen right and left. You've got Colonel Dollmann and all of Via Tasso alerted, and all you've done is have yourself transported to a very secret address, where, behind a secret door, a beautiful blonde lay waiting for you on an enormous bed. . . . How do you feel?"

Naturally I explained at great length that it was not so at all. But the idea, as I analyzed it in the coldness of the "hole," gave me something to think about other than the nightmare that was happening on the beachhead.

14 PLANS FOR PSYCHOLOGICAL WARFARE

PERHAPS THE MOST SUCCINCT yet comprehensive account of what happened to the February 16 attack is provided by Winston Churchill in his account of the Second World War:

The expected major effort to drive us back into the sea at Anzio opened on February 16 when the enemy employed over four divisions, supported by 450 guns, in a direct thrust southward from Campoleone. Hitler's special order of the day was read out to the troops before their attack. He demanded that our beachhead "Abscess" be eliminated in three days. . . . A deep, dangerous wedge was driven into our line, which was forced back here to the original beachhead. The artillery fire, which had embarrassed all the occupants of the beachhead since they landed, reached a new intensity. All hung in the balance. No further retreat was possible. Even a short advance would have given the enemy the power to use not merely their long-range guns in harassing fire upon the landing-stages and shipping, but to put down a proper field artillery barrage upon all intakes or departures. I had no illusions about the issue. It was life or death.

But fortune, hitherto baffling, rewarded the desperate valour of the British and American armies. Before Hitler's stipulated three days, the German attack was stopped. Then their own salient was counter-attacked in flank and cut out under fire from all our artillery and bombardment by every aircraft we could fly. The fighting was intense, losses on both sides were heavy, but the deadly battle was won.

General Westphal, Kesselring's Chief of Staff, attributed the German failure to eliminate the beachhead primarily to the strength of Allied and the weakness of German intelligence:

The assault . . . found the enemy ready, so that the surprise which would have increased the prospects of success was absent. Two days of heavy fighting resulted only in a slow and costly advance. German troops penetrated to within twelve kilometers of the beach, and some units still nearer, though these, left to themselves, must have been eventually overwhelmed, for there was no more news of them. The Army Group and Army commands decided that they could not be responsible for further heavy losses and called off the attack.

142

Then comes a telling remark about the importance of intelligence in warfare:

Naturally they [the German forces] would have kept up the pressure if they had known how things were going on the other side. But uncertainty of the condition and intentions of the enemy is one of the characteristics of warfare. We now know that the Allied command had in fact already decided on re-embarkation when the German pressure suddenly and unexpectedly ceased.

To indicate the magnitude and importance of the failure of the German offensive—on which depended not only the fate of the Italian front, but also the entire schedule of Allied invasion plans in Europe, and possibly the prolongation of the war—General Westphal used the following historic comparison: "Thus failed an undertaking which was launched with great hopes and an abundance of resources unknown on the German side since the capture of Sebastopol."

Though it was several days before we learned in detail what had happened at the beachhead, my message of the morning of the 16th started off: "Enemy less optimistic but still expecting success of big attack with arriving reinforcements. . . ." At the very height of the battle there was little we could do but concentrate on targets for the air force, the usual road and rail counts, and worry about our own particular problem.

Franco was now most preoccupied by the situation in the underground in Rome; its morale was suffering as much as ours from developments on the beachhead.

In Rome the Fascists were coming out more and more brazenly, sporting their black shirts and their daggers. The morale of the population was further depressed by the serious lack of food and heat, little or no gas or charcoal with which to cook, continuous lack of water, electricity and public transport (the last three deficiencies heightened by Allied air raids). To add to this miserable situation, Allied propaganda seemed to be set on aiding not us, but the enemy. The ingenuous broadcasts of Mayor La Guardia which filled the airwaves and constituted the Allies' prime weapon of psychological warfare, were, because of their political naïveté and total incomprehension of the realities of the situation, having an effect diametrically opposed to the one intended. The sermons of Colonel Stevens (the main Italian commentator on the BBC) were beginning to become monotonous, while reception of the Fifth Army's station on medium wave was still too disturbed and too weak. But the biggest gun of all in favor of the Nazi-Fascists was Mr. Churchill himself with his broadcast support of the "traitor-king," and the incongruous announcement of the ceding to Russia of Italian naval units.

What was urgently needed, Franco said, was a general boost to morale to brace up public opinion and strengthen rather than diminish activities of the partisans. Among his suggestions were a broadcast appeal to the partisan forces to redouble their efforts (little or no recognition had been given by the Allies to their efforts) and threatened action against traitors in pay of the Nazi-Fascists, but above all, the *tangible* boost of some parachute supplies and funds, so often promised and yet so far never materialized.

The partisans, mobilized now since the Anzio landings, had largely exhausted their stocks of food and money; a large percentage of them being workingmen or disbanded soldiers with families to support, they were now reduced to a meager meal a day, and that unheated. If they were to survive much longer some decision would have to be made by the Allies to help support them or at least give them arms and explosives with which to feed their morale by taking action against the Germans.

This, I knew, was a tricky point to be worked out carefully with the Allies; yet listening to Franco I realized that despite the situation at the beachhead, or rather because of it, I must again urge the base to make a parachute drop irrespective of the moon, the weather, or the dangers that might be involved. With the lowering of the morale of the population there was all the more need for equipment with which to intensify railway station sabotage in order to offset Allied bombing of these stations within the built-up areas of Rome which were causing very bad feelings against the Allies, especially when the planes missed their targets by sizable margins, massacring civilians.

Also, it seemed that the time had now come to implement a vital function of psychological warfare which I had been advocating since we landed in North Africa but which I had never managed to put into effect. If I could get another radio functioning—and thus not interfere with the regular flow of military intelligence—I could keep up a daily running commentary with my friends and former colleagues in the Psychological Warfare Section so that we might *really* play ducks and drakes with the Nazi-Fascists. My regular access to the Fascist daily papers alone would have sufficed to carry on a pretty effective operation, but my sources of political intelligence, were if anything even better than the military, and within the city of Rome there was very little of a political nature that was not quickly known to us.

Franco, and especially Giuliano Vassalli, were au courant with what passed in the top councils of the Committee of National Liberation, and therefore of the general pool of political information.

There was virtually no government office in the city—from the old ministries to the municipal garbage collectors—in which we did not have a man, either a Socialist or a member of one of the partisan groups, from whom information would be forwarded.

In all the large (and even in the small) hotels in Rome we had men reporting to us regularly, who, through their constant contact with the Germans, served not only as sources of itemized intelligence, but as barometers for gauging the daily and general morale of the Germans.

Soon after my arrival in Rome I had sent messages to our Allied diplomats closeted in the Vatican, to Sir D'Arcy Osborne, the British Minister to the Holy See, and Harold Tittman, career U.S. diplomat (who acted for Myron Taylor, President Roosevelt's Special Envoy to the Vatican), luckily both of them old and close friends of my family, whom I had known since childhood. The Tittmans were in fact just then eating off our family silver, whiling away the tedium of their imprisonment with volumes from our library (left there at the beginning of the war and which they were kind enough to take care of for us).

However, owing to the delicacy of their diplomatic positions, and the possibility that they might be involved in secret operations of their own, I decided to refrain from putting any further burden on them by asking favors, nor did I indicate to them the extent of my own operations. (Both of these moves were lucky, for it turned out that their codes were known to the Germans and what they filed was virtually in clear!)

We had, in any case, an excellent contact with the Vatican

145

in the form of Franco's uncle, a distinguished and delightful diplomat, at that time Chargé d'Affaires for the Sovereign Military Order of the Knights of Malta to the Holy See, whose chancery was the last house I had lived in in 1940.

Our man in the Fascist censorship office was so highly placed that little of interest passed through the mails that we did not get to know of. In fact, this industrious character would often forward actual letters to us to prove a point of interest. This channel afforded us information from other Axis and neutral countries, which, though seldom of immediate military value, was interesting from a morale point of view. His most useful function was passing on to us the contents of what is known in censorship parlance as a "submission sheet" containing the cream of counterintelligence data; it was amazing how extraordinarily careless people could be in their letters, giving away the location of Allied PWs, partisan groups in the hills, and, worst of all, their own political opinions. Thanks to our farsighted and generous friend, these submission sheets, destined for the German SD, would mysteriously vanish en route, and counterintelligence of interest to us about the neo-Fascists, and especially their double agents, wound up in our files, to be forwarded to the base or used for our own security.

Another man, most important to our security, worked in the Fascist republic's counterespionage organization, helping us avoid falling prey to their double agents, of which there were a great number always trying to pass themselves off as partisans and gain our confidence by handing out titbits of information.

In Regina Coeli, the main Italian jail in Rome, one of the wardens and one of the doctors worked directly for us. From Franco's SS pal Fruehling we had a good inside track into Via Tasso, the SD prison and torture chamber; so that once a man *was* caught we could usually know about it in a matter of hours, and could keep abreast of what happened to him. The padres who assisted partisans executed by the Germans were usually able to obtain the real names of the deceased, often unknown to the Germans themselves.

With these sources, with Cervo as a special assistant to the chief of police, Caruso, with Ottorino Borin at the Command of the Open City of Rome in liaison with Maeltzer, we were in a position to carry on some really amusing psychological warfare.

146

Only on the spot could the effect of Allied propaganda be evaluated properly. In Rome, with a vast network of sources and channels of communication, I could estimate for the Allies the effect their campaigns were having on the Germans, the Fascists, the police—individually and all together—the partisans, the Fascist or anti-Fascist sympathizers, the public in general. But most important—as such weapons are most often likely to backfire or be turned by the enemy against their employers—constant attention and instant communication with the Allies was essential.

So far the only MO—or Morale Operations—data I had felt I could afford to send had been of a counterespionage nature.

On February 14 I sent off fourteen names of the chiefs of the various police bureaus in the Ministry of the Interior, including the heads of branches of the OVRA or Italian secret police, which the base, possibly because so many names were liable to be garbled in transmission, requested we repeat.

On February 19 I sent off a long message indicating fifteen of the most notorious Italian agents working for the Germans (complete with addresses and even hotel room numbers). Here, at least, was a way not only of showing that the Allies were well informed about possible "traitors" and "war criminals," but by broadcasting their names I could spread the information publicly and force them into a sort of Coventry, thus hopefully inhibiting their denunciation of partisans and such innocent victims as Italian Jews, whom the Germans were hunting for their incinerators in Buchenwald and Dachau.

Apropos of this gruesome subject, the place now selected by Franco for the air drop of equipment—and we all dutifully made the sign of the horns when we mentioned it—was to be the Verano, Rome's mammoth cemetery on the edge of the city along the road to Tivoli. Not only would it be easily identifiable by the base when plotting a course for the plane, but Franco's partisans were assured of being undisturbed in lighting fires in the dead of night, thanks to the superstitious nature of Romans. In his note to me outlining the operation Franco pointed out that fifty of the more ostentatious mausoleums had already been selected as suitable for immediate hiding of the dropped equipment; thereafter the partisans could return, at their leisure, entering with bunches of flowers and exiting with explosives.

Thus four whole days dragged by while we coped with our organization, without much to keep up our morale but the laconic official communiqués of the belligerents. Then, February 20, five days after the launching of the German offensive, Franco brought me a bulletin with the first good news about the beachhead, indicating, to our great relief, that the offensive was on its way to failure.

It was evident now that the Germans would eventually be obliged to fall back north of Rome to other defensive positions. The first of these we had already established and informed the base of in detail; but it was only a holding line, and there would be others further north.

To spread our organization Ottorino Borin hit on the happy thought of getting himself assigned a police car with which to go on a junket up to northern Italy ostensibly for the Command of the Open City. He and Franco set off and having traveled as far north as the French frontier to make contact with other partisan groups returned with a packet of first-rate intelligence.

During their absence the regular bulletins, handled by Mario, were less copious, but one curious item foreshadowed the development of some surprise at the beachhead: a report to the effect that the Germans were building large numbers of tanks and guns *out of wood* in several carpenter shops in Rome.

Back from his travels, Franco obtained a clearer picture of this new German offensive, which was radically different from any of their previous efforts:

The Germans have deployed their forces to form two powerful spearheads of heavy tanks and armored vehicles with which to break through from each flank of the beachhead with the purpose of: (1) cutting the beachhead in two, laterally, thus surrounding a large part of the defending troops; (2) inhibiting the fire of Allied naval guns who would be unable to distinguish between their own troops and the Germans. At the same time pressure is to be maintained along the center of the front to permit successful attacks from the flanks.

This information, promptly radioed to the base, was followed by a solution of the mystery of the wooden tanks and guns, many more of which had been completed in the carpentry shops of Rome's largest motion picture studios at Cinecittà! They were to be placed at strategic spots at the center of the front to deceive Allied observers about the real deployment of German assault units.

On the heels of this bulletin came the exact location and number of the phony artillery and tanks: about sixty artillery pieces and approximately one hundred and eighty heavy and very heavy tanks had been set up on the slopes of the hills below Albano and Genzano in order to fool the Allies into believing the main German concentration was on the central front, whereas, in fact, it was deployed against the flanks of the beachhead—about one hundred real tanks and armored vehicles being hidden between Velletri and Cisterna, the principal area of German attack.

Once again the air force flew to the rescue! As their historian recounts it:

Although the weather was not good the air forces answered with around 800 bomber and fighter-bomber sorties and 900 tons of bombs: heavies flew more than 600 sorties against targets along the front, mediums and light bombers hit targets around Cisterna, Carroceto, Campoleone, and Velletri, fighter-bombers smashed gun positions, and fighters of the RAF destroyed 61 vehicles between Rome and the beachhead. The bombing pinned down enemy troops, wrecked communications, broke up units and installations, and materially disorganized the enemy's plans to continue the offensive. When on 3 March he attempted to exploit his earlier gains an Allied counterattack, strongly supported by MATAF's planes, wiped out the effort, and on the 4th the Germans took up defensive positions.

Franco's bulletin of March 5 contained the following textual remark: "The Germans no longer consider attacks against the beachhead worth while."

From that day on we reported no further activity on the beachhead.

With the stabilizing of the front there and at Cassino virtually all the Allied planes which had been employed in support of the ground forces were now freed to operate against targets elsewhere in Italy—and against Rome's rail centers, which became major targets March 3, 7, 8, 10, and 14.

On March 3 (in one of the longest messages ever sent to the base, covering not only the situation at the beachhead but ranging all over Italy) we reported the presence in Rome's Ostiense station of twenty-eight freight cars full of explosives, several trainloads of supplies in Rome's Littorio station, and seventy rail cars, mostly open, carrying light tanks and armored cars ten kilometers north of Rome on the

Salaria, urging the air force to act quickly before the Germans got a chance to move them.

When the B-26s came over they succeeded in centering the ammunition trains in the Ostiense, and the sound of the explosion was so terrific many Romans thought the Allies had made another landing and had reached the gates of the city.

Unfortunately these raids were causing a large number of civilian victims (near the Ostiense a factory was destroyed and 250 workmen were reported buried in the ruins). Although this time it had been clear to all concerned that the German ammunition and supply trains had been the justifiable military targets, I wished, for the sake of morale, that the air force would do its interdicting out of town. Nevertheless we had to continue indicating targets and reporting on the sad results—ironically enough, often at the expense of our own people.

After the raids of March 7 and 8, there was a curt note attached to Franco's bulletin to the effect that the road counts on the Ostiense and Magliana were incomplete because our observers were in the process of moving their bombed-out families!

15 WE EXTEND OUR OPERATIONS

DURING THE LAST TWO WEEKS OF FEBRUARY, Coniglio had been away on a trip to Florence and other northern points, so I had no contact with and was spared any trouble from him.

Early in March he returned to Rome and sent me a message to be forwarded to the base saying that the half-dozen Italian agents sent into northern Italy by Captain A. were crooked, refused to obey his orders, were not getting in touch with the base, and were generally making a mess of things.

At the same time we kept hearing through various underground sources that it was Coniglio who was impossible to work with, that he gave himself airs and antagonized everyone, and that though he insisted he was chief of the OSS for all Italy, he never gave proper or specific orders.

From Cervo we learned that several unfortunate occurrences had taken place in the organization outside Rome which Coniglio was supposed to be taking care of. The radio at the landing zone had for some time gone off the air; Germans were encamped in the area. Word from Genova was that up there one of Captain A.'s agents and the radio had been captured by the Germans. Two operators, whose code names were Siria and Iris, and who had never been able to get into contact with the base had now been abandoned by their local mission chief without money or orders. A radio dropped by parachute near the landing zone had never been recovered.

I was annoyed too because the message Coniglio wished transmitted to the base contained a lot of political "intelligence" to the effect that the CNL in northern Italy was inferior in numbers, organization, and technical proficiency to the forces loyal to Badoglio and the king—"intelligence" in no way corroborated by any of my other sources (it was, in fact, grossly tendentious)—which led me to believe that Coniglio had been more preoccupied with politicking in northern Italy than with getting agents to contact the base and file information.

On the other hand, this whole political argument was one I did not wish to become involved in. But to avoid doing so I would have to take an unpleasant stand. So far, I had categorically refused all comers the use of radio Vittoria as a channel for partisan political messages; now I would have to do likewise for Coniglio (whose previous messages I had forwarded verbatim). I therefore edited out the politics and sent along the service messages and the small amount of military data he had gleaned.

It was a moment of life and death for the Badoglio and former SIM services, who were fighting for their political existence and needed to give as rosy a picture as possible of their own forces and as misleading a picture as possible of the democratic anti-Fascist parties in northern Italy, for President Roosevelt had finally decided that the Allies should switch their support from the Badogliani to the parties of the CNL.*

On the other hand the king and Badoglio continued to fight with every means, overt and covert, to hang on, counting (apart from the personal support of Winston Churchill) primarily on control of the Italian armed forces, control of clandestine communications between north and south, and disparagement of the CNL throughout Italy.

For my part, I made it clear to all involved that despite my own political prejudices (which I was careful not to voice) I was interested only in military intelligence for the Allies (or psychological intelligence to be used against the Nazi-Fascists) and would have nothing to do, one way or the other, with intramural Italian political factions.

The mere fact, however, that I had gotten control of the radio, thus preventing Coniglio and his gang from controlling the clandestine media of communication with the south for their own political purposes, must have been considered by Coniglio an act of political discrimination against them—despite the fact that I filed nothing against them personally or politically and absolutely nothing in favor of any other party or parties. In any case that is the line they took.

* On March 13 Roosevelt cabled Churchill: "The political situation in Italy has developed rapidly since our earlier messages. . . . In the present situation the Commander-in-Chief and his political advisors, both British and American, have recommended that we give immediate support to the program of the six Opposition Parties. . . . I cannot for the life of me understand why we should hesitate any longer in supporting a policy so admirably suited to our common military and political aims. American public opinion would never understand our continued tolerance and apparent support of Victor Emmanuel."

Certainly it must have been infuriating to Coniglio to be saddled with an American who insisted on having sources of his own, and who could not be spoon fed, as had been done so successfully with non-Italian-speaking Allied officers in Bari, Brindisi, Taranto and Naples.

Finally, to add confusion—and a touch of irony—to the already confused situation, Coniglio complained (as usual via Cervo) that some new character had appeared on the scene, passing himself off as General Clark's "personal political representative," who was assiduously trying to contact the various clandestine political parties, saying that he intended to "teach these people what to do and not to do."

As Coniglio had been spreading the rumor that *he* was Clark's personal representative and that his Unione Democratica was the *only* party officially recognized by the Allies (though in fact not a party at all) he was even more infuriated by the arrival of this new impostor, and confusion round town was considerable.

Through Franco's *tuyaux* I soon established the identity of the newcomer, and was then myself astounded by the irony of the situation (and even inclined to believe that it was perhaps an advantage to have so many imposters, who might succeed, if in nothing else, in confusing the Germans).

Among the several hundred agents I had considered sending on missions across the lines while recruiting in Naples, I had come across a certain Captain Enrico Sorrentino, generally known as the *"Ingeniere."* For a long time (while I kept him under surveillance in a castle north of Naples or at my headquarters in Via Crispi) I had studied his character without being able to make up my mind whether he was an honest Italian patriot of no particular political affiliation, a compulsive agent (with a pronounced persecution mania) of the type who have to get money and boast of a secret mission, or, worst of all (and about this I was seriously worried), a German double agent specifically hired to join our organization and then be sent back across the lines by us. (It must be remembered—amazing as it may sound—that at that time in Italy we had no counterespionage organization of our own and that I had to supply this service myself as best I could, just as I supplied my own phony documents.)

So puzzled was I that one night I went so far as to stage a sort of Gestapo trick, bursting in on him with my two sergeants at three

153

o'clock in the morning, drawing a .45 and threatening him with immediate death if he did not reveal his accomplices.

Unfortunately, or perhaps fortunately, being constitutionally unable to carry out such scenes, I could not keep a straight face very long, and, after a few minutes of the charade, had to pat him on the back and inform him it was all just a test to establish his nerve and security. I decided, however, categorically against using him as an agent, paid him off, and (madness of madnesses, there being no OSS organization to take care of unwanted or "burnt" agents, despite my daily clamoring for such a branch) had to turn him loose on the streets of Naples, where he had been promptly recruited by Captain A. and sent across the lines!

From Cervo I then learned that Sorrentino was furious at Coniglio, whom he could not get hold of and whom he accused of misappropriating fourteen million lire, a sum he maintained had been brought to Coniglio from Naples (presumably in the suitcases of the two saboteurs who had landed with me) and which was to have been split between them.

To add to the confusion Cervo said that the two saboteurs who had landed with me claimed to have handed over to Coniglio ten million lire in paper and three million in gold, and that one of them, Mario, had written a letter to Sorrentino. In this he complained he had received no orders since he landed, that his situation was desperate and that he was in great danger of imminent arrest by the Germans; he requested 100,000 lire in cash and asked whether it would not be better if he were to leave for Florence or Milan if required to do any sabotage!

Every day it became clearer that Coniglio's whole approach to the problem had never been to furnish the Fifth Army with intelligence— his sources weren't providing any and he wasn't even getting his agents into contact with the base—and it looked more and more as if he and Gambareri and Company were in effect political agents sent to infiltrate, not the enemy, but the OSS, so as to assure control of the various intelligence organizations in Italy. But what was still an enigma was why Captain A. should have been so obviously in on the deal—unless it was to the interest of the old French S.R. to infiltrate American intelligence, and this was an easy way to do so, reviving perhaps some past association such as Cagoule-SIM.

In any case the intrigue was so thick and the situation was becoming so damaging, not only to our organization, but to the Allied and partisan causes in general, that I sent a message to the base asking that the whole thing be clarified officially.

By return message the base radioed that obviously *I* was in charge in Rome, that Coniglio was to go north and take care of the recalcitrant agents up there, and that, for my personal security, the base would see to it that all stray agents and saboteurs avoided the Rome area.

At last the situation should have been clear to all. Cervo and Franco, though they had never voiced any doubts, were delighted.

But when Cervo showed the message to Coniglio, Coniglio declared, with the straightest of faces, that if I were in charge in Rome it meant that I was his subordinate, he being OSS head for all Italy!

To remind Coniglio that I was an American citizen and that OSS networks were not built on Fascist hierarchical levels, and also to get him to obey the base's orders to go north and see to the nonfunctioning radios (over which he could file any damned kind of "intelligence" or political mumbo-jumbo that might please his contorted spirit) I arranged a personal meeting with him uptown.

He came. We talked at some length. But though polite and agreeable, he paid no attention to what I said or to the orders from the base.

As one cannot exert authority in enemy territory except at the point of a gun—and this I was unwilling to do, let alone have someone else do for me—I decided to try to laugh the whole thing off, trusting that once the Allies arrived the situation would quickly be resolved.

On March 12 the base repeated its orders to Coniglio to leave Rome immediately and take care of the agents up north, giving specific instructions that Mario and Camillo (the two saboteurs) go to Castiglione della Pescaia.

Then something happened to cheer me up: Cervo learned that Coniglio had managed to salvage a radio which had been hidden near the landing spot but for which he had no operator and therefore no use. Neither he nor his henchmen knew how to operate a transmitter. I therefore requested Cervo to get the radio from Coniglio and bring it to me as soon as possible.

My first thought was to set it up in our own headquarters in the Palazzo Lovatelli and do the coding and transmitting myself on the basis of my own private codes (previously established with the base) which I could set up by informing them of the necessary times, frequencies, call signs and code, over radio Vittoria.

Though better than nothing, this was by no means an optimum solution; the mere mechanics of setting up a transmitter, coding and decoding messages, especially considering their length, would be almost a full-time and highly technical job. Transmitting from our headquarters would also raise rather than diminish the risks we were running; and I was doubtful of the physical situation of the house (almost in the shadow of the Capitoline Hill) for good transmission.

Then came a great bit of luck—indicative also of the scope and sensitiveness of our ramified network which enabled us to keep tabs on any new contact made with any of the various partisan organizations. Cervo appeared with a long and miserable letter from a character who signed himself romantically but foolishly with the code X-1, who was trying to establish contact with someone who could get him in touch with the Fifth Army. From the letter it was clear he was one of the radio operators landed with Sorrentino who had not been able to get in touch with Sorrentino for over a month, had never made contact with the base owing to an irreparably defective transformer in his set, had been left for several weeks without money, clothes or even sufficient food, and who, quite naturally, was complaining bitterly.

All we needed now was to get hold of him, feed him, get him a house, provide him with the radio which was useless to Coniglio, and thus establish a second channel of communication with the base. By keeping them separate, without knowledge of each other, with no one person in the entire organization knowing the exact address of both, with luck we might have maximum security and an emergency means of communication in case of accident or disaster.

Cervo agreed to go to work on the plan immediately, and when he left me I felt elated at the prospect ahead of us.

16 A PACT WITH THE COMMUNIST PARTY

I've been here almost seven weeks now. I've been in this room with the striped pink walls, its big soft sofas, and the soft-petaled flowers brought by Maria, it seems almost forever. As for getting in and out of bed in my cold, ridiculous bedroom, each time I do it, I feel as if I had always done it. But the moments of panic are fewer and further between nowadays.

Though physically life is somewhat of a routine it could hardly be called monotonous. From the small hit-or-miss system of the early days, I now have a vast organization of hundreds of strange people in hundreds of the strangest positions gathering libraries of assorted information, and it all heads up here through its series of watertight compartments so that a steady flow of information goes out across the air. And there is so much of it, and it is so varied, and the situations created by its gathering are so tricky, that there is never a dull moment. What with checking up on the bombed targets we indicate, cutting all traces when one of our men is caught, helping informants when they are bombed out or lose a member of their family, avoiding Coniglio's two saboteurs who have threatened to report us to the Gestapo unless we give them half a million lire by March 15, trying to keep from being liquidated by Coniglio, or the Badogliani, checking and double-checking on double agents, creating and erasing contacts in practically every party, ministry, agency, class or form of activity, falsifying quantities of documents, not to mention keeping in contact with the various military, partisan and resistance groups all over Italy, life is never dull. There are so many things, so many strange people, and above all the personal intricacies and relationships are so incongruous they defy description.

Life here with Baldo, Lele and Maria has not changed much since I arrived. We get up late, stay up till four, or five, or six in the morning. My hours of work are pleasant because they last just exactly as long as there is work to do, which varies from day to day, and after that I can play cutthroat bridge or do what I am doing now. And always there is good music on the radio, and thanks to Franco's care, a bottle of brandy to be soaked up slowly through the night.

In a way it is a pleasant life, if it weren't for the nightmare of knowing that all the time we are being hunted, and wishing the time would come when we can go out and really do the job for which I came—but that too, pray God, will come some day.

I still go out as little as possible, and only for meetings which are absolutely necessary. But the days are getting long and warm and sunny; you can smell the spring where the sun warms the damp mossy stones of the walls in this ancient part of Rome, and I'm beginning to toy with Lele's idea of going out to lunch with a couple of starlets, one of these days, and have a little fun!

TWO DAYS LATER, MARCH 13, I WROTE:

The sun is beating down on the ocher terrace, and its pale green new wisteria leaves. The sea of roofs around us, soft and old and dominated by the cupola of Santa Teresa, are clear-cut against the Roman sky. Somewhere someone is playing softly on a concertina. He plays it well, with that langorous Gypsy wail; the chords are smooth and full, and they are some of my favorite tunes. Looking over the high wall I can just see that it is a girl in a red negligee, her lips painted, which is odd, because she is on the terrace of a tenement, her audience a handful of ragged but spellbound brats, none of them over six. Now she is playing "Lili Marlene," which will always remind me of these months, if ever there is an always!

God, but spring is wonderful in Rome, or anywhere else, I guess. Just to lie out in the sun and read or write for hours without the nightmare of always being hunted, listening for every suspicious sound, wondering if we have made a mistake, if someone has slipped up and they have found us out! Silly business. And apropos of business, it is slack today. It usually is on Mondays—God knows why!

Yesterday the Pope spoke to the crowds of refugees jammed into St. Peter's Square under a gray and almost drizzly sky. The people in the square cheered as if it were a political speech and shouted "Pace

Pacelli!" (the *Pace* almost with the same rhythm they had once shouted *Duce*). The left-wing parties were there shouting "The devil with peace!" and "Throw out the Germans!" which to us was encouraging.

One ardent partisan, dressed as a monk, was caught distributing leaflets; and that was sad.

Our cook, whose theft of the Count's bread ration card we had just exposed, rushed off to attend the ceremony and presumably be purified in the blood of the lamb. Out of curiosity we weighed the usual piece of autarchic almond cake she stopped for on her way back. She had removed 80 grams—to keep her hand in, I suppose. Poor woman, if only she realized that we would treat her more generously if only we could trust her discretion; but that with things as they are, we must strictly maintain the pretense to her that we are nothing but normal Italians hiding from the Germans. If only she were dear Virginia, how helpful she could be, and what a joy it would be to have her.

I wonder how much longer our life will go on the way it is. So far there is no sign from the beachhead they intend to move anywhere very fast, any time in the near future. There are a few signs about town though that may indicate the Germans might be planning to disengage. An armored division—possibly the Hermann Goering, we're not sure yet—left the beachhead area and is moving north; which is something. And Kesselring has ordered no more military traffic through Rome after March 20. *Chi lo sa?*

ON MARCH 14 I WROTE:

Once again I was awakened by the sound of bursting bombs. Outside the sun shone brightly in a clear blue sky. From the terrace I watched the formations, neat little groups of six, circling for their targets. They were lower than usual, but the few scattered puffs of flak didn't seem to bother them. It was almost pleasant to hear the deep full thud of the explosions and know they were ours. At the same time I was worried about the bombs that missed and murdered people without refuge. It isn't because they get killed. For some reason that does not seem to have the least effect on me—but it is because they miss the target so often, and sometimes by quite some distance, and the people of Rome are angry, and it creates a wave of hatred and bad feeling which isn't worth the candle—especially as I still don't believe that the rail yards and stations of Rome are an effective target, when they could interrupt traffic more effectively, and with no loss of civilian lives (and prestige) outside the city.

But the raid was soon over, and I turned to other problems: I was to go out to lunch with Franco and the head of the Communist military underground, Giorgio Amendola. Franco had suggested it was time Amendola and I had a talk because of the unpleasant situation caused by Coniglio and Sorrentino among the various partisan organizations. With the other parties my position was always clear; but now, since the cynical deal in southern Italy between Badoglio and Togliatti, the Badoglio underground and SIM agents were making overtures to the Communists, offering them funds and special facilities, and Coniglio had been busy informing them that I had no authority whatsoever and was in fact nothing but a cheap impostor!

Then Mario arrived from Franco's place with the morning bulletin and a very worried look on his features. In Mario this was an extraordinary sign, and I sensed that something terrible had happened.

"I'm afraid you won't be able to go out to lunch," Mario started off calmly enough, then finished with emotion: "The SS have captured our entire information headquarters!"

At my bewildered expression he quickly added: "Oh no, not Franco and us. The center where the stuff comes in from the various section heads."

When I pumped him for details, he shook his head. That was all he had heard. I would have to wait for the arrival of Franco, if indeed he were still free to come, to get more details.

To keep my mind from formulating imaginary pictures of what might have happened I took the morning's bulletin from Mario and began to study the various items which, in other circumstances, would have made me cheerful. The German High Command appeared to be skeptical about any further Allied landings north of Rome and estimated that the next one would be in France. No further troops were to be sent into southern Italy, and, in case of developments in France, central Italy was to be evacuated to the Spezia-Rimini line, which was now being hastily improved, the one just north of Rome being purely a holding line. The whole matter had, according to Franco's high-level sources, been thrashed out at Kesselring's headquarters and it was now only a question of the eventual time for putting the plan into operation.

A few minutes later Primo arrived to collect the day's message for the base which I hastily threw together before sitting down to an unpalatable lunch and an unpleasant vigil for Franco.

When he arrived he clapped me on the back, his features wearing a broad and reassuring smile; but his eyes looked worried, and I sensed he was putting up a front.

"The SS came to our general headquarters at eleven this morning, asking for one of our key men. Don't worry. They didn't get him, or anyone else; nor did they find any information. But we've had some serious losses in the peripheral sections."

As his story developed it appeared that the Germans had caught forty-seven of our people, including several women, many of them with written information on them. But like a general whose forces have suffered heavy casualties, yet hold their position, Franco was putting on a show of relief, not because he and I and the others had survived, but because the information service had not been seriously touched.

As far as we could make out from the scattered intelligence that had come in, and principally the testimony of one of our men who had managed to get away from Via Tasso, the SS must have been following one of Franco's men who had gone to the station to reconnoiter an ammunition train to be blown up that evening, and had then walked in on him at home while he was preparing the charges. With him they had caught another man and his wife. Then, as bad luck would have it, a messenger, a young boy merely used as a courier, had arrived, and under threat of torture the youth had agreed to phone the section leader and go to an appointment—with four SS men trailing him. From then on an SS man had impersonated the section leader and caught dozens of our informers in a sort of chain as they came in with their bits of information, including a couple of people who had nothing to do with the operation whatever.

For the last twenty-four hours the SS had been interrogating them at Via Tasso. Luckily there was only one man among them who knew the next step in the ladder of where the information was taken. At Via Tasso they apparently distrusted him more than the others and put him in a private cell with a regular window instead of the bricked-up ones. There he was informed by a tough, shirt-sleeved SS guard that the least he could expect would be to be shot, but that he might save himself a lot of pain and trouble if he chose to talk.

Standing by the window, breathing in the fresh evening air, our man noticed that the guard—like many of the SS—had a captured American .45 which protruded from his pocket. For several minutes our man pretended to be willing to talk, doing so at random, while the SS guard became more and more interested. Then, at what he hoped was the psychological moment, our man stretched out his hand, made a grab for the .45, jammed it into the German's ribs and whispered: "I'm bound to die. It means nothing to me to shoot you. You'd better keep quiet."

Moving back a pace, he slammed the butt into the German's skull, put down the gun, opened the door, slipped into the hall, saluted a couple of plain-clothes SS, walked down two flights of stairs, stopped nonchalantly before the sentries on guard to light a cigarette, walked out as leisurely as he could toward the corner, rounded it—ran like hell till he was safe!

To Franco he described what he had seen and heard at Via Tasso while he was there. Five of our men had already been beaten about the head with clubs so hard and so long they could only groan. But so far none of them appeared to have talked.

When Franco had finished his tale he said we were to go out and meet Amendola for coffee instead of for lunch. Just beyond the sun-filled piazzetta the Open City police car was waiting at its usual spot by the Antici Mattei; (it was never driven to the actual piazza so that we could not be traced from its presence) and Franco and I climbed in with the driver.

MY DIARY RECORDS THE TRIP AS FOLLOWS:

It is always strange and pleasant to drive through the streets of Rome on a sunny day in early spring—even if one is somewhat hunted.

Piazza Venezia and all of Via Nazionale were crowded, causing me to spend half my time noting German insignia and the other half following pretty girls.

We passed the station—or what was left of it—and went to make a tour of the spots that had been bombed in the morning. It is odd to look at your own fresh bomb damage. Off the Via Nomentana we passed the house where Gayda and his family had been killed a few hours earlier, and it reminded me of all the stories I had filed as a journalist, based on his daily column when he was Mussolini's mouthpiece.

Actually this little tour of Allied bomb damage was being fostered by the Command of the Open City of Rome, behind which organization a few spirited Italians had been trying by means of the Vatican and the Swiss to have Rome officially recognized by both belligerent sides as a truly neutral city *not* to be bombed. Now they wanted me to advise the Allies officially of how far astray from military targets their bombs were being dropped.

As far as I was concerned the tour was more for the record—to satisfy Colonel Bonzani of the Open City of my intercession with the Allies—and for a little air and sunlight. I had far better information as to what went on in Rome through our information service than I could possibly have established by touring the city for a week.

But the ride was quite enjoyable.

As we approached Via Veneto we left the car and walked a while in the sunny afternoon till the exact hour for our rendezvous with Amendola. Then Franco pointed across the street, and there he was, the head of the Communist military underground, just walking out of a small restaurant, newspaper under his arm—a heavy-set, well-built, youngish looking man, entirely unperturbed. As I watched him from across the street I could not help thinking of his father, the liberal anti-Fascist, who had died from internal injuries caused by a beating administered by Fascist thugs. No wonder his son had turned to extremes.

Nodding casually to each other we walked across Via Veneto and into Franco's building. Though it was Tuesday there was no one in the front office or anywhere else in the headquarters that I could see, and I presumed Franco must have given them all the day off. Sitting down we began to talk.

First we discussed the Coniglio-Sorrentino situation and I did my best to give sensible answers to Amendola about why the Fifth Army sent such curious Italian agents to Rome, all of whom were passing themselves off as General Clark's personal political representatives; and why Coniglio spoke so badly of me.

Though I had never used the Communists as agents, or to go on any missions (for the simple reason that they were usually more preoccupied with their own affairs than with anyone else's), I had been in close contact with their leaders since North Africa and had established what I hoped was an "ethical rapport" with them to help each other against the common enemy and do each other no dirt behind the scenes. In Allied territory I had always kept my side of this arbitrary bargain—as Amendola could easily check—and I now hoped that he would do likewise for me in enemy territory.

We then went on to discuss the partisan situation in general. Franco was worried by the way the Allies were already openly treating the genuinely anti-Fascist partisans almost as enemies instead of as the only people who were unselfishly giving their work and their lives, not only for the Allies, but for the principles we claimed to be fighting for.

In my diary I noted the following personal reaction to the conversation:

I cannot understand how any American can fail to see that political freedom and the mechanics of democracy, once people are forcibly deprived of them, can only be recovered by force, and that it is as ridiculous to try to prevent this coming about in Europe as it would be to try to defeat the Nazis without using force.

By the time we were through discussing the various details of operations the sun was casting long shadows across Via Veneto, lighting up the yellow walls of the Excelsior. As we came downstairs and out into the street an SS car pulled up before us. As the SS men alighted, armed with short Sten guns, I got a close glimpse of the deaths-head insignia on their caps, the *SS* on their collars. Had someone betrayed us? Were they after the head of the Communists? The head of the Socialist military underground? The American OSS agent!

164

But instead of retreating we used the old standby of "When in doubt, attack!" Skirting the car, like suspicious dogs, we stopped plumb in front of it and ceremoniously lit three cigarettes. All was well, at least for us; they had come to arrest someone else. Slowly we walked toward the corner, bid Amendola goodbye, then Franco and I set off to walk across Rome to Piazza Lovatelli.

Sauntering down Via Veneto and across Piazza Barberini in the last red rays of sunlight we tried to keep our minds off our worries by joking about how easy it would be to organize a racket after the war, on the basis of the techniques we had picked up in clandestine living. It seemed a reasonable deduction that if by any chance we were to survive there would be no cop anywhere who could scare us, or trick us. But the doubt was already in our minds that it could not be so; that what was keeping us alive, alert and operative was the power derived from knowing what we were doing was *for* society, not the opposite.

As we crossed the Tritone—perhaps because of the proximity of Via delle Avignonesi and its ancient brothel—the subject changed to women. Only later, as we approached our palazzo, did I realize that one subject appeared to be strictly taboo: the men of our organization who had been captured, who would be tortured, who would stand a 90 per cent chance of ending up with *douze balles dans la tête*.

Such things are not helped by discussion, yet through both our minds ran the constant problem: how could we get them out?

Somehow a raid must be planned.

17 MORE SUCCESS AND MORE DISASTER

MARCH 15, owing to the disruption of the information service, there were only three items of intelligence in the morning bulletin. But when Franco came to dinner that evening bringing a brand-new ricotta he was in a better mood. The Germans at Via Tasso seemed to be having difficulty getting anything out of the men they had caught. All other watertight compartments had held, and the information service was on the way to filling the gaps in its ranks.

But our plan to raid Via Tasso to try to release the prisoners had been forestalled by the Germans: they had placed machine guns and barbed wire to control all the approaches. If, however, we could get the Allied air force to make a pinpoint raid on the block with small-sized bombs, enough damage and confusion might be caused to enable some of the prisoners to escape while partisans in the neighborhood covered them. Doomed as they were to almost certain death, we felt sure our men would prefer to risk their chances in the air raid. And such a raid would be psychologically effective, highlighting the fact that the Allies knew what the Germans were up to, and showing the partisans, both in and out of jail, that the Allies were giving them support whenever possible.

As we discussed how best to give assistance on the spot to such a raid, the bell rang six times and Cervo came in in his usual excited manner.

I was annoyed by his unexpected visit (they were becoming too frequent for security, and his presence made Maria nervous), but this time Cervo had some really worth-while problems to discuss. He had located the Sorrentino operator, made an arrangement with him for a daily rendezvous in front of the Palace of Justice, and simultaneously managed to get the radio from Coniglio.

Unfortunately the operator had lost his cipher system. Now he could get in contact with the base only if I set up a new one for him—which would take a minimum of forty-eight hours.

The problem was to find a house for him. For this I decided the

166

time had come to cash in on the benny to whom I had given instructions to rent an apartment, lie low and wait for orders.

With Cervo I made arrangements to have the operator moved there as soon as possible. Next Cervo informed me that he had found a penthouse apartment on Via Flaminia with a large terrace thick with potted plants, ideal for the Vittoria radio and its operator, but the man who owned the apartment would not rent unless Cervo bought the furniture at an exorbitant price. As an indication of how foolishly puritanical one is capable of being, I too was stunned by the sum—a mere $1,000—and worried about Special Funds approving, till I realized that we could always sell the damned stuff after the liberation, and that whatever loss was entailed would be nominal in comparison with the use we could make of the apartment in the meantime. So I authorized the expenditure.

Cervo then said he would try to get the place within the next two days because of a possibly dangerous incident which had occurred. Two days earlier, Enzo, the Vittoria radio operator, had been accosted by a man in the street and asked if he were still transmitting with a secret radio! The man, known as Franco di Walter, had been introduced to him when first he had arrived in Rome, by Paolo, the fourth member of the original Coniglio team, the one later reportedly shot as a double agent while trying to escape from an OSS compound in Naples. Di Walter had left a note in the bar regularly frequented by the Vittoria operator asking for an urgent appointment. The waiter, who had passed on the note, warned the Vittoria operator that the man was known to be a phony Communist and almost certainly a Nazi agent provocateur.

Once again I felt like strangling Coniglio, Paolo, Morris and dear old Captain A. for such staggering insecurity, but instead, controlling my temper, asked Cervo to give the Vittoria operator strict orders on no condition to leave his apartment, that all his food be brought to him till we could transfer him to the new apartment to be rented by Cervo.

Cervo nodded, and agreed to act immediately.

But just as he was going out the door he turned and asked if I would like to meet his father, who was in town for a couple of days.

What an odd sort of meeting, I thought. But in the back of my mind I had been playing with the idea of seeing if we could infiltrate the

Nazi-Fascist setup in Bologna through Cervo's father by getting him to enroll an agent of ours among his paid informers; so I made a date to see him at Cervo's apartment the following afternoon at four, wondering as I did so what it would be like to have tea with a man who for years had been one of the heads of the Fascist secret police!

When Cervo had gone, and while we sat around waiting for Maria to cook the pea soup we were anticipating for dinner, Franco and I took advantage of the pause to curse again the fools who had hired such incompetent and dangerous agents as Coniglio and Paolo to try to do serious work, and this brought on the subject of the next day's operation, when Franco was to bring me a young partisan leader from Turin who had already established a courier service into Switzerland and whom Franco thought capable of organizing a network in Turin such as we had organized in Rome. If satisfied with his qualifications I was to give him the necessary instructions and money with which to get his organization started.

By lunchtime the next day, when the young man arrived, I had much of the work prepared, and discussed the details with him for a couple of hours, asking him to return the following day with any questions he might have.

It was almost time for my meeting with Cervo's father, and I had to hurriedly don my hat and coat and the phony glasses I wore in the streets for disguise, so as to slip across the piazza in order to be punctual for the appointment.

At the usual place, by the Antici Mattei, instead of Cervo's Topolino as I had expected, Cervo was waiting with the old familiar motorcycle, and I thought to myself as I climbed on behind him, How many more times will I have to ride this contraption before we are through, one way or the other?

Setting off down Via de' Funari we passed the Turtle Fountain (despoiled of turtles) and were heading for Campo de' Fiori when I whispered to Cervo that it was too near the Palazzo Ricci for safety, and got him to steer away toward the Corso Vittorio.

The mid-March sun gave color to the streets and I noticed gaily dressed young girls along the Tiber as we crossed the Ponte Vittorio. Looking up toward St. Peter's I thought of D'Arcy Osborne, four years a prisoner in the Vatican, and the dreary building he was housed

168

in. Had there been any sense to it, I could have waved to him from the *salita* that goes up toward the Gianiculum.

Instead we skirted the monstrous Ministry of Justice (the sight alone of which should have kept many an Italian from crime), bumped across the trolley tracks of Piazza Adriana, and entered upon the geometric concrete wastes of Prati toward the little square where Cervo lived.

Reaching it I caught a glimpse down the road of the Fascist militia guarding their barracks, and dismounted even faster than usual to seek refuge in the hall of Cervo's building. A short, well-dressed man about fifty, with thick black spectacles and an even blacker Homburg, stretched out his hand and mumbled something incomprehensible. Doing likewise I followed him into the lift.

In Cervo's flat we were welcomed, with the usual warmth, by Cervo's mother and sister, on their way out to visit the hairdresser or some such female errand, that we might talk uninhibitedly.

To my surprise Cervo's father turned out to be a Neapolitan, not at all frightening or even impressive. I did notice a certain southern shrewdness, but on the whole he struck me as a good citizen who had chosen the police as a career and must therefore continue to earn a living for himself and his families (of which he had two—one with Cervo's mother, from whom he was separated, and another with a paramour in Bologna—supporting them both through thick and thin) with no ideological influence other than a certain sense of humanity toward his fellows, whether criminal or otherwise.

After talking about things in general I got the conversation going along the lines I wanted, suggesting to Cervo's father that in spite of what he was doing for his son (keeping the secret of his clandestine operations), once the Allies finally got to Bologna, his own position as head of the local OVRA might prove embarrassing unless he could bring forth really concrete evidence of his sympathies for the Allied and partisan causes.

Pretty soon I got all the details of the OVRA organization I needed, including types and numbers of passes issued by the Germans, complete with samples of the German signatures and stamps; before I was through I got him to agree to enroll an agent of mine as an agent of his to be carried on his books, working the scheme out down to the details of conventional phrases and recognition signs before I would let him go.

When it was time to break up the meeting, to be home before the curfew, and I was in the midst of shaking his hand, he suddenly leaned forward and, in the Latin manner for expressing friendship or some honorable action undertaken together, kissed me on both cheeks. A little embarrassed by the unexpectedness of the gesture, I was, however, quite touched; it seemed to me he was a man who, in his own particular way, was both honest and humane, and for whom life had not been simple.

That night in bed, as I reviewed the day's work, I was pleased with the thought that despite Coniglio and his gang we might soon have the beginnings of a network to supply the Allies with information from other Italian cities as thorough and precise as the one we had set up in Rome, which, if all went well, would itself be greatly expanded within the next forty-eight hours by the addition of a second radio.

But though I went to sleep pleasantly, I was roused by a pounding on the secret hatch—always a frightening experience, especially that early in the morning.

It was Cervo. "The Vittoria operator hasn't been seen since last night," he explained all in one breath. "We're worried something has happened to him."

"How the devil," I asked, "could anything happen to him if he's been sitting in his apartment as ordered?"

Cervo shrugged, looking down at his feet, evidently as distressed by what he had to say as I was at having to hear it. The operator had disobeyed his orders and gone down to the café. After that no one had seen him again.

"I'm worried about the radios," Cervo added. "I better get them moved to a safe place right away."

"Couldn't you do it through a cut-out?" I asked.

Cervo shook his head. The man on the river boat had categoric orders to let no one into the locker but Cervo or the operator. Furthermore, he added, it had always been his job to handle the radios, and he wanted it kept that way.

Warning him to be excessively careful and to explore every move before making it, I arranged for a conventional phrase to be phoned to us by his sister if anything went seriously wrong.

With that he rushed off, excited as ever, and I just had time to dress before Mario arrived with a batch of intelligence from the reorganized network. This I made up into a message for the base, cursing the operator for disobeying orders, wondering what had happened to him and how long the message would now be delayed before he was found and it could be gotten off.

A little later the young man for Turin turned up and I was able to keep my mind off other problems by going over the codes I had prepared for him and discussing the final details of his operation.

As we were talking he suddenly wrinkled his brow and said: "I know you. You used to be at the Foreign Press Club." He then mentioned the Swiss correspondent who had introduced us.

For answer, I swallowed, wondering whether to deny the whole thing or admit the truth; then, judging it would make little difference his knowing who I was once he was on his way to Turin, and to show that I trusted him, I nodded. But it gave me a turn to think that a man who had met me only once, three years earlier, had recognized me so easily.

At any rate we parted the best of friends, and I had an intuitive feeling he knew what he was up to and would do well for us in organizing his network in Turin (which in fact he did).

Later in the evening Franco came in and I was so pleased to see him I brought out the last bottle of gin from our makeshift cellar and mixed some really stupendous martinis. As Maria was a little late with dinner we decided to play a proper rubber of bridge—Baldo, Lele, Franco and I.

Picking up a hand with a mess of hearts, I was about to bid when the phone rang. We listened, cards in hand, for the four calls. It was not a conventional ring, so we let it go. It continued, however, so persistently that Maria, who had come up from the kitchen, picked up the whole phone on its long extension and moved it through the door into the big living room. Still it continued to ring. Finally, with a frown, I nodded to Maria to answer. There was a pause, then she poked her head round the door with a surprised look on her face. "The sister wants to know if I have bought her any honey! What shall I say?"

"Say that you will let her know," I answered.

Maria did so, and hung up; but the others must have sensed that something was wrong. They were all staring at me apprehensively.

"They've got Cervo," I said. "That was the conventional phrase."

Immediately we began to clear the card table, remove the glasses, put everything in order.

"But it can't be anything," said Maria. "The sister's voice was so calm and natural."

"Perhaps it isn't anything serious," I answered. Then I began to wonder if Cervo might have misunderstood the conventional phrase and thought he was to mention the honey if everything were all right, not if something were wrong.

I said so to the others, and it seemed to cheer them up. Then the phone rang again: two and two—the danger signal—followed by silence.

Looking around I saw that the others looked as frightened as I felt. Franco glanced at his watch, and so did I. It was well past the curfew hour. Debating what to do we went about systematically collecting and burning and obliterating all evidence of our presence in the apartment.

There was no longer any doubt in our minds that something had happened to Cervo, and there would be no way of knowing whether he could resist under torture, and if so, for how long. In any case his sister had the phone number of our apartment and through it our address could be traced. We would have to get out, and fast.

Because of his curfew pass, Franco decided to go straight to his flat on Via Veneto and burn everything there that might be compromising. I also had a pass and decided to go with him, partly because Baldo, Lele and Maria would have an easier job pleading their innocence without me to cope with, and partly because if the police were to get Franco they would get us both, which I, for one, would have preferred.

But on second thoughts we decided it would be easier for Franco to risk it alone, and that the rest of us might stand a better chance of survival if we locked ourselves in the "hole" armed with hand grenades, and were either undiscovered or made a fight for it.

If all went well, when the curfew lifted, we would slip out into the Ghetto and scatter, Maria to stay with some friends who knew nothing of her clandestine operations, the rest of us to meet at Baldo's place whenever possible.

Luckily Franco had decided, just a few days earlier, that the whole organization might be seriously jeopardized if everyone's sex life continued to be neglected, not for itself but because one of the basic

172

requirements of an agent was to be able to account for a normal life when interrogated by the Sicherheitsdienst. An Italian who could not prove he had been with a girl in the past six weeks must obviously be up to something queer or subversive. We had therefore planned to have a "curfew party" at Baldo's place and invite several girls. Owing to the curfew limitations which enforced the closing at dusk of all cinemas, restaurants and night clubs, and forced civilians—unemployed by the Germans—to be off the streets, the custom had developed among the good burghers of Rome of organizing "curfew parties" which lasted till the curfew was lifted, and to which even "nice" girls were allowed by their mothers to go—under the notion, I fear me misguided, that numbers would serve them as chaperones!

At that moment none of us felt the least like a party, but Franco insisted that our best possible camouflage and alibi in case anything went seriously wrong was to be caught wenching with several young females in a typical *garçonnière*.

By a great piece of luck a new sports jacket and pair of gray flannels had arrived for me that very day from Lele's tailor—an ex-cutter of Caraceni's called Mondati—who had cleverly made them from measurements without a fitting. At last I could discard the miserable suit in which I had crossed the lines and which by now made me look and feel like an auxiliary policeman, whether I chose to or not. Sartorially, I could assume a brand-new role.

Bidding Franco good luck we watched him walk down the cold marble stairway and out into the night.

In the sitting room we were just collecting the last odds and ends in a neat little pile on the floor in order to be able to escape to the "hole" at a second's notice when we heard a truck draw up in the piazza, followed by German voices shouting in the alley. This time we were positive it must be for us, and the knowledge was paralyzing.

Hats and coats on, suitcase in one hand, automatic in the other, we stood around in a circle, unable to move. Then Baldo, for the first time since I had known him, instead of moving calmly, rushed toward the far window in Maria's room to see how many there were and which way they were deploying. Lele followed, then came back very pale.

"What is it?" I asked, trying to hide the tremor in my voice, as well as in my hands. "How many are there?"

173

"I don't know," Lele stammered. "Baldo is very excited. He's fallen down."

Then Baldo came back, rubbing his knee. "I didn't realize there wasn't a sill to that window. It's a goddamn truck full of Nazis, but they haven't come for us. They're loading something across the street again."

"Gesu-Maria!" said Lele. "What really frightened me was seeing the Count in such a fluster. When I saw him on the floor I thought surely the game was up."

A chorus of deep sighs made us all laugh, and with the laughter a little of the color returned to our cheeks.

To fill in the emotional vacuum that followed on what we all agreed had been the most frightening experience yet, we decided to put something in our stomachs while we still had the chance, then play bridge and wait for the dawn.

"If there is another dawn," said Baldo morosely.

In the kitchen, by the pale glare of the lone bulb, hats and coats still on, bread and cheese in one hand, wine in the other, our automatics on the table, we stood around a joint bowl of salad too nervous to enjoy our food, feeling rather like Strasbourg geese: stuffed and ready for the ax.

Back in what had once been our snug pink room, cold now and smokeless so as to leave no trace of human habitation, we played bridge, sitting on the edge of our chairs, bundled in coats, sadly sipping the bottle of very extra-special Otard we'd been saving for the day the Allies entered Rome.

Two more chores lay ahead—to be done in the small hours of the morning when the porter was most likely to be in his deepest sleep and when there was least chance of anyone in the palazzo being able to overhear us: first, the routine business of packing several dozen eggs, several kilos of flour and a shank of mountain ham from our larder into two large suitcases, partly so as to have the excuse, if picked up on the streets, of being black marketers, and partly so as to have food for the "curfew party" and any emergency which might follow; second, the burying of all our secret files and compromising equipment deep in the medieval cellar.

This routine ordeal I hated more than anything I had had to go through behind the lines. It required exposing oneself in the courtyard

174

outside the kitchen where one could be easily spotted from the neighboring houses; it meant going down a long narrow corridor where one could run into almost anyone, and which the Germans used when they visited the Rossi sisters who lived beneath us. Then came the problem of inserting an iron key, about five inches long, into an ancient iron door in order to get it to open without the sort of blood-curdling noises made by a rack being drawn. After which came the psychological horror of counting one's way down varied flights of steps into the damp, lugubrious, pitch-black medieval cellar of the old palazzo. As an added hazard, side and cross beams had been added at irregular intervals to brace the vaulted ceilings as a makeshift air raid shelter: and on these one was mathematically bound to bump one's shins. Thereafter, to find one's way through the catacombic labyrinth of passages one had to *feel* along the corroded cobwebbed walls—alive with scorpions, six-inch slugs and spiders the size of walnuts—crawl on all fours through a maze of rat-infested crates till one found the other "secret hole," barely wide enough to squeeze through, which led into a small cavelike space redolent of the *cloaca maxima* where one had to bury one's equipment entirely by touch lest one be seen or overheard by the policemen whose local station at the back of the palazzo was but a few steps away, visible through a small barred sewer a dozen feet above the ground.

By the time the job was done it was nearly dawn. Only then did we realize we had forgotten an important factor. The maid was due to arrive at nine; there was no telling what she might think—let alone do—on finding the house abandoned. It was therefore decided that, risky as it might be, Lele should stay and keep Maria company till the maid arrived, in order to tell her, with the help of a solid tip, that we would be gone for about three weeks.

This settled, the first yellow rays of sunlight broke across the terrace, lighting the living room. We hated leaving Lele and Maria almost in pawn, for the next would be the dangerous hours, but the time had come for Baldo and me to exchange one set of risks for another: so we said goodbye, rather formally, put on our hats, picked up our heavy black-marketers' suitcases and prepared to start across town the moment the curfew lifted, headed toward a prospect only slightly less frightening than staying where we were.

175

PART THREE

ON
THE
RUN

18 *CHEMIN DE FER* WITH THE SICHERHEITSDIENST

BALDO AND I AGREED TO LEAVE a few minutes apart, so that if something went wrong, or if the police were waiting, one of us might get away and warn the others.

Bespectacled, loaded down with two heavy suitcases, trying to look as *louche* a black marketer as possible I peered round the *portone* into the cobbled piazzetta, then eased it closed behind me. Though the sun was already up it was cool outside; some early risers were on their way to work, but nothing seemed unusual. Turning left I set off briskly down the lane that led to the Portico d'Ottavia. It was the first time I had left the building by that route, and when I reached the narrow passage between the cracked Corinthian columns I realized how close we had been all this time to the back of the Theater of Marcellus.

By the river, near the narrow bridge of the Four Heads across whose gentle 2000-year-old arches a horse-drawn cart was jogging toward the island, I had to wait for the Circular streetcar. But on which side of the trolley tracks should I stand? So beset by security had we suddenly become that I did not know where Baldo lived!

From the near side I could look down at the river breaking against the travertine flanks of its namesake island; from the other I could look up at the leafless plane trees round the Palazzo Sermoneta, the Orsini bears above the gate.

Putting down the heavier bag I lit one of Lele's Macedonias, which, despite its foulness, inhibited my trembling.

Strangely, there was something reassuring about the neighborhood. Most of the inhabitants were Jews, who must have felt as hunted as I.

But I was worried now about the arrival of either Baldo or the trolley, and the appearance I was giving of indecision. Folly perhaps, but just such an appearance could lead to one's being asked for one's papers.

After what seemed like an eternity, Baldo appeared through the columns of Octavia, weighted down by his suitcases, looking peculiarly like a decadent aristocrat, a faraway look in his eyes, as if hopefully pretending to pass for a man transporting ham and eggs from A to Z in quantities reasonable enough to eke out a living.

Looking downriver toward an oncoming trolley—a "Black Sinister Circular" as it was known to the Romans—Baldo approached.

As I followed him onto the rear platform, to steady my nerves, I addressed the ticket collector in the thickest Roman accent I could muster, concentrating so much on my own part I did not register his answer.

Then I realized what was making me nervous. The pneumatic doors had closed and we were trapped, at the mercy of the conductor. Also my Capri shoes—which I had worn for the metamorphosis of the coming evening—were out of key with the rest of my outfit. It wasn't so much fear of their being noticed as it was fear of the effect they were having on my behavior.

In Piazza Adriana we changed to another trolley—an antiquated affair of the Toonerville species—with an airy *open* platform, and the openness made me feel better.

At last, after wandering halfway round the city, we came to a final stop high in the Parioli district near Piazzo Pittagora. From there it was a kilometer's walk to Baldo's place.

By this time I was so nervous, so physically worn out by the long night, so weighted down by the heavy bags, that I would have been happy to be almost anywhere off the streets—even in jail.

Baldo's apartment, on the ground floor of a new white building giving onto a small garden, was not what I had imagined. Yet despite Baldo's proprietary assurances that it did not look its best in the morning light, inside it had a lot of atmosphere. There seemed to be an exuberance of fireplaces and double beds for such an incredibly restricted area. The bath was nice and modern, as was the kitchen, and there were exotic odds and ends of Baldo's such as guitars, huaraches, and a wallful of well chosen books which gave the place a livable feeling.

After a good hot bath we disappeared into separate rooms and I might have slept forever had not Lele awakened me at 3 P.M. in the midst of an Allied air raid. He too had managed to get away from the Palazzo Lovatelli, but when he had left, at 10:30 A.M., four policemen had been waiting in the piazzetta—luckily so deep in discussion they had not noticed him go! Almost too lucky to be chance, yet it was an indication they could not seriously be looking for *us*, at least not yet.

Either because we were rested, and for the first time in weeks had no specific work to do, or because the worry about Cervo could only be overcome by gaiety, no matter how shallow, we all three acted as if we were in the best of moods, ordering a dozen bottles of wine from a wineshop round the corner, only to leap as if electrocuted at the sound of the doorbell when a pint-sized Roman appeared with the basket of bottles.

Baldo and Lele wanted to go out to get haircuts and buy some essential toilet articles. This I did not yet have the courage to do, so I stayed and shaved and spruced myself up as best I could. My tailor-fresh clothes with one of Baldo's better silk shirts made me feel like a totally different person. And my quick meal of bread and cheese and wine before the sitting-room fire tasted more delicious than anything I had eaten in months.

It was almost dark, time for the curfew, when Franco arrived, looking very perturbed.

"It's bad," he said, then took my arm. "Promise me one thing. When the Allies come, don't ever let them send such people behind the lines again. Such swine! You know what happened? That filthy operator took the police to the spot where the radio was hidden on the river boat and set a trap for Cervo. The operator squealed to save himself. The rat! As if they won't shoot him just the same. . . . And now poor Cervo's caught!"

The doorbell rang, and Franco let go my arm. "Now we must be gay and pretend that nothing in the world is wrong. Here come the girls."

They were pretty, well dressed, with sexy sheer stockings and soft French perfumes. Just before introducing me, Franco and I had a rapid conference during which I picked a name, at random, for the evening—not too well known, not too unknown, with members of the family on both sides of the lines whom I could claim as relatives: Roberto Berlingieri.

With the girls came two young men, friends of Baldo's and Lele's

—one of them a gay type with Spanish-looking eyes called Piero Piccione—invited purposely to give verisimilitude to the party and to confuse the police in case there was a raid.

As everyone sat round the fire I opened the first of four bottles of good English gin wisely produced by Franco from his cornucopial brief case. Though we had nothing to mix with it we unanimously proclaimed it good enough to be taken straight. To ease my nervous tension and block out the thought of Cervo I led the way by drinking a couple of long straight draughts.

But not wanting to become too deeply involved in conversation with the newcomers I retired to the kitchen, lit a charcoal fire, and began to prepare crisp bread and ham—a recipe dictated by the larder— and within the hour was making mountains of omelettes à la Mont Saint Michel (or so they seemed to me in the heat of the charcoal and Old Tom gin) which were devoured as fast as I could make them.

The party was quick to liven up and the others started dancing to the radio. Soon they began to telephone other girls in the neighborhood, as we always seemed to be just one short. Then Franco, who had been wandering in and out of the kitchen, keeping pace both with the omelettes and the gin, said he would go down to the Tritone (into the center of town) to get another girl, there being no one else to fetch her who had the necessary curfew pass.

After that, things became a little vague and I was fully occupied beating eggs, blowing on the fire, drinking too many draughts of good straight gin.

I don't know how the idea started, but the first I remember was a girl talking on the phone to another girl in a nearby house who wanted to join our party and bring along a German captain! There was a moment's silence while some grimaces were exchanged, then everyone said yes. What else could one say! My own reaction was that if the bastard was to come I'd best go fetch him.

"What sort of a German captain is it?" I asked.

There was a pause while the girl repeated the question over the phone, then came the answer: "An SS Captain."

That settled it.

With Baldo's overcoat over my shoulders (my own being much too disreputable), a long thin kitchen knife in my pocket, I took Lele

182

by one arm and a girl called L. by the other and we headed up the cool dark street. We passed a German car parked by the curb; but there was no one inside it. Lele turned into a doorway. We had not walked far. Across the street I noticed a long Mercedes.

In the lift I closed my eyes and tried not to think. The next thing I knew I was being ushered into a big warm living room where dozens of strange eyes focused on me. At the far end of the room a woman lay on a sofa wrapped in furs. A German officer sat beside her holding her hand. One look into her snakelike eyes was enough to tell me she was doped. The Italian host was as slimy as a salamander and his clothes expensive, but very, very loud.

Luckily Lele seemed to know several of the people, mostly the women. By now he was a little tight and shook everyone by the hand, patting some of them fondly on the back. Our hostess' eyes were also glassy from dope; but in a way she was striking, with vivid blond hair.

Then I realized where we were. She was a well-known movie actress; he, the slimy one, her husband, a well-known racketeer and Nazi collaborator.

More strange people shook me by the hand.

Lele, who I now realized was a little tighter than I had thought, kept patting me on the back and saying: "Funny you don't know my friend Berlingieri! Known him all my life. Sure you don't know him? Must have seen him around. . . ." Whereupon he repeated my name, calling me sometimes Pietro and sometimes Roberto.

The host offered me a cigarette. "Brother of Antonio?" he asked. "No . . . no . . ." I stammered. "Cousin."

A small brown spaniel pawed at my legs. Falling to one knee so as to disguise my nerves I began to pet the dog and talk to it in a mixture of Roman and Florentine dialect so as to establish my origin.

One obstacle was surmounted.

A moment later the German officer rose, came toward me, introduced himself, looked me fixedly in the eyes.

I thought to myself, good God, man, what are you doing shaking hands with a Gestapo captain, and why the devil did you ever cross the lines! I was so perturbed I couldn't concentrate on what I was saying but only on how I must have looked bursting into an unknown house, well after the curfew, in a camel's-hair coat and open shirt collar—which no Italian usually wears, at least not at that season.

I had a feeling I was in a trap and would not be able to keep up my façade long enough to get out.

Both the SS Captain and another bird (whom I later discovered to be an oculist who had helped his mistress denounce her husband to the Sicherheitsdienst as a partisan) were staring at me intently.

The host, I realized, had slipped out to phone. Now I was sure I was trapped, that the end had come. Looking round for Lele I saw him in the next room with the hostess putting a record on the phonograph. In desperation I asked the girl who had come with us to dance.

Pirouetting round the room I could keep an eye on what was happening and felt a little safer; then I whispered in her ear that she must make a move to get back to the other party.

But the agony went on and on; another record was put on the machine and my nerve was about to give way when I noticed people were preparing to leave, and that the trap had not yet sprung. Following them out we found ourselves in the street on the way to the other party.

No sooner was I reinstalled in Baldo's kitchen than the SS Captain appeared, eyeing the proceedings with approval. Thanks to the heated pan and a bowl of broken eggs I had somewhat recovered my nerve and could smile and wink at him, putting all my skill, and a good deal of mental venom, into one of the evening's more perfect samples— which the poor man devoured as if he had not eaten in months.

A moment later he was fondling our ex-hostess with one hand while consuming large gulps of brandy from a double snifter with the other.

Then our ex-host came in, asking for an omelette, and two decks of cards with which to play *chemin de fer*. Another piece of luck; there were by now neither eggs nor cards, and I was able to induce him to return to his own, and better furnished, house for more supplies.

The idea of *chemin de fer,* seconded loudly by a small and infamous creature who passed himself off as a baron, but who was clearly a crook, pleased me greatly, for it was the ideal kind of prop to enable me to be nervous in a normal manner, speak when I chose, yet observe the others' reactions closely.

The gambling, once our ex-host had returned with the necessary cards, turned out to be a monotonous but soothing affair, during which, as usual, I was winning. (It seems to be part of the psychological claptrap of this planet that one can almost invariably win when *not* required to, and *not* win when required to.) Lele, who would have been only too happy to win (his personal finances being sorely strained by months of professional inactivity), was losing heavily; being a little drunk, he insisted on fighting it out with me instead of with the opposition. At first I was annoyed by this apparent lack of wit, for I felt it a cinch to take his money, but later I realized it was indeed a happy coincidence, for the venomous little "baron" was much attached to his own, and beginning to look as if he could get quite spiteful if separated from too much of it in a single evening. All through the game I had the sensation I had seen him before, and, what was worse, the impression that he had seen me too, and knew my real identity. At one tragic moment I let slip a phrase in Italian which was incorrect, then, to make things worse, repeated it in a moment of dead silence, before I realized the *gaffe*. I was just about to correct it, in a nonchalant semidrunken manner, when someone interrupted, and thank goodness, I had been correct the first time.

In the meantime Franco, who had been stopped twice by the PAI, a girl on each arm, but had managed to avoid arrest by the curt and authoritative manner of his answers, had returned and placed himself near the game where he was chatting busily with the Nazi captain in his most fluent German, making me wonder what the German thought of finding someone who spoke his language that well. As I overheard snatches of what they were saying it amused me that Franco was discussing the situation at the beachhead.

Eventually the game broke up and all the new arrivals prepared to go, leaving the original gang. The host and the "baron" came over and shook me firmly by the hand saying "Goodbye, friend Berlingieri"; the SS Captain again clicked his heels, bowing slightly; and that, I hoped, was that.

The relief, when they had gone, was general.

From then on, though it was close to four in the morning, the party became gayer. After we had danced the bad taste of our recent guests well out of our systems, the lights began to go off and, one by one, couples could be heard in various corners making affectionate noises.

Soon there was no light but the flickering fire, and no sound but the subdued music of the record player.

In the morning, when the girls got up and left, I turned over where I was and went back to sleep in the pale half light.

It was close to noon before Baldo, Lele and I finally pulled ourselves awake. The thought of the SS Captain did not mix well with our hangovers. The house was in a terrible mess, the kitchen devastated, my legs so full of gin and brandy I found it hard to walk. The only thing Baldo had managed to save from the locusts of the night before was a small package of tea and some sugar. So we each drank half a dozen cups of tea and began to feel better.

"How do you think it went off?" I asked.

"As a party," said Baldo, "or otherwise?"

"As a party there isn't any question about it," said Lele. "It was fine. The only trouble is that when you get full of gin you not only look, but dance and behave in a manner so patently American that you might as well have a sign on your back: *U.S.A.*! Luckily our friend Erich [the SS Captain] wanted to make that girl so badly and was too busy grabbing at her breasts I don't think he noticed very much."

"The hell he didn't!" said Baldo. "The last thing he did before leaving was ask me who the young man with the mustache really was. Luckily Franco was nearby and described—with great speed and some fascinating detail—what a no-good playboy you were, that he had known you for years, and that the only things you cared about were gambling and women!"

At which point the whole of my last conversation with Franco, just before he had left, came back in a miasma of horror.

"Do you know who that SS Captain is?" he had asked as he stood in the door.

"No," I answered. "Who?"

"Hauptmann Erich Priebke."

"Well?"

"He's the Sicherheitsdienst officer at Via Tasso in charge of uncovering and eliminating enemy agents and key partisan leaders!"

"You mean the one under Kappler?" I asked. "How do you know?"

"Because it was he who arrested me six months ago and kept me for a week at Via Tasso when someone falsely denounced me as a Badoglio parachutist."

By daylight the irony of the situation in which we had entertained the German counterespionage security officer whose principal job was to track us down seemed to have paled considerably.

We must decamp as rapidly as possible.

But where to?

Lele suggested his sister's apartment in a new part of Rome at the end of Via Salaria, where he had hidden for two or three days right after the armistice. Though his sister wasn't there, he had left some clothing in a closet, still had a key, and could use the clothing as an excuse with the superintendent for going back and spending a night. At least it would give us a chance to find out if Priebke had any intention of returning to Baldo's flat to investigate what we were up to.

What I did not know then, and did not learn till later, was that some months previously, at the time the German Secret Service had planned the successful escape to Germany of the entire Ciano family, it had been this same Captain Priebke who, presenting himself at Villa Ciano in civilian clothes, had received from Edda the remains of her jewelry which he had then personally handed over for safekeeping to Donna Lola Giovanelli *Berlingieri*!

That accounted partly for Priebke's special interest in me the night before. But there was more to it than that, which I was to discover later.

Having packed our combs, toothbrushes and razors into separate brief cases, along with an essential supply of tea, sugar, salt and olive oil, we closed the flat, slipped out the back window, and set off, at as brisk a pace as our hangovers permitted, in the direction of Via Salaria.

19 THE NIGHTMARE OF BEING HUNTED

IT WAS A SUNNY SUNDAY AFTERNOON—March 19, to be exact—as Baldo and I walked along Via Panama toward Via Salaria, the air faintly resined by the tall umbrella pines, the streets crowded with people, enjoying, or pretending to enjoy, those few hours of enforced leisure, undisturbed by the manhunts of the Germans and the raids of Allied planes.

As the clean fresh air cut through the mists of my hangover I was able, for the first time since Franco had told me that Cervo had definitely been caught, to think about our problem. Did the Germans have him? Or the Italians? And if so, where? Before any definite plans could be made the answers to these questions would have to be obtained.

Next an urgent message would have to be sent to the base to warn them that our signal plan was blown and might be being used by the enemy. Though I was sure that after an interval of forty-eight hours in our transmissions—the first since I had arrived—the base would guess that something was wrong, and be wary, especially if they were then to receive a message not in my particular style; I must nevertheless try to get a message through to them. For this our only hope was a British agent—known to us familiarly as "our cousin"—who had a transmitter (used mostly for high-level political messages) with whom we had established indirect relations.

It was infuriating to think that if for just one more day the operator had obeyed his orders we would have had another set of our own already in operation, and would not be in this quandary; but more than anything I was annoyed that our whole information service had been upset because of the indiscretion of fools who should never have been recruited to begin with.

As we strolled along, clutching our brief cases, passing German soldiers out on their Sunday passes, occasionally in the company of girls, we decided, both for our own morale and for appearances, to try to look less glum. For this the only method we could think of was to look at the funny side of last night's party. The incident which made us laugh the most, in retrospect, was that when I was dancing with one of the girls, and with Hauptmann Priebke but a few feet away, the pretty thing had repeatedly remarked to me that I did not seem Italian, that there was something in the way I danced that wasn't Italian. After the third or fourth attack, as my embarrassment was about to get the better of me, I had had the happy thought of answering boldly: "But of course! Can't you see? I'm an American!"

This had saved the day; the more I insisted I was an American the more the girl would laugh and beg me not to tease her. But Baldo, who had danced into earshot, had danced away without hearing the ending, concluding that the strain (or the gin) had been too much for me, and that I had lost my reason.

As we approached our destination, an ugly apartment house on the corner of Via Trasone, we saw that luck was against us; in the middle of the doorway stood the building's superintendent. We wished Lele were with us to give some pretext for our presence. Instead we walked twice round the block—only to find the superintendent immobile at his post. To have continued our carousel would have been even more suspicious, so we decided to brazen it out, walk right past him up the stairs and into the building.

Nothing happened; he didn't even blink.

But at the door of Lele's sister's apartment, we were in for an unpleasant surprise. It was occupied by an evil-looking creature, small but well muscled, who claimed to have the house in trust, and refused to allow us in.

Too tired to argue, and with no other refuge to retire to, Baldo and I pushed our way past him, lay down on the first available couches, and hoped that Lele would soon arrive to convince the creature that we were fully in our rights, at least as much as he, and entitled to occupy and inhabit the apartment.

What most preoccupied us, apart from the man's evident state of nerves, was the harangue he chose to give us, indicating, both by content and tone, that he was a petty officer in Italy's navy, and in excellent standing with the Fascist party.

Finally Lele arrived and managed to reassure the sailor, at least to the extent that it was his own sister's flat, by displaying his own clothes—luckily still hanging in an unused closet. But this only helped a little. The sailor insisted we could spend only one night and no more.

As his company, even for that length of time, appealed to none of us, we decided to go out and get a meal and study the problem of decamping the following morning.

Lele knew of a good restaurant only a short distance away, on the very edge of town, where he thought we might manage to get a black-market meal.

The restaurant, when we reached it, looked more like a farmhouse, with a rambling garden and overhanging trees. Since it was a Sunday afternoon, and nearly five o'clock, the stove had been allowed to go out. But recognizing Lele from the days of the armistice and realizing he must be in hiding, the young owner provided us with some eggs, salad, salami and a large bottle of ice-cold wine.

Not till much later did we discover him to be a Communist partisan, who, when his father was later arrested and kept at Via Tasso as a hostage (because of some hidden hand grenades) presented himself in accordance with the Germans' promise to exchange him for his father. Neither, of course, was ever seen again.

As we sat there at a marble-topped table, watching the light begin to fade, I felt more frightened and hopeless—despite the good white wine—than I had ever before, and could not keep it out of my mind that poor Cervo was caught, that the combined Italian and German police would soon be scouring the city for us. The terror of being hunted and the knowledge that if you are caught you will be horribly tortured, perhaps for days, is a most unpleasant sensation. A specific job, no matter how dangerous, can be worked up to, and the terror mitigated by action and the knowledge that there will be an end, one way or the other. But being hunted, with nothing you can do about it, except jump at every sound, suspect everyone who looks at you, and feel trapped no matter where you are, is a slow, steady form of torture, worthy of the most fiendish of inventors. To cap it, the thought that the Allies would not arrive for weeks, and that the torture, at best, would drag on without respite, made the whole thing almost unbearable.

Eventually, as the shadows of evening added their depressing tones to the already dismal picture, the innkeeper was obliged to drive us out—with the kind consideration of a parcel containing a half-dozen eggs and some remnants of bread—toward no better prospect of distraction than an evening of cutthroat bridge in our new "home," to which was added, later on, another and unexpected ordeal, in the form of some fiend in the neighborhood who insisted on throwing hand grenades at intervals throughout the night, so that Lele and I, already at a psychological disadvantage in his sister's narrow double bed, were jerked awake by the explosions, only to revert to nightmares of torture and persecution.

The next day's problems were finding out, if possible, the details of Cervo's capture, seeing whether the police had raided the Palazzo Lovatelli, or Baldo's apartment, and if Maria could find us some sort of refuge for the coming night.

Early in the morning Lele got up to go see Mario and Ottorino and carry a short message I had written to be relayed by our British "cousin" to OSS Caserta, which I had made as short and concise as possible, knowing from experience what a burden it is to have one's channel used by others.

I was to make contact with the Sorrentino operator at the fixed daily appointment in front of the Ministry of War, so as to start re-organizing our own channel, but at the last minute Franco insisted it was too dangerous so soon after Cervo's capture. So instead I roused Baldo, who seemed, in moments of acutest danger, to be able to withdraw into a private hibernating cave of his own, and we set off for the restaurant to get ourselves a meal.

Though it was Monday, there was a table of frolicking collaborationist black marketeers next to ours who joked and made stupid conversation; but, miserable as I was, I did not envy them their existence. And though food repelled me I forced myself to eat as much as possible of the rare black-market *fettuccine*, suspecting it might be the last real meal I would get for some time. I had a feeling that a quiet, mustachioed man sitting alone in a corner was eyeing me suspiciously. Altogether the situation was unbearable and as quickly as we could, we left.

Parting at the door, Baldo set off on an errand previously assigned to him by Franco of seeing if he could obtain for himself a refuge with one of his many well-heeled fiancées while I walked back toward the apartment, feeling more alone than a small boy being dispatched a thousand miles to a strange school.

Looking up at our windows in the apartment to see if there were any plausible means of exit from the back, I noticed that our sailor companion was making signals toward a window in a neighboring building! Was it a trap? Would the SS be there waiting when I entered? Or was it nothing worse than romantic signals to a nearby chambermaid?

Having nowhere to go, at least not till my six o'clock appointment with the others, there was nothing for it but to go on up and see. The moment I entered our sailor friend showed signs of extreme nervousness; needless to say, so did I.

In a few moments I became almost panicky, noticing odd things about the house: the drawers in the room where I had slept were half open and empty; the sailor had changed his clothes and prepared a parcel wrapped in a blanket; he said he had to go out right away to take a book to a nearby house.

Then suddenly I noticed the toilet had not been properly flushed and remembered the small slip of paper with the message I had prepared for the base to warn them our ciphers and frequencies were blown. In order to condense it to the utmost and yet have it perfectly clear I had had to rewrite it two or three times. Then, rushed and nervous, I had done something—for the first time since I had landed —which I had in previous weeks given Lele hell for doing: instead of burning every incriminating scrap of paper, crumbling it, and washing it away down the drain, I had torn the paper into small pieces and thrown them into the bowl.

All the sailor would have needed was to spot a fragment of a word to realize that we were up to something shady.

The thought of pacing up and down in a house with only one exit for more than four hours before I could take a bus to my six o'clock appointment with the others was a prospect which came close to driving me crazy. Inspecting the drainpipe from the courtyard window I figured that in an absolute pinch I might make it down, but could not close the window behind me; furthermore the house was so isolated I would be bound to be seen. The only thing to do was get out as fast as possible and bury myself in some neighborhood movie where

I would have to rely on my false identity papers in case it was raided —almost a certainty in those days of constant searching for men of military age.

Just as I was preparing my things I noticed the sailor coming down the street. He was alone, no longer had the book, and did not seem to be looking or acting as if it were an ambush. After a moment's hesitation I decided to let him in. He was still very nervous, but sat down and turned on the news from London. This, though it might have been interpreted as a sign he was pro-Allied, was in no way the case: he knew, as did most Italians, that there was better news and more of it from London at 2 P.M. than from any other station. When we heard the usual "nothing to report on the Cassino front" I asked if he knew of any movie theater in the neighborhood—an unlikely hope, as the neighborhood was still in its early stages of construction. To which he answered that he too had been thinking of going to a movie with his fiancée, but that she had had to go shopping with her mother. The nearest theater, he said, was the Excelsior near Piazza Fiume (two blocks from where I was to meet the others).

Looking in the morning paper I saw that an old Hungarian film was playing. We decided to go to it together.

Once on the sunny streets the sailor, knowing that I would not be back to bother him that night, became more polite, insisting on carrying for me my usual brief case of bread, salt, eggs and half a chicken saved from lunch. As we walked toward the center of town he asked if I were Roman, saying I sounded so from my accent, but that at times I had strains of a northern, and even of a southern intonation. At a loss for a better story I told him I was a traveling salesman born in Tuscany, which, for the moment, seemed to satisfy him.

At length we reached the movie, paid and ducked in. At first I could hardly see the screen as my glasses were doing funny things to my eyes. Later I got used to them, and rather wished I could not see the film, which, as was to be expected in those days when much of the supply came from the Balkans instead of blockaded Hollywood, was superlatively dreadful; nothing, however, to compare with the horror that followed close on the main feature. The whole place was suddenly illuminated by multicolored floodlights for what purported to be a vaudeville show—horrible not so much because of the extremely poor

193

quality of the talent, but because the floodlights, which were defective, made sitting in the audience like being pilloried in the middle of town at high noon.

To add to my discomfort, the sailor insisted on moving up to the front, like baldheads at the Old Howard, for the perverted pleasure of admiring the shaggy flanks of what passed for ballerinas; and I, having spotted an emergency exit near the front, was induced to follow him.

"*L'avessi mai fatto!*" as the Romans say. My friend chose to sit directly in front of a pair of Fascist militiamen in uniform, and their presence sent gooseflesh up and down my neck. Then I sensed that someone else in uniform was sitting beside me. Out of the corner of my eye I saw that it was a security policeman, who, instead of admiring the legs of the ballerinas, had riveted his attention onto me. As if this weren't enough, several Vigili del Fuoco, in their SA-like, ordure-colored uniforms, came in and sat directly ahead of us, and I began to feel that I was being deliberately surrounded.

The show went on, getting lousier and lousier, making me almost as nervous as the night I had landed; a mixture, I suppose, of accumulated nervous tension and the certainty of an impending raid.

Then I knew the game was up. Without turning I heard the heavy footsteps of booted motorcycle guards as they marched down the aisle, unmistakably Caruso's men, with black leather helmets and submachine guns, searching up and down the rows of seats. I wanted to scream and was afraid I would faint, but they passed my row, went over to the emergency exit, felt to see if it was locked, which it was, then marched back up the way they had come just as two PAI corporals with tommy guns disappeared backstage. Now I *knew* a roundup was about to start!

The comedian on stage went right on cracking lousy jokes and I noticed the drummer had aristocratic features and was uncommonly well dressed. He too had an eye on the guards, and must have been in hiding.

Then, to my enormous relief, the vaudeville ended, the lights went out, the screen was lowered, and the feature started again. Never did this happen in Italian theaters; there was always an endless intermission between one show and the next. Had the projectionist or the management, foreseeing the impending raid, rushed the show so as to avoid it?

Looking at my watch, and seeing that I still had an hour to wait before my appointment, I decided that any risk was better in the dark than on the open streets. People were moving round to better seats or making for the exits. As we got to our former seats the sailor suddenly handed me my brief case, saying goodbye, that he had to leave. I was surprised but relieved. Now the film began to get on my nerves, its familiar scenes mingling incongruously with images of the last few days' events and fantasies of what was happening to Cervo.

Then someone stood beside me.

I did not dare turn to look, but sat frozen, too terrified to tremble. Whoever it was stood equally still. Even my imagination stopped. Then I saw the shadow edging forward, dark Homburg, well cut dark blue coat, unmistakably Cervo's father. In my mind I unraveled the reason: he had guaranteed to turn me over to the police if they would spare his son. I wasn't the least surprised he had tracked me to the theater; it had been his specialty for twenty years, and this time the incentive was clearly stronger. As he did not move, and I dared not turn my face and thus reveal my features by the light of the screen, I sat immobile. And still he did not budge.

Could he possibly miss me, nearsighted, unaccustomed to the darkness? It was getting time for my appointment with the others. If I were to miss them they would never find me, or I them. There was nothing for it but to take the risk. With my heart in my mouth, I stood up, ostentatiously blew my nose so as to cover my face, moved rapidly toward the exit. I was sure now that the police were waiting for me at the door, guns pointed, car ready, and I hoped, though there was little chance of it, they would fire on sight instead of carting me off to endless torture. From her glassed-in cage the ticket girl looked at me curiously. Then I was out. In the light of the street there was no policeman. Was it a trap for me to lead them to the others?

I walked away slowly, turned the corner, turned again, then again, till at the end of a narrow deserted street I slipped into a doorway and glanced behind me. No one was following. I looked at my watch; it was five past six.

Then I remembered I had to buy an evening newspaper to hold

in my left hand as I went to the appointment to indicate I wasn't being followed. The first newsstand I passed had no change and I had to struggle all through my pockets to find the few small coppers. But with the paper safely in my hand I realized that in my efforts to shake off any pursuers I had lost my bearings. Time was ticking away and I felt panic at the prospect of missing the others and being left alone in Rome.

After going two blocks in what I thought was the right direction I stopped an elderly man and asked the way to Piazza Fiume, but the words stuck in my throat. I cursed myself. The man looked at me curiously, then hurried away without a word. At length I found a small boy from whom I had the courage to obtain a vague direction which led me back to one of the main streets, thronged with people on their way home from work.

Hurrying along, looking at my feet, I wished the days had not grown so long. With every car or trolley that passed I would look the other way, convinced that by some wild chance the face of Cervo's father, or the radio operator, or Hauptmann Priebke would be staring at me in terrifying recognition. At last, turning the corner, I saw the piazza open up ahead of me. And there they were: Franco, Lele and Mario, standing like a rescuing island by the bus stop, alone, each with a paper in his hand; and a wave of relief poured through me.

As we walked off, bound by an aura of warm fraternity, they recounted to me their own adventures, which, though possibly less frightening than my own, were certainly more fantastic.

20   AT LAST—NEWS OF CERVO!

"WE'VE BEEN TO SICHERHEITSDIENST HEADQUARTERS at Via Tasso," said Franco nonchalantly.

"Good God, what for?" I asked.

At my look of puzzlement the others smiled.

"Oh . . . Ottorino, Mario and I had to take a friend there. Remember Fruehling? We had a little drinking party at the Biblioteca Valle, at four in the afternoon."

"We spent four hours drinking white wine while the orchestra played sticky German-Neapolitan songs and he got maudlin drunk. Then, just as we were leaving, he developed a yen for somebody's wife and reached for his Luger. Luckily he was so drunk it skidded along the floor. After that we had to drag him across Piazza Venezia while he shouted that Mussolini and Hitler were a pair of *"Schweinehunde"*! It was all we could do to get him into a *carrozza* and to Via Tasso where we deposited him in the arms of his *Kameraden*—cab fare compliments of General Donovan!"

Franco winked, and I couldn't resist a smile.

Turning down a side street Franco continued: "Unfortunately, at that very moment his commanding officer walked in. You should have seen the freezing look he threw at Fruehling. But we were thanked profusely by all concerned. Funny, no! I suppose it is the first time in history that an SS NCO has been dragged to Via Tasso—by three subversive elements!"

As I smiled, a little wryly, I managed at last to ask the question that was weighing on my mind—and the one that had obviously prompted their sortie: "What about Cervo?"

Franco shook his head. "He's not at Via Tasso. But we have some news."

Franco then described how he'd arranged a meeting between Maria and Cervo's sister in a nearby church which he had had surrounded by plenty of guns. Maria had arrived dressed in mourning, heavily veiled. Cervo's sister had managed to come without being followed. In a dark corner they had exchanged a few words. From Cervo's sister Maria learned that a police commissioner had phoned Cervo's home to say that Cervo was all right, and on duty out of town. The family hadn't fallen for this though, suspecting it to be a trick. Later they had received a message in Cervo's writing asking for bread and honey and cigarettes. But as we all know he doesn't smoke, and honey was the conventional word through which we learned of his capture, the family assumed the message to be a warning of danger. After that, nothing more. Finally, Franco added, Cervo's fiancée had left for Bologna to see if she could get his father to help.

We were just then passing the moving picture theater where I had spent the afternoon and I now wondered if the man I had seen was really Cervo's father, or just some figment of an overwrought imagination!

One thing in Franco's story appeared to be greatly in our favor. It looked as if Cervo had been captured by an Italian counterpartisan gang and that the Germans weren't yet in on the affair. It so, we might stand a chance of organizing a rescuing raid. But for this we would have to discover exactly where he was being held, and how heavily he was guarded.

It was still not established whether Piazza Lovatelli or Baldo's house had been raided, but Maria had managed to find us another hideout for the night. How long, I wondered, would this wandering last! By now we had reached the neighborhood of Mario's house, too small and too dangerous because of the neighbors, to afford us a refuge even in such an emergency; so we bid him good night and moved on through the growing darkness toward an address in the newish part of Parioli near Via Bruxelles.

As we approached the building, Lele, who had the keys, went ahead and opened the door for us into a one-room ground floor apartment decorated like a boudoir in a call house, normally used by a lone woman as an occasional *garçonnière*.

The furniture consisted of an enormous bed (surrounded by mirrors at suitably salacious angles); so we deposited ourselves on this *piazza d'armi*, speaking in muffled whispers—the walls being so thin we could hear distinctly what was happening in the neighboring apartments— while we passed around a glass of brandy-and-water and I spread out a rudimentary meal from what I had salvaged from lunch. One thing that could be said for our escapades was that someone always managed, at whatever risk, to see there was a handy bottle of "medicinal" Cognac Stock—this particular bottle having been obtained by Lele during the afternoon from our private resources through a series of contacts and cut-outs almost as complicated as required for hand grenades or secret intelligence.

Then the doorbell rang and we all sat up with a start despite the fact that we had been expecting Baldo to arrive from round the corner where he had managed to find refuge in the house of the mother of one of his numerous fiancées.

He and Lele and I were obliged to sit around the bed with our hat and coats on (to keep warm) and play cutthroat bridge by sign language—business being out of the question owing to the thinness of the walls—while Franco lay on the far side of the bed catching up on two nights' lost sleep. Later on Baldo slipped out and back to his dowager countess to be fed and tended by solicitous ladies hopeful of sealing his charms into their signet.

About two in the morning I woke up with the solution to a means of combining two signal plans I had been carrying in my head; but so as not to repeat the mistake I had made in the house with the sailor, I lit a match to burn my jotted notes, inadvertently setting fire to a frilly lampshade of pink celluloid on the bedside table. There was a burst of flame as if someone had ignited magnesium and the two bodies beside me rose simultaneously like corpses from the grave, the whole scene repeated ad infinitum in the maze of mirrors.

Miraculously we got the fire out without raising the household, but I was worried about what the landlady would think of the damage. Luckily, or so Lele assured me, there was little chance of her returning to the scene, as she was then recovering from a minor operation to remedy a condition contracted, we presumed, in the very bed wherein we lay.

As I fell off to sleep I wondered how, with human garrulity being what it is, we had managed to keep anything at all secure in our organization.

Very early in the morning Maria arrived, dressed all in black, and looking quite different, to warn us that though the landlady was incapacitated we would nevertheless have to move because her lover was likely to appear for extracurricular pastimes of his own. The others rushed off in different directions to see if they could find a new refuge for the night, leaving me to curse the Latin temperament and climate.

Having cleaned the apartment I lay on the bed fully clothed and overcoated, ready to flee through the window at the least indication of trouble. But my nerves were, if possible, in an even worse condition than the previous day. What's more, the flat itself was a form of torture —footsteps three floors up resounding as if they were inside my head. Then the doorbell rang, not in the conventional manner, and the effect —a quick beating of the heart followed by a sinking feeling in the solar plexus—was in no way diminished by the certain knowledge that it could *not* be the Gestapo.

Putting on my false glasses, and the most annoyed expression I could muster, I opened the door to find two small boys begging for money.

An hour later, to set me jumping in a different way, the phone bell rang, each insistent ring giving a deeper twist to my nerves, till at last it stopped and my nerves slowly unraveled.

The next time the doorbell rang properly, and I opened up for Lele. He and Baldo had been to Piazza Lovatelli, had walked in from opposite ends, crossed its courtyard and turned and disappeared into the side lane that led to the Portico d'Ottavia. They had been quite prepared to go down into the medieval cellar to get the hundred thousand lire we needed so urgently, but there had been two policemen stationed at each *portone,* who had eyed them fixedly, and with marked interest, from the moment they had come into sight.

Baldo had now gone to see if his apartment were being watched, and Maria to see if they had traced her to her father's house, which, since his death, had been uninhabited except by the servants, but which, if raided, would give us the clue that she, and therefore we, were being personally sought.

Meanwhile Lele informed me he had managed to get my message to the contact for our British "cousin," and trusted it would soon be on its way, but that he must now rush out to see about another house belonging to a friend of his that might afford us refuge. So he left, handing me a small piece of bread on which to chew for consolation.

The rest of the afternoon I lay on the bed reading *Arrowsmith* in Italian, not the most suitable literature for the occasion, but all I could find to keep me from the matted skein of nightmares that pursued me.

Finally, in desperation, I got up and made myself some tea. Just as I was about to pour it the doorbell rang. It was Maria looking worn and miserable. Her nightmares must have been even more painful than ours; her whole world of the last few months had crumbled, leaving her with nothing but anxiety. She was having a hard time finding anyone to hide with because it was too great an imposition on the friends she knew least, and she had to keep away from the ones she knew best, for the police might be looking for her there. She had, however, found a convent that would take her for a week or so, and there she was going to disappear till we knew how things really stood.

When it was time for her to go I held her hand tightly, kissed her on the cheek and led her quickly to the door. She had been extremely brave these last few days of trouble, but the strain was beginning to be too much for her high-strung nature, and I realized that Franco had not been exaggerating when he had said that after her meeting in the church with Cervo's sister she had danced through the streets half laughing, half crying, uttering uncoordinated phrases, trying to buy a horse and buggy and a bunch of flowers.

When she had gone I made the place spotless, packed and prepared myself with hat and coat for the scheduled arrival of Baldo at six-fifteen to take me to wherever we were to spend the night. The curfew was for seven.

At six-thirty there was still no sign of him, and I began to be seriously worried. If he didn't come something awful must have happened. What was worse, I would now be totally alone, and would have to go out into the city and seek refuge as best I could. In such circumstances one is usually driven to find some place utterly new and unlikely. But, even if I could have thought of a good one, my choice was limited by what I could reach before the curfew. Only one solution seemed possible: an old servant of ours whom I had not seen in years who had been with us fifteen years earlier on Lake Maggiore and who was now the porter of a building near Piazza del Popolo. No one in Rome knew that I knew him; but by a strange set of circumstances he and his wife, who had then been our butler and maid, had acted as godparents for me in the baptistry of the Chiesa del Jesu in Pallanza where I had been baptized at the age of nine.

By six-thirty-five I was extremely nervous and could not decide whether to leave immediately and make a dash for the new hideout or wait for the early morning. But the thought of a whole night alone in that flat in the state I was in, not knowing what had happened to the others, was more than I could stand. Any risk would be better. Yet I was obliged, by logic, to stay where I was. It was the only place where any of the others might still get in touch with me.

At six-forty-five, with fifteen minutes to go, I heard the doorbell and Lele appeared, white and very nervous—more than anything, it developed, because Franco, who had always been punctual to the second, had turned up fifteen minutes late to his appointment, making Lele really sweat.

But all seemed well. In the last red rays of evening we set out for an empty apartment belonging to the brother of the girl who had the lease on the Palazza Lovatelli, a boy called Emanuele de Seta who had gone south at the moment of the Anzio landings to try to cross the lines.

Passing a wine shop, just before it closed, we replenished our supplies for the evening, then turned onto Viale Parioli. By a small gate Lele stopped, looked around, motioned me into a garden, quickened his step toward the back of a reddish house with a sharp-slanting roof. From a small side door a red-faced woman with a pleasant smile appeared like a cuckoo from a clock—Emanuele's Swiss nurse. Climbing numerous flights of narrow marble steps we finally emerged into a top-floor apartment with a charming atmosphere. Sensi, the nurse, brought forth sheets and towels and plates and glasses, while I wandered happily around looking at the books, feeling the softness of the beds, relieved at being out of the constricting house of assignation where we had spent the last twenty-four hours.

In the sitting room we pulled in the shutters of the huge French windows that gave onto a terrace overlooking the Villa Borghese, turned on the radio, prepared a meal of cheese and omelettes and fresh bread and wine, then played gin rummy till it was time for bed. It was a strange feeling of relief to lie once more in soft clean sheets and think that for one night at least we were comparatively safe.

But the next day Franco brought news of yet another disaster. One

202

of our men, fresh back from our partisan friends in the mountains round Visso, had drawn up a long and detailed report on the parachute drop of men and equipment that had finally taken place on the night of March 14 to 15, and which had turned out to be another catastrophe directly attributable to the type of agent recruited in the south.

Though the BBC had failed to give the signal "The Stars Are Shining," which was to warn that the operation would take place that night, the partisans had heard the planes and lit the fires. Ten men and two radio operators under the command of a twenty-three-year-old Italian lieutenant of Slovene origin by the name of Italo had been successfully dropped along with thirty-odd containers of equipment. All of the equipment, according to the lieutenant, had been safely recovered, with the exception of a radio set and two million lire (presumably ours).

Senior partisan officers had soon reached the area and warned the lieutenant that once the equipment was safely hidden he and his men should move with the rest of the partisans to a safer area higher in the mountains because the Germans were bound to get wind of the drop and scour the area.

The lieutenant refused to listen, insisting he had a personal mission to carry out and would stay where he was.

Several times the partisans entreated him to change his mind, offering him scouts and armed support for any operation he might wish to carry out, pointing out to him that they knew the area intimately whereas he had no knowledge whatsoever of the territory. Still the lieutenant refused to move.

On the afternoon of March 18, at five o'clock, twenty-five Germans had arrived, caught Italo eating dinner in a farmer's house right near the spot where they had dropped him. In a short battle they had killed Italo and two of the parachutists with him, capturing the other two.

None of the rest, who had escaped, knew what to do, affirming that only their leader knew of their assignment (just like the night I had landed). All insisted on trying to get back to the Allied lines as soon as possible.

But that, sad as it was, was not all the bad news of the day. We received more details of Cervo's imprisonment thanks to the appearance of a young boy at the home of Cervo's parents. The boy had been arrested with an old professor, blindfolded and taken to a strange apartment full of frightful men and women. There he had heard people howl and scream and had seen Cervo stripped of his lieutenant's insignia, his face badly bruised and beaten, minus several teeth. He also reported having seen Cervo's orderly with him and that he too had been beaten. The boy said that Cervo had begged him—were he to manage to escape or be released—to go to his family.

Cervo's mother and sister were afraid, however, that it might be a trap; and we were inclined to agree. From the description of the place we figured that poor Cervo must have fallen into the hands of another bunch of brutes like Bardi and Pollastrini, the organizers of a Fascist torture chamber in the Palazzo Braschi which had been broken up as being too awful even for the Germans.

It was a relief though to know, pretty well for certain, that the Germans, as yet, had nothing to do with Cervo's arrest, and that once Franco's men had carefully reconnoitered the place we might proceed with our next operation of attempting to get him out with an armed *coup de main.*

Then Baldo came in, fresh from a reconnaissance at Piazza Lovatelli. The police had called five times in our absence and finding no one in the apartment were now planning to break down the door—not, so it seemed, in a search for us, but to requisition the place for bombed-out civilian refugees in case the apartment was really uninhabited.

Or was this a ruse, we wondered, to get the purported owner or tenant to come forward to save the property, and thus trap us all?

21 PLANS FOR A *COUP DE MAIN*

THE NEXT MORNING, March 23, Franco reported that his men had located the place where Cervo was being kept a prisoner—an apartment in a dismal gray building in one of the ugliest parts of Rome near the Termini Station: Via Principe Amedeo 2. Since his men had been watching they had seen what appeared to be three corpses taken from the building, and neighbors complained of frightful screams and gunfire late into the night.

About a dozen men, well armed with submachine guns, were reported in and out of the apartment; to make a frontal assault would be costly and almost certainly useless. Yet something must be done, and soon, to liberate Cervo.

Finally we decided that if at any time there were less than fifteen men in the apartment we would attempt a direct assault. Both Franco and I felt we owed it to Cervo to be there personally when we tried to pull it off. Meanwhile Franco had requested his men to discover what was in the apartment immediately below the one in which Cervo was being held.

Primo had managed to see Cervo's sister (they lived almost across the street) without being followed and had recovered four hundred thousand lire from the funds hidden in Cervo's house; with this we could now pay the men of the information service, who had been without funds for several days and in immediate danger of being picked up by the police.

In the evening, as I sat on the terrace watching the first of the swallows, Lele came rushing in, out of breath. Someone had thrown a bomb or a series of bombs in a side street called Via Rasella (a narrow street running steeply down from the Palazzo Barberini to the end of the Traforo tunnel) and had killed about thirty German MPs. The whole area was in a turmoil. German police and Fascists had opened fire, and it was rumored that as many as 200 civilians had been injured or killed in the shootings. The Fascists had then gone from house to house beating anyone they could lay hands on, arresting all men in the area, lining them up along the walls of buildings with their arms above their heads, carting them off to jail irrespective of identity.

Our first reaction was that there was no point in killing thirty non-descript German MPs! Why hadn't whoever was responsible for the attack risked his courage against Via Tasso, or picked off Kappler and his gang of butchers? Now there was no telling what the German reaction might be; certainly it boded no good for the underground in the city. What saddened us even more was to contemplate the beauty and precision of the attack the organization of which appeared to have been damned near perfect!

The next afternoon, March 24, Franco had scheduled another of our incongruous pastimes: a tea party at Baldo's with the girls whom we had invited the night of SS Captain Priebke's arrival. The purpose of the party was to establish whether it was safe to reoccupy Baldo's flat, and to convince the superintendent of our purpose for doing so.

As usual I didn't feel like leaving the comfort and apparent security of the flat I was in, but Franco insisted. So we set off about four in the afternoon, loaded with good French brandy and a couple of dozen pastries. Owing to the attack on Via Rasella there was a rumor the curfew had been advanced to 4 P.M. But there were still people on the streets and we walked through Parioli undisturbed.

At Baldo's I lit a fire with the only wood available; stray bits of furniture and a washboard. The girls arrived and we sat around the fire consuming tea and cakes and brandy. Soon I began to forget the realities of the world outside and enjoy the company of the girls, especially the one called L., with whom I had been to fetch Captain Priebke, and who was now eyeing me curiously.

By seven o'clock, the proper curfew hour, we had perforce to part. I was unwilling to, and Baldo and I decided to walk L. home—a risk we should not have taken, but which, with the aid of so much brandy so early in the evening, I managed almost to enjoy.

When at last we regained our own flat we discovered that the Germans had threatened to shoot three hundred hostages, ten for each German soldier killed at Via Rasella the previous afternoon. According to rumor, there were 150 men available in the main jail and they intended to take the rest wherever they could find them.

From Sensi, the good Swiss nurse, we obtained, along with the latest rumor, a small roast beef, which we washed down with a bottle of good red wine while heatedly discussing the most effective way to get Cervo out of the hands of the brigands who were holding him prisoner.

According to Franco's latest reports there were seldom less than fifteen well-armed guards in or around the apartment at Via Principe Amedeo 2, but one of Franco's men had discovered the apartment beneath it to be empty. Franco had therefore planned for a partisan locksmith to go there the next day, make an entry, and plant enough dynamite to collapse the floor of the hall of the apartment above. In the ensuing confusion we would stand a better chance of overcoming the guards and freeing the prisoners.

The next morning, March 25, I had a hangover from the brandy and good red wine; to ease it I drank several glasses of that appetizing but nauseatingly labeled Roman beverage known as Acqua Marcia— or Rotten Water. In the light of day, and without benefit of exhilarating brandy, the operation to free Cervo seemed more problematical; nevertheless it was the best that we could hope for. Franco was to bring news of the hour and final disposition for the raid we were to stage.

Late in the afternoon Lele arrived with a rare delicacy: a pork chop!—followed shortly by Maria with a small bunch of flowers and news of her own adventures during the last few days.

Still there was no sign of Franco.

Suddenly a fuse blew and I was obliged to go down to the cellar, where, with one of the refugees who lived on the ground floor, a lanky fellow with a bastard hunting dog, but a first-rate electrician, we managed to remedy the defect in one of the most prehistoric lighting systems ever installed in the twentieth century.

As we worked he informed me he had just heard from the maid of the bombed-out police commissioner who lived on the floor below us the latest information on Via Rasella.

It was the first I had heard of any such person living below us, and my blood ran cold at the thought, only to be chilled even further as I heard the rumor that 320 hostages had been shot the previous afternoon for the death of the thirty-two Germans killed at Via Rasella.

Upstairs, just as I was putting on the water for some tea, Franco arrived—bereft of his usual smile.

"Hello," he said, not at all in his usual voice; then enunciated slowly: "They have shot Cervo. And eleven of our men."

Only then did I notice how pale he was and that there were small bloodshot veins in his eyes.

"We will kill a lot of guilty Fascists," he said, gripping my arm.

I nodded. "All who are guilty," I said. But for some reason I could not feel sad or depressed, as if my emotions had been novocained. I was a little scared, but more than anything—horrible as it may seem upon analysis—relieved. Cervo's death appeared to me to be a release *for him* from what must have been almost unbearable torture, *for us* from the constant fear that he might not be able to refrain from giving us away; and behind all this was the warm, glowing realization that a human being had achieved one of the highest peaks within his limits.

"How do you know?" was all I could bring myself to say.

Then Franco told me that a degraded lieutenant of the PS (Security Police) had been seen at Regina Coeli too weak and too battered to stand alone, and that he had been carried away with the others.

Having cleaned out Via Tasso the Germans had gone to Regina Coeli and asked for 250 more men at random. Neither the prisoners nor some of the authorities apparently knew that the men were to be shot, thinking they were to be taken to forced labor. Some asked to take their canteen cups and blankets, and it was not till they were loaded onto trucks, hands tied, with the Germans holding tommy guns to their ribs that they realized what was in store for them. Some tried to jump from the trucks, but too late. They were rushed out to some catacombs near San Callisto where they were thrown at random into one of the caves and shot individually in the back of the neck, the living climbing higher on the pile of dead. And when the dead and wounded lay in a vast heap, the Germans exploded half a dozen mines, burying the living and the dead under the collapsing cave.

Only later, from Cervo's orderly, who was arrested with him but miraculously escaped execution, we got the following full report of what had happened to Cervo since the day, a week earlier, when he had rushed out of the "hole" to move the radio by the river.

March 17, 1944 at about 1430 hours I was asked by Lieutenant Maurizio Giglio to accompany him to the neighborhood of the Risorgimento Bridge on the corner of Piazza Monte Grappa.

We went there on a motorcycle driven by the lieutenant.

He then ordered me to watch the motorcycle, saying he was going down to the river boat of the Ministry of Finance for a few minutes, adding that, were he to be much delayed, I was to return the motorcycle to our barracks and inform his mother, Mrs. Anna Giglio, and then absent myself. He indicated that the delay might be caused by an arrest.

I knew quite well that the lieutenant was involved in daring patriotic activities and that he was in contact with the South.

I waited about twenty minutes. As the lieutenant did not appear I moved the motorcycle to a more advantageous position to see what was happening on the river boat.

From my new observation post I saw several civilians, all of them young, enter and leave, at intervals, over a period of an hour and ten minutes.

I was very much worried about what might have happened to the lieutenant. I therefore decided to go down to the river boat, charging a young fourteen-year-old student (whom I later discovered to be the son of an air force colonel in hiding) to watch the motorcycle.

As I was moving toward the river boat I was approached by two individuals who had just left it. They invited me to follow them in order to report to a Commissioner of Public Security into whose presence they brought me: he was standing, about 1.82 meters tall, thin, with a striped brown suit, dark complexion, beardless but with a short mustache, black eyes, smooth black hair, no identifying marks, very white, closely-set teeth. I categorically denied knowing Lieutenant Giglio, also because I did not know whether the interrogators were authorized or not.

With the so-called commissioner, whom I later learned to be the ill-famed Dr. Koch, were other agents also in civilians, who said they belonged to the Fascist Republican Police.

Among them was a confidant of Dr. Koch, named Walter, born 1916, 1.65 meters tall, olive-skinned, wavy black hair, longish ascetic face, heavy beard, short brushy mustache, normal head, no identifying marks that I can remember, always wearing a raincoat.

Apart from these, all those present, as I was later to learn, took turns at Via Tasso and other torture chambers at Via Principe Amedeo 2, and later in Via Romagna.

At my request Koch displayed a bilingual, stamped pass, indicating that he belonged to the Fascist Republican Police.

I was disarmed, and, owing to my insisting that I did not know Lieutenant Giglio, ordered to follow them.

Before letting me out they closed the door so as to first remove my officer. He was put into a Fiat 1100 while I was loaded onto another car, a short distance behind, along with the boy to whom I had entrusted the motorcycle, who, not seeing me return, had come down to the river boat and also been arrested.

We were taken to Via Principe Amedeo 2, near the Hotel Diana, up to the top floor, the lieutenant in the elevator, the boy and I on foot, escorted by armed guards. Walter and Koch were with the lieutenant. In the apartment we were put in separate rooms. It was now about 1630.

1st Interrogation: At 1700 the lieutenant was interrogated. I did not see or hear him being tortured. At 1630 I was interrogated. I insisted that I did not know my superior. They began to ill-treat me. Koch, Walter and three others were present, and to these five, others were later added, called in by Koch to take a hand. They were all armed: some with pistols, others with knives. One by one they would point these weapons at my mouth, my temples, my ribs, my kidneys. They then started punching my chest, my jaws as if I were a punching bag.

At this point they called in the lieutenant to confront me. Receiving an order from him to admit to the fact that I knew him, I admitted the truth on this point, declaring myself to be his orderly.

I was bleeding from mouth and nose.

Knocked along the walls of a corridor I was thrown into a room where there were other prisoners: among them Professor Albertarelli and Lieutenant Carlo Costantini. I do not remember the names of the other seven. All had been tortured. Professor Albertarelli had his ribs crushed and was bandaged round the chest. With the exception of Costantini, the faces of all the others were swollen. A traitor—Enzo, formerly a comrade and confidant of the lieutenant—was in perfect physical shape: medium height, born in 1917, radio telegraphist in the Signal Corps, olive-skinned, smooth chestnut hair, chestnut eyes, no particular distinguishing marks, gray suit.

2nd Interrogation: During the night of 17th to 18th at midnight. Before interrogating me, they interrogated Lieutenant Giglio. I could hear Walter and the others beating him in the corridor. He was put back in his cell, after which I was interrogated.

Koch, Walter and ten to fifteen cutthroats armed with pistols and knives were present. Koch asked me if it were true that I took messages to the British, if I distributed pamphlets, if I hid hand grenades and munitions. As I remained silent they beat me and tortured me, worse than the first time, lasting an hour and a half.

At 2 A.M. of the 18th the lieutenant was brought back to Koch, where he signed a paper. He was then brought into our cell, bleeding from the mouth, nose, and with his face all swollen. He had lost several teeth.

3rd Interrogation: Lieutenant Giglio was interrogated first. He was tortured for several minutes, then taken back to his cell by the torturer Walter. He was bleeding, complaining mostly about his ribs. Enzo, the traitor, tried to comfort him. After talking with him, Enzo would go straight to Walter to report on the conversation. He would then return smoking a cigarette or eating some food.

I was called, and for half an hour invited to tell what I knew. To persuade me they pulled out my whiskers, attached two steel points to my temples drawn together by a band of steel. I felt as if my eyes were popping out. When I was on the point of unconsciousness the grip would be loosened. They wanted me to say who were the lieutenant's collaborators, where arms and munitions were hidden, what jobs I fulfilled for the organization. I remained silent.

I was then taken back to the communal cell, bleeding profusely. The walls against which I was thrown were smeared and thick with it.

From eleven o'clock of the 18th till 2200 of the 20th we were not interrogated. Our food consisted solely of a small plate of overcooked rice in some diluted filthy broth. No bread.

The night of Sunday the 19th Enzo was taken away. He said goodbye to Lieutenant Giglio, wishing him well. Overhearing them, Walter said to the lieutenant that he would not see him again.

4th Interrogation: Toward 2115 of the 20th Lieutenant Giglio was interrogated, it lasting about forty minutes. Ten minutes later I was called. Covered with blood I returned to the cell, in the presence of Koch, Walter and the Chief of Police Caruso.

Lieutenant Giglio informed me that he had been tortured in the presence of and with the consent of Caruso, and that Walter, throwing his head forward, had given him a violent blow on the nape of the neck.

Brought to the torture chamber I was seated on a chair. An electric current was run through my body. I paled, nearly fainting, covered by a cold sweat.

With Caruso's consent Koch beat me savagely. Walter, in a tone as if to help, put a handkerchief under my nose, saying: "Poor boy, wipe yourself!" at the same time hitting me on the nape of the neck.

As I went out Caruso said: "Blackened soul! Try to go straight!" To which I answered that my soul was clean, cleaner than that of some others. This let loose a storm. I don't quite remember how. I only know that I was dragged to the cell and tied, with handcuffs on my wrists, to a bar about 1.70 meters from the floor.

The lieutenant found the strength to give me a little water and a few slices of potato which had been left to us by the charity of Professor Albertarelli, who had been taken to Regina Coeli, so they told me, about 1700 that afternoon. Our other comrades of ill fortune were distributed in other jails; so that night, the 20th to 21st, the lieutenant and I were alone.

After about six or seven hours, thanks to the lieutenant's efforts with one of the guards, I was untied. The remainder of the night we tried to get some rest.

5th Interrogation: 2300 hours of the 21st in the presence of Koch, Walter and others armed with pistols and knives.

The interrogation lasted about half an hour. A pistol was pointed at my mouth and another at my temple and I was invited to speak. I remained obdurate, telling them it was unjust so to torture a man. Two or three shots were fired through the window to intimidate me.

In the face of my determined stand Koch suggested the application of a new method. A wooden frame was brought into the room onto which was attached a board thirty centimeters by one meter with six rows of long, well-sharpened nails. Naked, I was stretched out on this frame with my back against this sort of "wool-carder," my arms folded across my chest and a steel bar on a hinge drawn across me and fastened so that my body was forced onto the pointed nails.

In a frenzy, Walter and the fiercer of the others slapped me, pulled out my whiskers, my eyebrows, fired pistols, pushed me from right to left so that flesh was ripped away by the nails. After twenty minutes I was thrown back into my cell by Walter.

With the little strength I had left, I recounted to the lieutenant what had happened. As always, grieving and sad, and running his hands through his hair, he whispered: "Poor Scottu, how much you are suffering because of me."

Trying to cheer him up, I said that it was nothing.

Then Koch came in, smiling and impudent, and asked how we were.

Closing the door he said: "This is nothing! Now we will bring you some company."

Between two and five o'clock of the 22nd several new arrivals were introduced into our cell: two cloth merchants whose names I do not remember, one about fifty years old, fattish, short, with sparse white hair; the other of medium height, with a lot of dark hair, who looked about thirty; both from Rome. Then a tailor whose home and workshop, as far as I could gather, were in Via Milano: tall, olive-skinned, bushy mustache, followed by a shoemaker and an oil and wine merchant with a shop between Centocelle and Porta Maggiore. The shoemaker was deformed owing to a fall in gymnastic exercises with the GIL. Lastly, a young professor of twenty-four, tall, thin, long-faced, olive-skinned, brown suit with stripes, goatee and whiskers.

All of them were marched in with scorn and insults, their eyes swollen, their faces bruised from the first blows received. All were bleeding from nose and mouth.

At noon, special treatment: spaghetti, apparently ordered through the charity of Caruso. No bread. The usual bottle of water for an entire day. The cell, three meters by three, was furnished with a double bed and two cots, all with mattresses, two of wool, two of dried grass. No sanitary facilities; for this purpose a waterless basin was used. The air was fetid, unbreathable. The shutters were blocked by iron bars fastened by six padlocks. This to avoid the possibility that despair might lead us to suicide, last custodian of our faith and of our actions.

Professor Albertarelli had been stopped by the legs just as he had tried to go to his Maker, out of love for his neighbor and for his country.

The night of the 22nd Professor Ascensione arrived, whose first name I do not remember. He was accompanied by a boy of twelve or thirteen who had been with him at the moment of arrest, but who was, however, released on the morning of the 23rd.

All through the 22nd and till almost 2300 of the 23rd, neither the lieutenant nor I was interrogated.

Toward 1400 hours of the 23rd, however, Walter approached Lieutenant Giglio and said to him that he sincerely regretted having had him captured, offered him a cigarette and some chocolate, flattered him and promised him a rosy future. He then reminded him of their former pretended friendship. Quietly the lieutenant answered: "Walter, you are like Judas!"

Toward 1800 on the 23rd, the doors suddenly opened and seven or eight of Koch's agents rushed in and started to beat, kick and punch those present, covering us with spittle and insults because of the news of the Via Rasella attack and the death of thirty-two of their "German comrades." Walter was among the more active, but neither the lieutenant nor I was touched during the outburst.

6th Interrogation: From 2200 to about 2240 of the 23rd, I was interrogated in the presence of Koch, Walter, ten to fifteen guards and a Doctor or Lieutenant Tela of the Fascist Republican Police who wore glasses, about 1.70 meters tall, smooth chestnut hair, gray suit, clean shaven, olive-skinned, no distinguishing marks.

Lieutenant Giglio was interrogated for about twenty minutes, coming back, his face disfigured, tottering and worn out. Walter punched him in the mouth. Blood flowed from his cracked lips. As he sat on the bed wiping the blood with his handkerchief he weakly called out for his mother. At that moment Walter, like a beast, raised his foot and brought it down with all the weight of his body, kicking him in the pubic region.

The lieutenant, at the end of his strength, uttered a weak cry: "Mamma, Mamma, they've killed me!" As he tried weakly to turn onto his side Walter let go another kick, as hard as the first, striking him between the kidneys and the sacroiliac.

It was all that was needed.

The lieutenant turned white as a corpse. I tried to help him, get him onto the bed. I bathed his lips with a little water. But Walter and a Tuscan guard considered my sympathy a crime, kicking me and throwing a bucket of water into my face. In fact the episode brought on another interrogation. Same old story. They accused me of unpatriotic activities such as distributing leaflets, indicating to the Allies places to bomb, etc.

I re-entered the cell at about 2300. That night and all of the 24th the lieutenant was between life and death.

When I tried to give him a spoonful of soup, lifting his head from the pillow, Walter threw the dish away, spilling the soup onto me, insulting me as he did so.

At 1450 Walter informed us of an order that we were to be turned over to the German SS and that each of us might send a last note to his family.

Everyone was crying.

Only the lieutenant whispered words of encouragement to all.

I helped him to the toilet, but he could only pass blood. Seeing us, Walter knocked us both to the ground.

A woman, acting as maid because her husband, a Communist, had managed to avoid Koch's agents, took pity on the lieutenant and brought him a glass of milk.

But no sooner had he drunk it than it brought on a crisis, and he fainted. One of the guards threw a canteen of water into his face and the lieutenant revived.

He was then carried bodily out of the cell and taken to Regina Coeli jail. I now know that he lies buried with his companions, victims of German ferocity.

My fate was like the others': I was taken to the same jail, but, arriving late, was not included among those who were taken away to be shot as hostages.

As a postscript to this account, Scottu added:

214

During some of the interrogations two young women were present, one a stenographer, short, dark-skinned, black-eyed, with loose black hair, white teeth; the other chestnut, taller and better built. The stenographer, I am told, was the mistress of Koch.

Both of them, present at a couple of our interrogations, laughed at the sight of our torment and spilled blood. They slept in the apartment with the male personnel.

Two pitiful figures occasionally appeared on the scene of our misfortunes: the two spinsters who ran the *pensione* adapted by Koch into a headquarters for his operations. One, by the name of Mimma, about 1.60 meters tall, black hair, combed straight back, black eyes, with a Roman accent; the other, whose name I don't know, taller and stronger, between thirty and thirty-two years old.

I am in a position to recognize any survivors, and to identify, on seeing them, one by one, all those who tortured me.

Signed and sworn to:

GIOVANNI SCOTTU*
Public Security Agent

Then we learned—a circumstance quite unusual in such cases—that if Cervo had wished to talk and reveal our names and addresses he could have saved himself. Owing to his father's position in the OVRA it would have been easy to pass off the story that he had been a double agent *all along,* working to ferret us out. By keeping his silence and sacrificing himself Cervo had saved every one of us and the organization too.

As we looked out at a storm of Allied fighters high in the Roman sky, I realized dispassionately that at the height of his ordeal, while they had stood him up to be shot, we, his friends, had been drinking brandy in the apartment of a Palatine count in the arms of beautiful girls; but all I could conclude was that *even if* we could have felt his loss more keenly, or had known the moment he was to die, we might have but drunk deeper, danced later into the night.

---

* Married to an American citizen some years after the war, poor Scottu was forbidden entry to the U.S. to join his wife, on the grounds that he was tubercular. Nor was there anything I could do with the immigration authorities to help him.

In my diary I wrote:

If there is any avenging to do I would personally prefer to do it constructively, if possible, for it seems to me the only way to build a better world. Nevertheless we are planning a little surprise for the brutes that torture people at Via Principe Amedeo 2, in the form of eighty pounds of dynamite, and it does not displease me to think that if the job comes off successfully in some small way we will have avenged the hours of torture that Cervo suffered at their hands.

The next morning I noticed a small paid announcement in the obit column of the morning paper. Cervo's parents, "torn with grief, request that their friends neither call nor send messages of condolence."

It was odd to see the name bordered in black, and the words announcing: "At only twenty-three the life of a young lieutenant and doctor of law, a volunteer, wounded in action, and decorated, has most suddenly been extinguished."

22 WE REORGANIZE FOR COVER

WITH THE DEATH OF CERVO, and his courageous silence, we realized it should now be safe to contact the radio operator with whom he had set up a daily rendezvous outside the Ministry of War. It was essential however, lest the operator be suspicious of his unknown interlocutor, that someone go to the meeting who was familiar with the OSS on the Allied side of the lines in order to convince him he would, in fact, be working for the organization which had hired him. It was therefore decided that I go myself.

The information service was to be recognized along more compact lines, based on fewer, and only the most reliable and experienced, of our men. Such large-scale operations as the road-watching—now that Kesselring appeared to be serious about rerouting German traffic around rather than through the city—could be sizably reduced. It was ironic, in this connection, to note that the Germans' decision seemed to have been influenced by their discovery—when they caught so many of our road-spotters *in flagrante*—that the Allies had a vast and effective espionage network in the city watching their every move.

The next most vital problem was for each of us to acquire, establish, and maintain some decent sort of cover that would protect us in case of random arrest, and enable us to move about the city on our various jobs with reasonable assurance.

As luck would have it, Ottorino was about to be reassigned as liaison officer from the Open City directly to Kesselring's headquarters in Monte Soratte—constituting, we trusted, a most remarkable source of daily information.

Franco was to try to become a liaison officer between his uncle's chancery of the Knights of Malta and the Vatican.

Baldo, being the possessor of a genuine Palatine title, we hoped to get enrolled in the Palatine Guard!

Lele, who was by profession a doctor, and had been an intern at the Polyclinic, was now, thanks to the good offices of a doctor friend, to start going regularly to the hospital so that his papers as a practicing doctor would be sufficiently in order to give him an explanation for where he spent his days.

Maria, now that Cervo had died without revealing the secret of the Palazzo Lovatelli, could have reoccupied our old headquarters, but we decided it would be better for her to establish residence in her father's place, and have Mario, who had authentic papers as a refugee, live in the Palazzo Lovatelli with his wife and child, thus giving us two safe addresses and avoiding the Palazzo Lovatelli's being filled by the police with authentic refugees. If possible we wished to retain possession of the place, not only because of the "hole," but also because of our equipment in the cellar.

The remaining problem was to find a proper solution for my own status—and a radical one at that. With the defection of Enzo, the Vittorio radio operator, the Fascist Security Police (and by now almost certainly the German SD), must have been aware of the presence in the city of an American major by the code name of Pietro in charge of an espionage network.

I therefore decided my first security step would be to kill off Pietro, spreading the news throughout the underground that with the death of Cervo, Pietro had vanished. To replace him, another agent had appeared, by the code name of Roberto—the first name that went with my new identity of Roberto Berlingieri.

Though apparently amateurish, the device, in the long run, was to prove all too effective.

As the chances of getting me any really authentic papers seemed remote, we discussed various places in which I might hide. Though I knew a friendly Swiss diplomat, I did not want to embarrass him except as the very last resort. In answer to a note sent into the Vatican to our minister Harold Tittman about seeking refuge there, I received an urgent warning that the Holy See had become, at least geographically speaking, a sort of goldfish bowl carefully scrutinized by the Germans (arousing in my imagination the picture of a feline and myopic Himmler leering at a bowl of $\iota\chi\theta\nu s$). We even discussed, in case of emergency, putting me into a convent (along with Messrs. Nenni, Bonomi Bencivenga and Company) while Franco took over the organization— a prospect which pleased me not at all, and which was immediately discarded, my knowledge of OSS procedures and intelligence reporting still being essential enough to the organization for Franco to promise to do his utmost to find a solution for my cover and identity.

Then, on March 26, just before noon of a bright sunny day, as I was about to leave the apartment to go to the rendezvous in front of the Ministry of War, Lele, as always out of breath, came rushing in with a startling piece of news.

The doctor friend of his, a partisan in the Partito d'Azione, who worked at the Polyclinic Hospital, had just told him of being contacted by the representative of a group of three agents and two radio operators who claimed to have been sent to Rome by the Fifth Army, where they had lost confidence in their mission leader, and wished to get in touch with the Fifth Army in order to get back to work.

Truly an exciting bit of news! But who could they be, and how could we put them to work? Certainly they had nothing to do with Coniglio, or that would have come to the fore. Suspecting them to be the agents who had landed with Sorrentino and then argued with him, I decided to investigate them further before meeting the operator at the Ministry of War. Were these operators in possession of radios and crystals, with apartments from which to operate, we should be able to re-establish communications with the base much faster and better; and once this was done, set up other channels more easily.

I therefore got Lele to go straight back to his doctor friend and have him ask the representative of the agents if the words "Siria" and "Iris" meant anything to them.

If they turned out to be whom I suspected, our whole lives might take a turn for the better—unless of course it was a trap!

As I paced the apartment, looking out across the terrace at a formation of Allied bombers, listening to the miserable news, or lack of it, from the southern front, wondering how long it would be before I got an answer through Lele, Franco turned up to relieve me of my agonizing vigil with a good bit of news of his own. He had a scheme whereby he might obtain for me something even better than paper credentials— the real cover of a uniform in a branch of the Italian army!

For some time he had been in contact with a lieutenant in the PAI (Italian African Police)—the one who had obtained for us the police plates to put on the stolen truck with which to go to Visso to collect the equipment which was to have been dropped for us. Now the lieutenant seemed willing to help us even further. Franco had cooked up a story for him to the effect that there was an Italian air force major in hiding in Rome whom the Allies were anxious to get hold of for the development of guided missiles, suggesting that if the lieutenant were really interested in doing the Allies a favor he might undertake to enroll this Italian major as an NCO in his own PAI company in order to keep him from the Germans. Espionage being still too heinous to admit—I was to be the Italian air force major!

The lieutenant agreed with the plan, providing he could obtain the tacit approval of the colonel commanding the whole PAI column, to enroll an Italian officer of field grade as an NCO in his company. For this Franco was to meet the colonel, and, to prove the bona fides of the Allies, arrange for a recognizable conventional phrase to be broadcast over the BBC.

I then told Franco about the development of the new agents, and, as the moment seemed propitious, opened a brand-new bottle of brandy with which to toast the dawning of what might be a whole new area of operations, with good cover, a streamlined organization, and the establishment of multiple contacts with the base!

Then Lele came in with enough good news to join us in another toast. The representative of the agents had been staggered that anyone could know their most secret code names, Siria and Iris. Were I satisfactorily to establish to them that I was from the OSS, Fifth Army, they would be only too anxious to get back to work and carry out the assignments for which they had crossed the lines.

We held a conference to decide on the next move. My guess about their identity had proved correct. Still, there was the vaguest chance they might be working for the Germans, trying to lure us into a trap. In either case, viewed quite cynically, it would be wise to bring Lele's doctor friend into our camp where he could serve as an excellent cut-out.

We therefore assigned him the code name of Marcello and I wrote out a note instructing him to inform the representative of the Siria and Iris radios that there was an OSS representative in Rome by the name of Roberto, that they should place themselves immediately at his orders if they wished to carry out the assignments for which they had crossed the lines.

The following day I received an answer through our cut-out, Marcello, from the representative of the agents now known by the code name Eugenio. They were most anxious to place themselves at the orders of a real OSS officer, providing, of course, this Roberto could satisfactorily establish his authority by answering a series of intimate questions about OSS personnel and establishments round Naples— which turned out to be mostly about the features and habits of Captain A.

I answered as follows:

Captain A. wears a French army uniform. He is stocky, almost fat, and rosy-cheeked. He lived first at Via Crispi 71, then at Arco Felice on the second floor of the red house, then at Villa Giudice at Baia. He does not drink wine with his meals, and never smokes. His assistant is an Italian of Levantine origin who wears an American uniform with U.S. insignia. Another, named Giulio, is Italian, tall, with sallow features, who dresses in civilians or in American uniform; Mike teaches radio communications.

Along with this I sent them specific orders about what to do with the radios, a warning that the Germans had brought detecting equipment into the city, and the categoric injunctions that no one other than the two operators should know where the radios were actually located, that no messages (other than QRX signals for establishing contact) were to be sent—except in case of emergency—unless signed by Roberto.

Dawn was breaking and I was very excited at the prospect of resuming work. Acres of information had been piling up at Franco's emergency headquarters since our radio had gone off the air, and I now started going over endless bits of multicolored paper bearing the results of the labors of hundreds of clandestine workers to see what was still valid and most urgently sendable to the base as soon as communication was re-established.

The next morning as I lay dozing—so as not to fret up and down the apartment waiting for Lele to arrive with the latest developments—I was roused by our good Swiss nurse, Sensi, and a really shocking piece of news. While Baldo and I had been lying in our respective beds, each playing possum from his own reality, the police had come to arrest the owner of the apartment! They were apparently combing the whole area for deserters and hidden officers.

What had saved us, it appeared, was a piece of luck that verged on

221

the miraculous: the bombed-out police commissioner who lived as a refugee on the floor below ours had decided—apparently for the first time in his twenty-odd years of service—not to go to work that morning. Furthermore, he had happened, also thanks to the *divina Providenza,* to be out on the landing in front of his door at the very moment the patrol of Italian and German police had come up the stairs on their way to our apartment on the upper floor. Being assured by this authentic police commissioner that the owner of the apartment had not been around for months and that it was entirely empty, the patrol had hesitated for a moment, then turned and gone back down the stairs. All this, it developed, simply because the commissioner's wife (with whom Sensi was on very good terms) had previously told her husband that we, upstairs, were really *"gente per bene,"* "nice people."

Hearing the story, and recounting it to sleepy-eyed Baldo, I had the sensation of having been strapped to an electric chair which had misfunctioned because of a faulty fuse.

Then Lele arrived to tell us that across the street the patrol had found an authentic Italian air force major and carted him off to Regina Coeli.

As for our new contacts, in answer to my most recent message, Eugenio now informed me that, though thoroughly satisfied as to my authority, it developed that Siria had lost his signal plan and Iris his crystals; neither could get in touch with the base.

For this there was but one solution. I must concoct new plans for both and send another message to the base via our British "cousin." Unfortunately, and infuriatingly, this would take at least several days to be relayed.

Then who should turn up on the scene but Coniglio! He too had found out, through the underground grapevine, of the presence of the Siria and Iris agents, and was anxious to get them to work for him. They, on the other hand, informed me ("Roberto") that they didn't trust Coniglio, and wished to have nothing whatsoever to do with him.

At the same time a message from Coniglio, addressed to Pietro, was passed on to me via Marcello, Lele's doctor friend, helpfully informing me of Cervo's death! Luckily Marcello had informed Coniglio that Pietro no longer existed. This, I decided, was probably all to the good, and might rid us of the importunities of Coniglio, at least for a while.

Then came the climax to this Molière mixup. No sooner had I gotten Eugenio, the representative of Siria and Iris, to agree to work for Roberto, without their suspecting for a moment that he had anything to do with Pietro (who to all intents and purposes was buried or had escaped across the lines) than they ran into a man—through underground channels—who purported to be a courier from the north with crystals and a signal plan and instructions for them to put themselves immediately at the disposal of an American officer called Tomsic (*sic*).

Now Eugenio sent me ("Roberto") an urgent message wanting to know what to do, that the agent from the north seemed convincing but was vague on certain points, occasionally contradicting himself, and they could not be sure it wasn't a trap, adding that in any case they were all set and anxious to work for me ("Roberto") and wanted to know what to do about this American officer!

It looked as if I had outsmarted myself and overloaded my own security circuit. One part of their story, however, was puzzling. According to Eugenio the emissary from the north claimed to have an appointment with the American officer (Tomsic) the next day at 10 A.M., and this, for obvious reasons, I knew could not be the case.

It was a serious problem. If the messenger turned out to be bona fide and had plans and crystals it meant we could get into contact with the base immediately. On the other hand it might be one of the most natural traps perpetrated by the men who had captured Cervo and the Vittoria radio operator, to lure me, or us, into exposing ourselves through the hope of re-establishing contact with the base. Or was it simply some crackpot scheme of Coniglio's to get me to reappear in the open!

In either case we would have to move extremely carefully, and ferret out the answer.

223

23 FROM A RANK TO A MAJOR DISGUISE

THE NEXT DAY Franco was to have his dangerous meeting with the colonel commanding the PAI in the hope of convincing him to accept "the Italian air force major" as a member of his column—dangerous because the colonel could weasel out of the deal, in case of trouble, by turning Franco over to the Germans.

All morning I was in a state of nerves waiting for the outcome. For the evening—no doubt to add quantitative as well as qualitative verisimilitude to our alibis—Franco had planned another all-night party, with different girls. I was beginning to wonder about these alibis, but Franco cut me short with a cynical smile and a shrug of his broad shoulders: "If we have to have alibis, and we do, we might as well get them in the pleasantest possible way."

Early in the afternoon it developed that the messenger from the north was in contact with Coniglio as well as with Eugenio, but said he would not turn over the plans and crystals to either. This seemed peculiar, so I sent him a note, through channels, telling him to ask any question he liked about the OSS, that it would be promptly answered in such a way as to prove that Roberto was an authentic OSS officer. But I was not particularly worried, as I expected to be able to contact the base almost any day now, through the message I had sent via the British, and then find out who this messenger really was.

Toward evening as I was silently preparing a picnic dinner for the forthcoming party—circumstances having unceremoniously forced me into the position of official cook and bottle-washer—Franco arrived with news of the interview.

We strode together along the streets of Parioli in the early evening, loaded with roast beef (the Swiss had great connections!) hard-boiled eggs, and a couple of bottles of prewar gin. As we walked Franco told me that his talk with the colonel, though an ordeal, in the end had been successful, the colonel standing at attention and saluting Franco—a mere civilian in his twenties, but backed by the political power of the CNL—and they had agreed on the deal. All was now set for my first interview with the PAI lieutenant who was to initiate my recruitment the next day at noon.

As we crossed Piazza Santiago del Chile to approach Baldo's place without passing the house where I'd run into Priebke, we planned my transformation from a captain on the staff of the Command of the Open City of Rome to that of a corporal in the PAI, throughout which performance I was to pretend to be an Italian air force major. It amused us to imagine the PAI colonel's expression when, and if ever, he found out who it was he was actually recruiting into his outfit.

At Baldo's, Piero Piccione turned up to enliven the party with his music, so again we found ourselves one girl short. To remedy this situation, Franco and I, a little full of gin, but with our papers now in better order than anyone else's, departed arm in arm. Our mission was to pick up what turned out to be three ravishing, rather high-class *poules* whom Maestro Piccione had strongly recommended.

Rounding a corner a German car appeared at the end of the road just ahead of us. Instead of waiting to test my curfew pass, I skipped over a wall and into an empty garage from which Franco, by means of a series of birdlike whistling noises, eventually recovered me.

I don't know who the three girls thought we were, but they seemed impressed, and later delighted, by the open fire, good victuals and really first-class music of the maestro, who, having no piano, performed admirably on Baldo's guitar.

It was a strange evening, partly due to the fact that there were more women than men and by early morning one could see figures draped about the house and mixed bathing in the bathtub.

At eight-thirty everyone but Baldo tiptoed out, and I made a whispered rendezvous with Franco for eleven o'clock at Ponte Garibaldi to go to my interview to be enlisted.

Only later, as I lay in the semidarkness by the fireplace, my head throbbing from the liquor of the night before, did I realize that the affair might be something of a trial. With the gin still pounding through my veins I tried to memorize countless invented details of mother, father, birthplace, education, dates of military service, promotions and campaigns, to go with my new personality.

After a while it became so complex I went to sleep, waking suddenly, as if jerked by a string, to find it was quarter to ten. Baldo was still asleep in the bed across the room, otherwise the place was deserted, smelling strongly of face powder and stale smoke.

As I scraped a dull blade back and forth across the stubble on my cheeks, trying to anticipate the questions that would be fired at me, I decided I must choose the most esoteric branch of the Italian air force if I was to stand any chance of passing. Luckily I had been obliged to associate with some of Italy's experts on radio-controlled planes, bombs and torpedoes while on another mission earlier in the war, and had acquired enough of the jargon to fool an amateur. So with a long swig of brandy to settle my nerves, stomach and hangover, I left Baldo to his dreams and set out to become a new identity.

Naturally the first person I spotted as I went out the door was the German agent of the first night's party. He was some way up the street and I just had time to double back into the doorway without being seen, only to go out again even more nervous than I had been the first time.

To add to my discomfort I had not only broken my disguising glasses but had struck a morning with no sun and could thus not wear my dark glasses without attracting even further attention; so I walked along, feeling excessively nude about the face, dreading an hour's trolley ride across town at that particular time of day.

Nor was it easy to keep two entirely different identities clearly in mind, one for the forthcoming interview, the other in case I was stopped on the trolley. There was no particular reason, I knew, why they should pick on my particular trolley, but somewhere in town it happened every hour of the day. To make things worse it was the rush hour for those poor people who had to travel halfway across Rome each day to snatch an early lunch from whatever meager black market gleanings other members of the family had managed to scrounge.

As we passed the spot where Cervo had been caught, then the gates of Regina Coeli from which they had carried him away, and then headed toward that part of the city where I was most likely to be recognized my mind went blank on both identities and my body clung like a zombie's to the window railing.

At last I saw my stop approaching. Jumping off I was swallowed in the crowd of the busy intersection. Then I felt an arm on my shoulder. Punctual as usual, there stood Franco. And just across the

Tiber in Trestevere, looking like any typical police station, stood the local PAI command post.

In the lieutenant's ground floor office I found a pleasant-looking fellow who clicked his heels and stood at attention, thinking, of course, he was dealing with a field grade officer of his own army.

It was an odd scene, but it went off pretty well. Sitting in a leather chair by his desk I answered question after question, skirting the more difficult ones, inventing a complicated military career, till, satisfied, the lieutenant issued me a small piece of paper vouchsafing my identity as that of a *sergeant* in the air force who was shortly to be enrolled as a corporal in the PAI, and was therefore at liberty to circulate freely in Rome.

I blanched at the thought of another identity to master—that of an air force sergeant, but it was essential for protocol, and the prospect was mitigated by the knowledge that at last I was in possession of an *authentic* bit of paper to proffer when asked for my credentials!

Back in the apartment at Viale Parioli I now had nothing to do but wait for the BBC to broadcast the conventional phrase I had requested: *"La richiesta e stata accettata,"* and for the great bureaucratic machine of the Italian army to grind away till I could be officially carried on the books.

THE NEXT DAY, APRIL FOOL'S DAY OF 1944, MY DIARY STARTED:

I got up as usual and made hot coffee and milk, then tidied up the room. It is a beautiful apartment, at times. Primo came, bringing a message from Eugenio. There is still no contact with the base, which is depressing. I can't figure out what has happened, unless our British "cousin" hasn't passed on the message as promised. After Primo left I sat in the sun and wrote. It is a pleasant existence, reading and writing and tanning in the sun, but I would willingly exchange it for a rifle in the front lines any time. More than anything I long for the days when I could work for hours over scattered and involved bits of information and then put them together into nice long juicy messages for the radio. Now there is a large bundle of multicolored bits of paper in a hollow bronze bust, and the goddamned base won't give a sign of life. Late in the afternoon Lele arrived and fell asleep on the long striped sofa. He has really been working hard these days.

He has done almost all the contacts with the new bunch, he stays up till all hours of the night, works from 8 A.M. to 2 P.M. at the hospital, then takes some ravishing young starlet out to lunch—partly to create our alibis, and partly, I think, because he really likes them. It is funny how he and Baldo have come round in the last few months from being frightened, rather lazy human beings, to reliable and self-sacrificing ones, who can be counted on to do a dangerous piece of work successfully. Getting Baldo out of bed is still somewhat of a problem, but if things keep up at the present rate, we will succeed there too.

IN THE MORNING I HAD SENT EUGENIO A MESSAGE:

Eugenio: If you haven't yet been able to contact the base it may be because of a misunderstanding about the time. The message I sent said 6:30, but the base may have interpreted it as GMT—that is to say 7:30 and 17:30 Italian time [there was further complication of two sets of daylight saving time on either side of the lines]. It will therefore be necessary to listen an hour later as well. As soon as you make contact send the message written on the back of this note [which read: "Absolutely vital my safety BBC say '*La richiesta e stata accettata*'—The request has been accepted"].

In due course Franco arrived and we set off with Lele for Baldo's place. Arriving there was always a pleasant sensation, perfume pricking at one's nostrils, the fire crackling in the hearth, the sound of ice tinkling in the martini shaker.

At first L. looked at me askance, as if she really didn't know me; but it turned out to be some feminine maneuver.

Eventually we all fell asleep by the fire. By nine in the morning, when I woke up, I found myself alone in the house with L. To my surprise she was a sweet, ingenuous child, insisting on whispering odd and somewhat romantic phrases to me in English, which, thanks to a childhood governess, she spoke very well, but which I, of course, pretended not to understand.

But by then she had to fly, running the risk of serious trouble with her mother if she could not rapidly acquire an alibi of her own—also by the use of an obliging girl friend.

228

Getting back to Emanuele's apartment on Viale Parioli was like coming home. Baldo was there, with his usual enigmatic expression. He had been down to the Palazzo Lovatelli to remove the small suitcase which contained our most vital files from its burying place in the dungeon. In a way I was annoyed, as I had decided it should stay there, hidden, until we could pull off the deal of letting Mario live there; but I gathered Franco had assigned Baldo the job partly to see if he would do it without a murmur, though it was dangerous, and partly because he needed a list of addresses of German agents which was in it.

For the rest of the day I lay in the sun relieving the shadow of a hangover with Acqua Maria and reading *The Communist Manifesto*. There was pleasant music on the radio, a sort of Sunday atmosphere (due, no doubt, to the fact that it was Sunday), and among the blossoms in the garden the birds sang cheerfully. All seemed calm and safely under control till Sensi, the Swiss nurse, came in looking extremely worried, followed shortly by Lele. The police commissioner who lived below wanted to see us immediately. As Lele seemed the most suitable envoy, his papers as a doctor being reasonably authentic, we sent him down.

When he came back he gave us the bad news.

Far from lightning not striking twice, the same police and German SS who had been around the day that Baldo and I had been calmly sleeping were now back in the area. They had the whole block under surveillance and were planning a large-scale raid the following day. What was worse, a plain-clothes cop who had seen us go out the previous evening had come up to the commissioner to ask who we were, especially the one with the black satchel and glasses—which was me!

Now the commissioner politely but firmly suggested that for his own sake as well as for ours we decamp as rapidly as possible.

Clearly there was nothing for it but to open a bottle of Otard—a brand of brandy which seemed predestined for such moments—and sit around for another miserable night, listening and waiting, just as we had done the night of Cervo's capture.

At dawn Sensi woke us, whereupon we set out, each in turn, to meet at Baldo's.

It seemed a crime to leave Emanuele's lovely flat, but the thought of the imminent arrival of the SS and the fact that it had only one exit somewhat smoothed along our departure.

I left first, walking—as if it were the plank—out into the brisk morning air, but succeeded in getting to Baldo's without being seen.

Eventually the others turned up. We had made it, largely, it seemed, because it was the first day of local daylight saving and no one had been on hand that early.

To keep from being too nervous while the others went off about their various chores, and in order to have some sort of excuse for being in the house in case of a routine checkup or raid, we decided I had better call L. and invite her to spend the afternoon. So I dozed on the couch while Baldo's part-time maid cleaned up, dreaming that I was being chased by the SS and that the black market bakery had run out of cakes for L.'s tea—and in my dreams I wasn't sure which was worse!

Later I woke up, bathed and shaved, while Baldo, with a wink, produced a package of cream-filled pastries he had thoughtfully gone out to buy. He then disappeared to a bridge party in the house of one of his richer fiancées where he was later to meet Lele and Franco —bridge-playing *borghesi* being the best sort of cover for organized subversives.

At three-thirty L. arrived, very excited and looking very nice. I had fixed the fire and prepared some drinks, and began to think that maybe there was something to Franco's method of obtaining alibis.

We drank quite a bit, playing many records in the firelight, and at 8 P.M. she left, cutting the curfew, which that day had been set for 8:30, just a little too close.

Then Franco came in, more nervous than I had ever seen him, his movements jerky, his eyes wandering back and forth, barely alighting on anything, like an animal at bay.

That afternoon the police had caught nine Communist regional leaders, discovered quantities of arms, had captured Peppino Craceva, the third member of the Socialist military triumvirate, after putting a bullet through his lung.

Then Franco gave me the details of a story I found it hard to believe. He and another friend had apparently walked up to a German vehicle on Via Veneto, gotten into it and driven off to the hospital where Peppino was having the bullet removed; with the connivance of the doctor they had slipped him out the side door, driven him to a cellar and abandoned the German car. Thereafter they had rigged up hand grenades behind the doors of the places where their most incriminating archives and arms deposits were hidden.

Later Franco had joined Lele and Baldo at their Parioli bridge party where he had tried to act as natural as possible. But things were getting out of hand: the Germans were now specifically hunting for a tall, well-dressed young man by the name of Franco.

The worst, however, had yet to come: Giuliano Vassalli, the young lawyer contact with the CNL who had put me straight about Coniglio's phony partisans the day of the landings, had now disappeared and no one knew what had happened to him. He had simply vanished between one rendezvous and the next—which meant that Franco was the last of the Mohicans.

It was too late now to accomplish anything so we sat around the fire dismally forcing food into ourselves, trying to drown our jitters with glass after glass of good red wine.

Then Baldo came in and brought me two cigars and a note from Maria, who, back in her father's house, assured us the place was safe. I felt guilty that despite the terror of the last two weeks the rest of us had at least been able to enjoy each other's company, while she had been forced to stay home alone.

As there was nothing I could do during the next few days while we waited for the BBC to broadcast our message and for the PAI lieutenant to push my induction papers through military channels, and before Mario could get himself established in the Palazzo Lovatelli, I decided I might spend two or three days with Maria to keep her company and let us cheer each other up; to this Franco agreed, pointing out that I would do well to get used to the house and the servants as it might turn out to be an extra refuge in case of emergency.

Franco then decided that he would go back to his own place that night, so that, if the Germans came for him, he would be able to face them with the most open and plausible denial, showing that he had no reason to move from the place where he was officially supposed to reside. It was a serious risk, like the time I had sent Cervo back with the camera, and I did not envy Franco the ordeal—though by now there was no telling from what direction danger might arrive.

In fact, as soon as Franco had gone, Baldo and I decided that if anyone were to come in the night I should be the one to answer the door, my papers—indicating I was about to be recruited into the PAI —being better than his. If it were a routine checkup he would slip out the back door. On the other hand if it were Captain Priebke coming specifically for me, he would come out shooting.

At eight in the morning the doorbell rang. At that moment—the police's favorite calling time—I was all for both of us scramming immediately through the back window, but, in deference to our agreement, went resolutely toward the door.

Three men with hats pulled over their eyes were there to greet me, and I knew it meant the end.

"Does Count Secco-Suardo live here?" one of them asked.

I nodded, too nervous to answer.

"Is he in?" asked another.

"Who . . . whoo . . . who wants him?" I stuttered.

"La Finanza," was the answer. "We're checking on owners of apartments for next year's taxes."

It was as if someone had dissolved the stiffening in my bones. Throwing open the door, I welcomed them in with effusion.

Baldo appeared from behind his curtain, wreathed in smiles, all for giving them a drink.

It was the first time in Italian history, I suppose, that anyone had been so nice to, or so genuinely pleased to see, the tax collector!

24 AN INTERIM WITH MARIA

AT SEVEN-THIRTY THE NEXT EVENING Lele came to show me the way to Maria's house. It was a cloudly, unpleasant evening, unusually chilly for the season, and I was sorry to have to leave the atmosphere, both physical and metaphysical, of Baldo's apartment. But I had made my decision and could no longer reverse it.

On the northeast corner of Viale Liegi and Via Salaria stood Maria, dressed in black, with a veil, acting rather nervous. In a slightly hysterical voice she whispered that two plain-clothes policemen had been patrolling the stretch before her house, that it was better I go ahead alone.

Maria's house was a *villino* of the type most common in the Piazza Quadrata area of Rome, surrounded by oleanders and the sort of shrubbery found in the garden of a *pensione*. There was no sign of any policeman, plain-clothed or otherwise, but a figure was approaching from across the street. With relief I realized it was Franco, only to be surprised at his cutting me.

Turning quickly at the gate I went up to the door wondering if a trap was about to be sprung. A quiet, well-trained servant answered the bell and led me up to the first-floor sitting room. The house was cold and uncomfortable, with little or no taste, but full to the rafters of books, which made it habitable.

A few moments later Franco and Maria followed me in and I gathered that Franco must also have been pretty nervous, for he said he had not even seen me outside. Added to this, Maria's hysterical laughter did nothing to put me at my ease, and it was only when she had brought out her last bottle of Saccony & Speed port, to soothe poor Franco, and to feast my arrival, that the tension was finally relieved.

Yet Franco was still in bad shape. As soon as Maria left the room to see about supper he rapidly told me that it looked as if our whole organization might crumble, that his political one was close to it, that he was practically the last military leader of importance not in jail.

233

That day he had had more than ten contacts to make, each time not knowing whether the man he was to meet had already been caught and the SD would be waiting in his stead. Yet he had been obliged to keep these appointments, putting his hand right into the fire, in the hope of cauterizing as many wounds as possible to save what could be saved.

For the first time since I had arrived in Rome he spoke seriously of the possibility of trying to get back across the lines as soon as he had tied up the stray ends of his organization. There would be little left for us to do, he pointed out, if many more of our men were blown. Almost a score had been executed and more were in Via Tasso waiting to be tortured and disposed of. There was no sign that the Allies had any intention of arriving for many weeks to come; yet every day, as more men were caught, our chances of survival diminished. Sooner or later some poor man would be forced, or trapped, into talking—and that would be the end. What was worse, Franco had a strong suspicion someone high up in the underground had been selling left-wing party members down the river. Too many things that had been far too secret had become known to the Germans, too many people had been suddenly arrested at appointments no one should have known about. I could not help thinking of Coniglio and his gang.

Then Franco left, and Maria went to bed, and I retired to my somewhat virginal room with a frilly dressing table and satiny bedcover neatly turned back by the quiet, dutiful servant.

The next morning Primo arrived with half a dozen oranges—a true rarity, cut off as we were from southern Italy—as well as a long message from Eugenio giving me a lot of details about the miserable condition of the agents who had been virtually abandoned by Sorrentino.

When Primo had gone, there was nothing for me to do—while praying that the base would give some sign of life—but pace up and down my room, glancing out through the windows at the oleanders in the garden below, at the occasional pedestrian who hurried along the unfrequented street.

In despair I turned to the bookshelves for solace. It was an odd and uninspiring collection of literature, either too light or too Fascistically distorted to be instructive or holding. Then I found a history of communism as seen through the eyes of a professor of political science at a Fascist university. Always a little ashamed of my ignorance of the background and development of communism, I decided that fate had put me squarely before the problem and that I had best get down to what at college I had found a subject conducive to nothing but sleep.

Later in the evening Maria came in and told me that Simonetta and Nina Cesaró had just been arrested and taken to the women's jail. My first reaction was of sympathy. I had known them since childhood and was fond of them, yet I couldn't help thinking that dabbling in underground activities was hardly their speed, that you cannot "play" at the game, no matter how good your intentions; and I thought back to the incident at the beginning of the war between Simonetta and an extremely young American Secretary of the Embassy. Or was it that I was prejudiced by Franco's tale that they had refused to let him hide a sack of grenades in their apartment at a time, soon after the armistice, when the struggling underground badly needed caches for its arms?

Maria brought in a tray of supper and we sat around chatting and drinking brandy. Perhaps due to its warming effect I developed a strong desire to telephone L., but wisely refrained from doing so. Eventually, after some quiet conversation, Maria and I retired to sleep, each in his own puritanical room.

Next morning Maria came in with a cup of tea, looking extremely puzzled. A man with a strong Neapolitan accent had called twice to try to make an appointment, saying he was a friend, yet Maria insisted she had never heard the voice before.

I wondered whether it might be Cervo's father, but Maria said she didn't think it could be. After some discussion we decided to do nothing about it.

Settling back I resumed my history of communism. Then Baldo came in with a curious expression.

"Good morning," he said. "Have you heard the news?"

"No," I said, "what news?"

"Ah, well, in that case you'll be amused!" And he drew up a chair. "Ottorino has discovered that both the German and Italian police are busy looking for a young man by the name of Peter Tompkins who used to be in Rome as a newspaperman and is now back as an officer in the Intelligence Service!" He paused and smiled. "It would appear they know about you in some detail!"

The news gave me a peculiar feeling in the stomach, much as if one were to discover there was someone else in the world with one's own identity.

Then Baldo went on. "It seems the Germans got the information from a double agent on the other side of the lines. They have your picture and they've got people on the streets, especially a woman called Magiotta, who apparently knew you before the war, to see if they can track you down."

The thought was far from pleasant, and I wished now that I had sent a second warning to D'Arcy Osborne in the Vatican to avoid this Magiotta woman, when Franco had originally warned me she was a double agent working for the Germans.

The idea of the Germans having my photograph brought a mental picture of a fourth-grade U.S. post office in the general store of a small rural community with the notice: WANTED FOR . . . $$$ REWARD!

The news, in fact, was so disturbing that I decided I had better call off the luncheon I had agreed to go to with the others at Lele's girl friend's house, where L. was also to be. If it hadn't been for the fact that her apartment was two blocks from the Foreign Press Club I might still have toyed with the idea; but too much was too much.

Then Baldo went away with a parting bit of news to the effect that Peppino Craceva had died in his cellar.

Sitting by the window I was overcome by a wave of depression and the premonition of terrible things to come. So positive was I that I was bound to be caught and killed, I became almost reconciled to the fact. I knew it made everything simpler, though no pleasanter. I regretted having left my automatic at Baldo's.

Looking down into the street I wondered if people who had not actually been faced with the imminent possibility of torture (and knew that the descriptions of its horrors, far from being exaggerated, were, if anything, underrated) had any appreciation of what an unpleasant prospect it could be. But what depressed me most was the thought that all the good work we had planned would go to pot, and that in all probability there would be no one else to carry on. I thought of all the names of German agents we had tucked away, of the methods we had learned so as to catch them, not torture them, but for once show them there must be some sort of manners in this miserable game.

Outside the sunlight fell upon the cherry tree. The room was warm and fragrant. Lying back on the pink and blue satin cushions of Maria's childhood room I swallowed a long draught of brandy. Jerry's Front—the German program for the Allied troops at Anzio— came on the air, and Axis Sally played "Lili Marlene." I thought of L., and of how pleasant life could be if one were able to absorb more of the subtleties of and the peculiar ways it goes about creating its beauties.

Later I phoned Baldo to send a large bunch of flowers to L., to prepare her for the news that I was obliged to leave suddenly for Florence and would not be able to see her again.

Returning to my history of communism I noted that, being written by a Fascist, it was intelligible only in the footnotes, and I was thus inclined to wish a pox on both their houses.

In the evening paper, as an alternative, there was a description of the Pope's Good Friday ceremony in the Sistine Chapel, "an incongruous performance," I noted in my diary, "in a war-torn world."

That night I did not sleep well. Every time a car passed, every inch of me was awake, and I came to the conclusion, twisting and turning in the crumpled sheets, that being hunted was as bad as being homesick or in love, or being permanently under an artillery barrage in which one's whole existence is wrapped up in the pitch of each damned howling shell.

The next morning Primo brought me another message from Eugenio saying there was still no word from the base, along with a pale blue, heavily scented envelope containing a photo of L.

When Primo had gone, I sat in a sort of maudlin stupor looking at the photo, only to be interrupted by Baldo on his way to the luncheon who had stopped off to cheer me up and give me a package of pastries to compensate for the undoubtedly Lucullan meal I would be missing.

These I ate, solemnly and alone, while reading Marx. In fact I spent the whole day buried in Marx and Engels, till, toward evening, to try to get away from the thorny politico-economic problems which chased through my brain, I put it all away and turned to brandy and

Dorothy Parker, being forced to admit, as I noted in my diary, "the brilliance of her puttering with squalid human beings." Obviously the brandy had not succeeded entirely in disposing the aftertaste of Marx.

Then Franco turned up, in worse shape than ever, with the news that Giuliano Vassalli was definitely at Via Tasso, arrested by the SS between two rendezvous near Via Tritone, but that Giuliano had managed to discard his brief case containing dangerous and damaging material, just before being arrested, and it had been safely recovered.

There must now have been twenty men in jail who knew Franco's real name. Yet Franco slept nightly at his proper address so as not to arouse suspicion and be able to maintain a semblance of innocence if arrested. Not a restful existence.

It was a real blow to learn of Giuliano's arrest and to think that he was bound to die: a young professor of law at twenty-seven, with a command of languages, he had been a pillar of the underground since the days of the Italian Armistice Commission in France.

The only positive news Franco brought was that I was at last to be inducted into the PAI on Monday morning, and that my enforced idleness would soon be over. Primo, and another faithful messenger called Vito, whom I had not yet seen, were to be recruited with me into the lieutenant's company in Trastevere. I would thus not only be able to move about freely with two well-armed bodyguards, but would have the very best of messengers beside me to enable me to keep in constant touch with the base.

Yet when Franco had left, my depression grew suddenly worse as I pondered the strange way in which periods of comparative peace and utter terror succeeded each other in the silly business of espionage. At times it appeared a matter of days or hours before one would die; then suddenly, on the flimsiest basis, we would go right on planning and daydreaming as if we would live forever.

25 OUR LAST REAL MEAL TOGETHER

THE NEXT DAY, Sunday April 9, was Easter—a day to be celebrated as no other in the Eternal City, no matter what the circumstances.

Franco woke me early with the usual satchel full of things to eat, including the rarest delicacy: a kilo and a half of bread. Then Primo came to collect a routine message for Eugenio, and they went off together about their various secret assignments, leaving me to my sunlit room, odd and peaceful, at least till Baldo and Lele arrived with a bottle of crème de menthe. As this particular liquid had a tendency, in Baldo's catalytic presence, to mix with brandy, we all decamped to the bathroom to imbibe a series of peacock-colored stingers while I took my bath. The bathroom in Maria's house was one of the nicer rooms, perhaps because of the trees immediately beneath the window —a huge mimosa and an equally imposing cherry tree, both in full bloom, spiced by the fragrance of sun-warmed pine. Lying back in the hot tub, stinger in one hand, scented soap in the other, sunbeams pouring through the latticed shades, I almost forgot the war.

Then Maria roused us from the clouds of steam and stingers to summon us to lunch, always a lavish affair on Easter day in Rome, but even more so on this particular one as it was my last day before enlisting in the PAI, the last time we would all be together for a long period, if not forever; and certainly the last good meal we were likely to eat.

And what a meal! The total contents of the larder! First an enormous *foie gras* with piles of toast and butter (thanks to Franco's foresight). With this a good white Bordeaux which I shocked Maria by mixing with our usual Frascati, a form of sacrilege soon emulated by the others when they discovered it to be, if not quite kosher, certainly delicious, taking away the sweetness from the French, adding aroma and flavor to the stark Italian.

Halfway through lunch we were all quite gay. By the time we'd finished the chicken, roasted to a turn (*abbacchio*, even with our contacts, being beyond the question), accompanied by hearts of lettuce

239

and followed by a huge tray of ricotta-filled *cannoli* to be polished off with a bottle of old and excellent Barolo, Lele had passed out. We tried to take him to the bathroom to make him put his fingers down his throat, but he was far too gone.

A sudden knocking on the door revived our sobriety. It was the owner of the flat on Via Paisiello, Emanuele de Seta, the air force pilot; he had failed to cross the lines, become disgusted and returned to Rome. He was an odd-looking fellow, very much the Sicilian baronetto, and we stared at each other with mutual curiosity. Recounting his adventures of the last three months, he told us he had spent the time mostly in a farmhouse near the front, anxiously and hopelessly awaiting the arrival of the Allies till he had finally been obliged to leave—largely, it seemed, because of the most jealous husband in the village. My first impression of him was that he was crazy, but Franco assured me all Stuka pilots were, so I decided to be tolerant.

The rest of the afternoon we alternated tea with brandy, till I saw that dusk was falling. As I had hidden a blank identity card for my new PAI adventure in a book at Baldo's, the name of which I could not remember, I must perforce spend the night at his place. A faint rain had started and the light was fading rapidly; having prepared my few belongings, and awakened Lele, we kissed Maria goodbye, tipped Oreste, the faithful butler, and set off for Baldo's house.

At the trolley stop Lele, still too drunk to reason, insisted upon arguing with the conductor that it was safer to get on from the front rather than the rear, and was thus left standing in a squall of rain. But he rejoined us later, somewhat sobered by his walk in the downpour, to set off for a night contact with his doctor friend Marcello.

As the door closed behind him the telephone rang and a couple of girls—as yet unknown to me—asked Baldo if they could come and spend the night with us. For a moment we played with the idea, but when we learned they could come only in the company of a major on Kesselring's staff we put them off, Baldo and I concurring that Kesselring was already as deeply infiltrated by us as he was ever likely to be (especially by brother Ottorino) and that we were more bent on acquiring cover than a surfeit of intelligence.

Then the phone rang to announce the immediate arrival of a Florentine friend of Baldo's vaguely associated with the Party of

Action, who lived on the floor above and who turned out to be doubly nervous because of a pregnant wife. He wished to establish an entrance to the building through Baldo's back door.

When the Florentine had gone, telling us he had received an anonymous danger signal, I stretched out on the familiar sofa by the fire and tried to sleep; but I could not, partly because I kept thinking of the walk I would have to take the following morning, right into the heart of town, to be recruited, and partly because of trucks which kept drawing up at intervals throughout the night while voices shouted in the darkness, making me sit up with a heart as big as a melon.

Eventually the dawn came and the alarm clock sounded in the dismal grayness. Dressing quickly I woke Lele and got him to fill out my new identity card, one that would make me older and from a different part of Italy so that my identity in the PAI would be as different as possible from any of my previous ones. The name I had decided on was Luigi Desideri, the surname being that of Virginia and Serafino, our old and faithful servants in the house to which I had gone the first day I had arrived. With that name I could pretend to be a distant relative of theirs, use their address in an emergency, and have an excuse for being in the Palazzo Ricci.

Then the phone rang, giving us all a fright. The Florentine with the pregnant wife had been out to see what was developing in the area only to discover the alarm was not for him, but general; the Germans were planning a large-scale roundup in Parioli that morning, based round Piazza Santiago del Chile—just where I had made my rendezvous with Primo, who should already be on his way!

Baldo and Lele were throwing on their clothes.

Afraid my Capri boots would attract attention at the recruiting office I borrowed a pair of Lele's shoes which did not fit, but which I trusted would soon be exchanged for a more solid pair of army-issue boots.

By the time I had bid them a quick farewell it was nearly eight o'clock. On the wide sidewalk of Viale Parioli, under the burgeoning plane trees, I spotted a *brigadiere* and a corporal of the PAI. They eyed me suspiciously as I passed, but I consoled myself with the thought that if all went well, I too would shortly be wearing the same uniform, and could—*Deo volente*—eye people with the same suspicion.

241

Primo was late for the appointment and I began to grow nervous, trying to walk up and down the piazza in a nonchalant manner, knowing quite well I cut the perfect figure of a conspirator, my only comfort being—as I spotted several other odd figures in raincoats and dark glasses, hats pulled over their eyes, clearly plain-clothes men preparing for the imminent roundup—that my demeanor was lurid enough to be mistaken for one of them.

Already my nerve was beginning to fail—like the first morning I had arrived—and I was on the point of panic when I saw Primo coming toward me across the piazza.

We walked, it seemed, for miles; each step nearer the center of town my nervousness increased, as did my nonexistent cold, causing me to blow my nose profusely in a vain attempt to obliterate my features. The thought of being caught now within hours of being able to wear a covering uniform added exasperation to the fear of what would happen at the induction center. The most exposed five minutes was on crowded Via Nazionale, but we managed to pass without being stopped. The recruiting office was on one of the short sloping streets that lead up from Via Nazionale toward the Quirinale; outside the four-story building we were greeted by Vito, the other messenger who was to enlist with us.

Passing through the typically barren waiting room, already crowded with young men in their twenties, we were ushered into a small office off the main corridor and told to wait. That we would have to do so thirty or forty minutes was my presumption, and I hoped our uniforms would be issued on the spot, but the very first rumor we heard was that they would have to be picked up across the river.

Eventually a *brigadiere* of the PAI appeared and ushered us into another small office where a clerk was installed behind a typewriter, and where we were obliged to start filling out papers. Luckily they started with Primo and Vito so that by the time it got around to me I had memorized most of the phony answers; yet it wasn't easy, and I consumed several kilowatts of energy in the hour it took to fill them out. During short intervals in this organized torment of Italian bureaucratics Vito and I made cigarettes out of writing paper and the remains of half a dozen butts collected from the floor. The poisonous results not only gave us an excuse to do something with our hands other than scratch, but, under the circumstances, tasted delicious.

After filling out every possible sort of questionnaire—outdoing even the form-thinker-uppers of O.N.I.—I thought we would be free, only to be caught in the snares of yet another trap: the physical exam.

Just as I removed my trousers—wishing earnestly that circumcision were not such a fetish with American hygienists—the doctor turned and asked point-blank how my father had died. As I stumbled in my pants leg, only just regaining my footing, I got a flash of my father lying on a mortuary slab and wondered how the devil the doctor had received the news; almost as fast came the realization of what he had meant, and I managed to produce the answer previously prepared for the lieutenant of the PAI. "In a car accident," I said, almost without hesitation.

"Where?" said the doctor. "What year?"

This I had not anticipated; but some guardian angel, chemical or metaphysical, came quickly to my rescue: "On the Milano-Sesto Calende Parkway, 1929."

I noticed with a certain satisfaction the quaintness of the date, which as I thought about it, was prompted by the instantaneous but rational computation that at that particular date my real father might easily have died on just that stretch of road.

No sooner out of the rough than a young and pimply assistant in civvies turned and addressed me: "Haven't I seen you in Naples?"

For a moment I had the nightmarish sensation he might have seen me there, and recently.

"S-sure," I stuttered.

"Where?" said the youth.

"What . . . er . . ." I mumbled.

"On what street did you live?" said the youth severely.

"Oh . . . oh . . ." I stuttered, hoping with one small truth to avoid the greater one. "On Via Crispi."

This seemed to satisfy him, though he continued to eye me suspiciously while scratching his acne.

At length, when the doctor had finished his more debasing probes, and we were again hopeful of being freed, we discovered to our distress that we still had an indefinite wait, and I was beginning to suspect something had gone wrong. From these worries I was startled by the sound of someone called, "Desideri, Luigi." Accustomed as I was to being Roberto Berlingieri, I nearly forgot to react.

Along with two unprepossessing new recruits we were prodded into the presence of the senior *brigadiere* who had helpfully advised me, during the earlier paper work, to say I was younger than the age indicated on my identity card and to emphasize that I had fought on the Albanian and Libyan fronts. He now handed us a covering letter addressed to the main barracks at the Foro Mussolini, where he said they would dress us. The paper work was apparently over, but the thought of crossing town at high noon was a shock.

"And don't get yourselves picked up by the Germans," added the *brigadiere*, correcting himself quickly to: "or whoever it is who picks people up in the streets—Bolsheviks, Demoplutocrats or North American spies!"

This last remark seemed rather pointed, but I realized it was merely jargon picked up from German propaganda.

So we left, feeling that our particular branch of the Republican Armed Forces might not be as terrible, seen from within, as it certainly appeared from without.

Already we were planning to play hooky and stop off at the lieutenant's to make sure we were assigned to his company that very afternoon, so as not to risk getting caught up in hierarchical red tape with someone who mistook us for regular recruits—such as the two distasteful characters who now insisted on accompanying us—and spoiling the plan.

In a whispered conference we decided that Primo hop off the trolley at Ponte Garibaldi, go see the lieutenant, then join us as soon as possible at the barracks.

The trolley was crowded, it being, as usual, the rush hour; to add to my discomfort Lele's shoes had raised three separate blisters, making me look forward much less happily to the army boots I expected to be issued.

Skirting the Colosseum in the heat and dust of noon, the overloaded streetcar screeched on its polished tracks like a thing alive. The stop I feared most was in front of the Palazzo Sermoneta but we got by it somehow and were careening past the synagogue on the way to Ponte Garibaldi, sweaty and suffering, when I noticed that just as Primo was maneuvering to make his descent from the rear platform, our sober-faced lieutenant of the PAI was about to get on at the front one (a courtesy allowed only the police and *grandes gueules cassées* of World War I).

I had already started a panic-stricken gesture to Primo but he too had spotted the lieutenant, and managed, in the nick of time, to accost him, then clamber back onto the trolley.

The lieutenant, in full-dress uniform, now stood beside me on the forward platform by the conductor, but either did not recognize me, or pretended, very ably, not to. In either case his presence gave me an encouraging sense of security. Were there to be a raid I would straightaway latch onto him, and, with my recruiting papers in my pocket, surely manage to make an effective front. I even stopped worrying about hiding my face at every shadow.

Primo approached and whispered in my ear that all was well, that the lieutenant would see the colonel after lunch and get us attached to his company in Trastevere as soon as we were uniformed.

Much relieved, and excited by the prospect, we proceeded on our way, changing streetcars, then walking along the broad, empty, sunswept streets that skirt the upper Tiber till Mussolini's obelisk and the marble buildings and statues of the forum appeared at the foot of Monte Mario against the green of Villa Madama.

Successfully passing the sentry with the aid of our written orders we climbed the steps of the headquarters building already anticipating with pleasure the idea of patrolling the secret alleys of Trastevere fully armed and uniformed.

The young guards in the building were all tall, most of them good looking, wearing their uniforms with a swagger, their cordovan boots and leggings, their riding breeches, bush jackets, topees and tinkling sky-blue lanyards as smart as anything the British ever wore in India.

At last I began to feel the situation was improving. It was some time, however, before anyone paid any attention to us, and when they did, it amounted to a curt order from a *brigadiere*, or sergeant, to sit and wait; which we did, for at least another hour. Looking up at the clock on the wall I saw that it was almost two, and realized I was hungry. The guards who worked as clerks in the big airy room off the lobby had already had their chow and from our queries about the daily ration of bread we discovered they received two large loaves— more than five times the regular civilian ration!

That, I thought to myself, will at least be one good problem solved for the next few weeks.

Glancing around the room I saw a poster on the wall of a wicked-faced man listening to the conversation of two stalwart soldiers, emblazoned with the flaming caption:

"Beware! The enemy is listening!"

Primo too had noticed it, as I could see by the twinkle in his eyes, and it was all I could do not to laugh aloud.

It amused me too to think that Vito, who had been faithfully and enthusiastically working for us for months, was now sitting beside me giving me the *"tu"* without the faintest idea I was the "Pietro" for whom he had carried so many messages.

At intervals between rereading the want ads in yesterday's paper I studied the other two recruits—one practically illiterate, the other short and obnoxious, with a suspicious habit of asking impertinent questions. Clearly they were Fascists. What I couldn't decide was whether this would prove advantageous or disastrous to whatever was in store for us; in any case I prayed we would soon be dressed and assigned to the healthier atmosphere of our own lieutenant's company. I was impatient to know if Eugenio had made contact with the base, and anxious to get to work.

At long last the *maresciallo* (company sergeant major) arrived and ordered one of the corporals to escort us across the forum to what was to be our barracks, seeming very surprised that we should count on being dressed that afternoon.

Crossing the forum, with its Fascist buildings, its young umbrella pines, its tall naked figures in Carrara marble that surrounded its arenas, I thought of the days I had watched Brugnon and Borotra fight it out on the sunken tennis courts with a backhanded Aussie.

In the building adjacent to the one with the huge mosaic pool (how often had I swum there!) we were led into a dusty room known in Italian army jargon as the *fureria,* or orderly room, where yet another surprise was in store for us in the form of a seven-foot *brigadiere* with a double-bass voice who lined us up and shouted for our documents. Trembling, we presented the slips of paper the lieutenant had given us three weeks before.

"No, no, no!" screamed the vile *brigadiere*. "Your identity cards!"

246

For a moment we all stood, knees buckling, looking at each other out of the corner of our eyes. Seeing that the other two recruits seemed as unhappy as we were, and that we could show a solid front, I piped up in as controlled a voice as I could that we'd been told at the recruiting station to come with nothing but these slips of paper.

There was a moment's silence while the *brigadiere* looked at us with a suspicious frown, then brusquely ordered the corporal of the day to start taking down our personal histories. In vain we protested we had done nothing else all morning. We were obliged to start again with birthplace and parents, military careers, etc.

At one moment, as the *brigadiere* fired questions and the corporal wrote them down, Vito (who had momentarily assumed one of his less exact aliases) gave his birthplace as a small town in central Italy, only to be bombarded with detailed questions about its neighboring villages.

Shaking in Lele's uncomfortable shoes I wondered if I were going to manage to pull through the ordeal; and the panic I thought I had left at the gates started pouring back. Would I ever be able to invent fast enough and well enough to convince this Rabelaisian monster!

When it finally came to my turn I had decided on the only military establishment in southern Italy the neighboring country of which I could well describe: Caserta, the recent HQ of our Fifth Army. But no sooner had I breathed the fatal word than the *brigadiere* hit the table with his fist.

"Ahhaaa! Just where I spent three years of my career! Now tell me . . ."

No sound would issue from my throat. I was on the point once more of throwing in the sponge when the door opened and some poor guard stood frozen to attention in the doorway to receive the flow of venom about to be directed at me.

By the time the *brigadiere* could get back to his original victim, most of what was necessary had been dutifully filled into my form by the corporal of the day, and we were dispatched to get mattress covers and the straw to fill them.

In the acrid concrete basement we were issued rough blankets, and bedding smelling strongly of brilliantine and urine, then marched past a line of guards who had been on duty during chow and were getting theirs late. After many prayers they condescended to give us a community bowl of the stock fare: saltless pea-and-macaroni soup, with which tasteless gruel we managed to ease the craving in our bellies.

Carrying our dusty mattresses up to a large windowed room filled with rudimentary double bunks, we were confronted by the regular soldiers strewn around the dormitory enjoying their hour of liberty, who, seeing us, burst into mocking jibes: "New recruits, hey! Plebes! Whatever made you do it!"

Those nearest our assigned bunks started asking our names, ages, jobs, and so on, to all of which I answered in the thickest possible Roman accent.

Though we would have liked to register a complaint we had no choice but to arrange our mattresses and blankets in the requisite order, as if we were really to spend the night: whereupon we were summoned to the hall again and informed the captain wished to see us.

Another long wait while every guard that passed made a wisecrack or asked an embarrassing question, till, almost to our relief, the corporal of the day announced in stentorian tones the commanding officer would condescend to receive us.

Lined up at attention in his office we each performed a snappy Fascist salute, answered perfunctorily by the captain, who set in on what seemed to be the inevitable routine of asking questions about our names, ages, birthplaces and military experience. More easily satisfied than the *brigadiere,* he switched to a pep talk which, as I listened, I swore to myself I would have him repeat verbatim if ever I got him safely behind the stockade of an Allied PW camp.

Toward the end, when he had told us what we were to do and not do while under his command, he added that above all we must forget any political ideas of whatever nature they might be, that our job was to be guardians of the public order. This, at least, was a ray of light; even if the discipline were tough, they could not all be rabid Fascists.

Once the captain had finished his spiel, and it was clear we would have to spend the night, I requested we be granted a few hours' pass to settle, as is customary in the Italian army, certain pressing family matters. Again the captain was obliging. With even snappier departing salutes we filed out, not stopping till we were beyond the outermost sentry and out of range of the damnable *brigadiere.*

248

Walking along the Tiber, with me limping to keep up, we realized we'd been quite shaken by the turn of events. I was relieved to be out of the prisonlike barracks, but almost immediately beset by the fear that always accompanied me in the open. I thought of the long trolley ride to the barracks and how I had prayed, at every stop, that we reach the barracks safely, and here I was happily leaving it behind. But where could we go?

Vito decided to call upon his family, so we parted, agreeing to meet again just before re-entering the barracks. My own first thought was to get some adhesive tape with which to patch the blisters on my feet. Primo's house, the nearest refuge, was right near Cervo's, and I became very nervous as we ducked into the street, not daring to look up in case one of the family was at the windows, and the sight of me, still alive and more or less free, should gall the wound they had so recently received. But we reached the cool hallway of Primo's house and a moment later I had both feet firmly planted in scalding water, solicitously administered by Primo's sweet and hard-working mother.

After that I lay on a soft bed and reviewed our miserable adventure, which, for a moment, seemed almost laughable, till thoughts about the information service, Coniglio, the men who were in jail, and the goddamn base that wouldn't answer, came pouring in to revive the pain and worry.

We had supper early at Primo's so as not to have to submit to the barracks chow, then set off in the late afternoon feeling refreshed and almost philosophical about the night ahead.

In the barracks we lounged around our dormitory, as is the habit with soldiers and schoolboys, smoking and chatting idly, till one of the younger guards, easily recognizable as a university student, took pity on us "new boys" and offered to show us the grounds.

Wandering among the not unpleasant monuments to Fascist culture we ended up by the largest stadium, where in the last rays of sunlight the guards were diverting themselves with a game of soccer. Among the players I noticed a colored PW and for a moment my heart stood still at the thought that it might be an American soldier; but it turned out to be "Louis," a South African prisoner of war. Still, it was an odd sensation to stand so near an ally and not be able to speak to him.

249

The sound of the bugle was carried on the resonant spring air. Our cicerone turned his head and listened intently, then shouted to the players: "Alarm, alarm!"

This time my blood began to tingle. The game broke up and the guards began running across the field tearing on their coats. It was obviously not an air raid, there being no trace or sound of Allied planes in the clear evening sky, and I wondered, as we ran, what could be causing the excitement. Primo said it was a rumor the Allies had landed at Fiumicino (by the mouth of the Tiber). Though the rumor was old, and I had heard too many false alarms, I felt exhilarated and almost happy. Trotting along behind the others we let our imagination run with lively stories of the joy it would be if they really had landed and things were about to happen.

But back in the dormitory we found out the company was to carry out an immediate roundup on behalf of the Germans, the rumor being that the Germans intended to collect 150,000 men. Even if the figure had been exaggerated from 15,000, the situation was likely to be unpleasant, and I was glad we were sleeping in the barracks, and that they *hadn't* yet issued us our clothing. I was pleased too to gather from the uninhibited remarks of several of the guards that they did not relish sending fellow citizens to concentration camps in Germany, one being outspoken enough to say: "I'll collect all the people whose documents are perfectly in order!" and another: "I'll rake in nothing but disabled veterans from the First World War!"

Reassured by what I heard I lay down on the upper part of my double bunk on a mattress full of what must have been rocks and fell into exhausted sleep. But not for long. The rotation of duty involved in the roundup continued all night long; men kept coming and going, dressing and undressing, shouting orders, or wasting oaths, and the last sensation I recorded was of a bayonet passing within an inch of my nose. Then the scene was mercifully obliterated.

26 SARTOR RESARTUS, OR, "JUST DESERT"

I HAD BARELY GOT TO SLEEP when the piercing notes of a bugle sounded the Italian version of reveille—a nerve-racking tune, and intended to be so—followed almost immediately by the sound of a U.S. Army reveille. Some fiend had attached to the company PA system Axis Sally's program directed at the U.S. troops round Anzio. It was 5:45 A.M.

The mixture of emotions this created in me at that time in the morning was almost more than I could bear. Outside the dormitory a melancholy corporal was issuing canteen cups of barley substitute, which, not having yet received our ration of bread, I was obliged to drink as it was—insipid but warming, while the other guards noisily dunked the remains of yesterday's bread ration into the liquid.

After "breakfast" we lolled around watching the others polish their boots and guns for imminent parade. Already the tall *brigadiere* was shouting himself hoarse, dispatching three poor guards to the guardhouse for no other reason than to assert an authority in no way natural to him.

Left alone, we weren't sure what to do, but were soon relieved of our worry by the corporal of the day who accompanied us across the area to a quartermaster depot, where, at long last, our dream of being covered by uniforms was quickly converted into a nightmare and the apparently endless issue of shelter-halves, tent poles, water canteens, one winter and one summer uniform, two pairs of boots with cordovan leggings, one overcoat, three pairs of drawers, undershirts, bush shirts, insignia, lanyards, buttons, chevrons, much of it with no possible sense or reason, considering the season, or the progress of the war, all of it invariably the one size that could not possibly fit.

Only one part of the affair turned out to be exhilarating: holding in one's hand a smoothly working general-issue Beretta light machine gun complete with fifty rounds of ammunition.

By the time we had staggered back to our bunks with this mountain of mismatched equipment the bugle sounded for midday chow and I

251

was relieved to see that as compensation for our newly acquired status we were being issued two enormous loaves of fresh and comparatively white bread. Lining up outside the barracks on the edge of the copse of umbrella pines, clutching our precious rations, we slowly inched forward to receive our complement of unpalatable pea-and-macaroni gruel, which, we learned from our comrades-in-arms, was to be the stock fare, morning and night, till the end of the war, making me think with a shadow of regret, of the times I had complained of the unsavory contents of a can of GI "meat and beans."

Then Primo discovered that in the middle of the park, well shaded by the taller pines, stood a kiosk where an old man sold black market wine and doughnuts, a luxury beyond the means of most of the impoverished guards, but one on which we glutted—while I offered a silent toast to the health of General D.

Stretched out on a marble flight of steps, just out of sight of the horrible *brigadiere,* absorbing the mildly stinging rays of April sun, we allowed the wine and doughnuts to pursue their satisfying course, I, for one, daydreaming of being by the fire in Baldo's room with some quiet female, away from all this martial madness.

Eventually, as the sun shifted and the effects of the wine wore off we struggled to our feet, and walked back to the barracks to collect our uniforms in the hope that we might find a tailor clever enough to remedy their more glaring faults.

Having partially succeeded, we decided to part company: Primo to find out what was happening to our organization, Vito to conclude our sartorial problems, I to have my hair trimmed before some company barber got his shears into it.

None was very successful: I managed to save only part of my hair; Vito found a tailor for the coats, but—such is the healthy fragmentation of skills among Italian craftsmen—not for the pants; Primo failed to make contact with anyone in our organization.

This was preoccupying, especially after the all-night roundup which had taken place, and because it was enervating to be stuck in the barracks without news of what was going on, let alone word from the lieutenant as to when we were likely to be sprung. Before giving up our passes I decided as a last resort to try to raise someone on the phone in the hope he could convey, at least by double talk, what was going on.

A quarter of a mile downstream from the forum we found an old farmhouse wineshop with a phone, but though I repeatedly tried to ring Franco, Mario, Lele and Baldo none of them answered.

Early next morning, as soon as we had consumed our bread and phony coffee, much preoccupied about how we could get in touch with our friends or transferred to the lieutenant's company, we sneaked out and hid again behind the kiosk in the sun. But our sentinel posting was deficient and at eleven o'clock we were caught by the *brigadiere,* who ordered us instantly into uniform.

Now, ironically, we were afraid of being properly outfitted. Only weekly passes were normally issued, and once in uniform we would no longer be able to get out of the barracks to contact our organization. So we pleaded that our uniforms were still at the tailor. Undaunted, as seems to be the habitual attitude of NCOs of any country, we were forthwith ordered to don our summer drills pending the arrival of our regular uniforms from the tailor.

Luckily, as we stood in line for chow, dressed in our spanking new summer outfits, a lieutenant caught sight of our heavy leggings, complained they were not regulation tint, and ordered us to dye them darker. Thus reprieved we climbed back into our civilians, deciding that Primo leave immediately to find out what was happening to the others while Vito and I dyed all the leggings.

Some four hours later, having finally obtained the proper tint, Vito and I decided to slip out and join Primo at his house for supper, only to be caught, just as we reached the main gate, by the *brigadiere* who informed us the captain wished to see us.

Again the whole bank of schoolboy emotions poured in on me. What did he want with us? Had something happened to Primo?

But we missed the captain—as well as our evening ration of gruel—and were forced instead to sit in the day room with the rest of the company, idle and hungry, wondering what the devil had happened to Primo.

As I lifted my eyes from tracing a groove in the desk, I saw him standing in the door with a peculiar expression. Hardly looking at us he edged his way to our last row of benches. I could see now that he was very pale and sensed that something must have gone very wrong.

Sitting beside me he stared silently ahead. When no one was looking, he leaned toward me and whispered: "They've caught the PAI lieutenant. He's at Via Tasso. The SS came for him last night!" He paused as a guard stared in our direction, then quickly went on: "Ottorino found out, by sheer luck, five minutes before Mario was to meet him. Things look pretty black. Franco says to stick it out tonight: he'll let us know at one o'clock tomorrow what to do."

I doubt if anyone could have brought more frightening news.

"What is he in for?" I asked.

Primo looked furtively round the room. "For aiding subversive elements," he whispered.

"Not us!" I asked, following his eyes.

In answer Primo merely grimaced.

Vito, on the other side of me, anxious as a schoolboy to be informed of our whispered conversation, had to wait for a suitable moment. When it came, and I repeated what I'd heard, poor Vito grabbed the desk to steady himself.

Once more a wave of terror ran through me. At the same time I was furious that what had been about to be a perfect scheme for cover was to be definitely wrecked. The sensation of frustration was almost as bad as the fear of what was now to happen to us.

Yet the full realization of the danger we were in did not come tumbling in on me till we were on our way back to our bunks and I realized that we were trapped for the night without possible exit. Then I thought of Franco; his name would come before ours. For all we knew he might already be caught.

Sitting on the bunk, arranging my cartridge belt and placing my machine gun beneath my pillow so as not to have it stolen in the night, I realized how useless these weapons had become. Then my blood ran cold. In the silence of the high-ceilinged hall three names had been shouted by the corporal of the day: our names, and no one else's.

Trembling, barely in control of my actions, I dressed quickly, watching Primo out of the corner of my eye as he betrayed a similar state of anxiety. Pulling on my boots I felt my blisters smarting, but I reflected, with the last bit of life left in me, that they would probably not hurt for long.

In the *fureria* the horrible *brigadiere* lined us up at attention; my heart pounded so loud I was afraid I would collapse.

"You're the new recruits . . ." said the *brigadiere* in his ominous bass. Digging into the drawer of his desk for what I knew would be an automatic he pulled out six green packages.

"Here," he said handing us two apiece. "Your weekly ration! Sixty a man. Not bad!" And his face contorted into the closest he had so far come to a smile.

Back on my bunk, boots removed, legs dangling, almost rejoicing in the pain of my blisters, I smoked, first one, then another of the rationed cigarettes down to the quick. Clearly they did not know yet! But could we, I wondered, last out the night?

Morning, with its plural reveilles, found us with the trap unsprung.

To keep out of uniform we hid by the tennis arena, ostensibly polishing our leggings, with only one thought: the appointment at 1 P.M. when we were to hear from Franco what best we should do—that is, if Franco were still around to tell us!

It was Primo's sister's birthday and his family was expecting us for lunch, poor people, unaware as yet that we were once again in serious trouble.

Then our flagrant act of goldbricking was interrupted by the *brigadiere*, who ordered us instantly into uniform, leggings or not. It was a delicate moment. Come what might, Primo must get out of the area and keep the 1 P.M. appointment. So we decided that Vito and I, uniformed and visibly present, should parade ostentatiously up and down the yard, in the hope that Primo might thus slip out unobserved. This we somehow managed, and Vito and I, immaculately outfitted, spent the afternoon marching about the grounds, counting the minutes till Primo's return.

As we moved about, lanyards dangling in the sun, highly polished boots and heavy-thonged leggings squeaking in a martial manner, Vito, who still had no inkling of my true identity, thinking me just another partisan hiding in the PAI on orders from Franco, stopped and shook his head. "You know" he said, "you wear that uniform as if you were an officer. Funny, you can always tell an officer by his manner and his movements. One of the boys at chow said you looked like a goddamn British colonel!"

Changing the subject as delicately as I could I maneuvered him over to the doughnut stand, wondering what I could do to amend my posture.

There was still no sign of Primo, and we were getting claustrophobic, searching the barbed wire which enclosed the entire area for any means of escape, either in or out of uniform. Just as we had found a spot behind an evergreen hedge—which in better times had protected heavy-breasted Roman girls sunbathing by the pool—a bad-tempered captain came riding by on a bicycle and ordered us forthwith to report to the orderly room to police the area for trash.

In our attempt to escape this fate we ran straight into the seven-foot *brigadiere,* who, seeing my hair line, now that I was wearing regulation headgear, ordered me forthwith to the company barber to have the back of my head shaved clean.

Considering, as I do, that a man's cut of hair is strictly a personal matter, and categorically wishing to avoid being branded by a military haircut, I realized that the affair was taking on the tragicomic aspects of a Laurel and Hardy feature when I was saved by an announcement from the corporal of the day that the captain wished to see us immediately.

More preoccupied now about my actual neck than any particular hairline, I doubled across the yard with Vito toward the captain's office, where, despite our promptness, we found the captain had left two minutes earlier. Now there was no power to save me from the barber, the results of whose efforts, though not as drastic as I had anticipated, left me smoldering with anger.

Down by the main entrance Primo appeared with a large newspaper parcel under his arm and I knew immediately by its obvious contents of bread and hard-boiled eggs that we would be obliged to spend another night. Disappearing with us out of sight of the rest of the company, Primo whispered the news: he had seen Mario, who had been in touch with Franco, who said that in view of the fact that the PAI colonel was also being strictly watched by the SS there was nothing he could do for us at the moment, suggesting we approach the colonel from within.

At which remark I felt like walking right out of the barracks and up to Franco to explain to him in six easy lessons the theory and practice of hierarchy in the Army, let alone the PAI. It was all we could do to get a word in edgewise with the corporal of the day! How in the name of heaven would we be able to reach the colonel, especially as we didn't even know where he was, and would create instant suspicion if we tried to find out?

It looked as if we would be arrested in a matter of hours, or, at best, spend the rest of the war in the ranks of the PAI, drilling, catching hell, patrolling Via Veneto and Corso d'Italia—where the Germans had their main headquarters—the areas normally assigned to our present company!

In either case, and for better or worse, we would have to continue our charade as guardians of the peace; so Primo went off to don his uniform, taking advantage of a moment when no one was looking to slip several tightly folded messages into the palm of my hand.

These I was unable even to glance at as the bugle had sounded for chow and some sort of commotion had started in the yard. Soon a rumor spread through the ranks that there was no salt *at all* in the soup (salt, coming almost entirely from southern Italy, was a rarity in the Fascist republic) and that we should all stand together and refuse to accept it. I was surprised, as I looked toward the head of the line, to see what a united front the boys were presenting; no one accepted the soup. What a position to find myself in! Either I accept my ration, and thus become a scab, or, refusing it, risk having my identity discovered because of a bowl of saltless gruel!

Luckily the entire line refused; and I didn't have to make much of a choice. Promptly we were confined to the day room, where a second lieutenant began to berate us on the consequence of mutiny. Luckily he turned out to be one of the more decent of his species, even letting some of the guards express an opinion; but the whole performance, as they argued back and forth about the bad food, the long hours of duty, the lack of passes, etc., struck me as quite fantastic. God, I thought, with a shudder, how twenty years of Fascism can drown a people's spirit.

But at length the arguments ceased, unresolved, and we were allowed to go. Again the corporal of the day—may the saints watch over him—announced, just as I hoped to get a squint at the messages brought by Primo, that the captain wanted to see us, immediately, and properly dressed. This special proviso set me to wondering as I straightened my uniform and gave an extra polish to my boots.

What transpired was an individual interrogation, the last stage before being fully incorporated into the company, and I had some anxious moments when the captain, in the presence of the *brigadiere* and the corporal of the day—who was taking notes—insisted once more on reviewing my military career with particular emphasis on what I had done at Caserta. Searching for a rare specialty with which to gain some slight advantage I was prompted by some spirit to say that I had been a sergeant radio operator at the Air Corps Academy; with this everyone was dutifully impressed except for a lieutenant who had so far been a silent witness to the proceedings but now asked how I liked the place.

I was about to reveal to him that my knowledge of the town was of extremely recent date and under the sole domain of General Clark when the bugle—that bugle which was beginning to be part of my existence—sounded retreat, and our release.

But the excitement wasn't over. As the eight o'clock guard came off duty a great commotion was started by the discovery in the soup of a rubber contraceptive! Chaos broke out in the dormitory as the trophy was rushed to the captain in the *fureria*. I don't think anyone was quite sure whether it had really been found in the soup or whether someone had placed it there on purpose, but there were long arguments about the degree of its translucency which tended to prove it had been boiled for quite some time. At any rate the satisfaction was general and a good deal of the lieutenant's lecture on mutiny went to the dogs.

The next morning I was again subjected to the emotional torment of two mutually exclusive reveilles, but the day's prospect got me out of my bunk and on my way to our hideout by the arena. We were all in uniform now, with no excuse to keep us from active duty other than sewing and unsewing an odd variety of buttons, lanyards and chevrons; we had now been promoted to corporals, there being, we discovered, no lower rank in the column!

About ten-thirty, feeling a definite yearning for food, we took advantage of some mysterious strands of fog that had appeared in the park round the base of the umbrella pines to reach the kiosk and obtain several glasses of sweet Aleatico into which we were dunking our sugared doughnuts when the word "*Brigadiere!*" spoiled the effect.

It was not the tall one, however, and we maneuvered, depending on the direction of the sergeant's footsteps and the doughnut vendor's solicitous instructions, till we were routed from behind by the corporal of the day.

"Where the devil have you been! The *brigadiere* wants you at the

258

stadium, this minute, and fully armed. He wants to know what the devil you mean by skipping drill!"

Meekly, our lanyards drooping, we paraded off to the dormitory to arm ourselves. Outside the main entrance we found the entire company lined up in the square. The moment he saw us the tall *brigadiere* let out a yell. Thereafter, and for several minutes, he swore incoherently while we stood at rigid attention. Catching sight of my hair, he insisted on being told why the devil it hadn't been cut, repeating the question several times at the top of his voice.

Presuming the question no longer to be rhetorical, I answered, still standing at attention, that I *had* had it cut.

"What do you mean you've had it cut!"

With my left hand—my right was preoccupied with balancing the Beretta submachine gun—I removed my cap. "I had it cut," I said again.

"Oh, so you've had it cut!" the *brigadiere* shouted, almost doubled up with fury. "Right! You'll have it shaved to nothing after drill. Corporal! Take their names. They are all confined to quarters!"

With that we fell in beside the rest of the company and began to march up and down sloping arms, turning to the right and to the left, doing all sorts of odd maneuvers which I did my best to imitate in approximately the same time and order as the others, for the first time in my life wishing I had paid more attention to what had seemed such futile training in the British OTC and the State of Georgia ROTC in those happy thirties when drilling was considered by civilized people fit for none but perhaps the Swiss guards with their halberds.

As if this were not enough, the captain caught sight of us and shouted to the *brigadiere* to get "those new recruits" out of the backward group, that by our records we were veterans of several campaigns and should be put at the head of the column to show the others how it was done.

I felt myself sinking. There was no way out now but to step forward as boldly as possible. "Captain, I'm an American agent. You can take this godforsaken weapon and you know what you can do with it!"

The whole scene was teetering on the verge of an abyss when I had the bright idea of nudging my neighbor and whispering rapidly that I

259

had been a specialist in the air corps, that in the air corps we'd never done such nonsense. In less than a second, while everything was in the balance, my neighbor stepped forward. The captain, not wishing to compound what was already an unmilitary situation with further remonstrances, let the matter stand, and a moment later I found our platoon assigned to the nice lieutenant, who, having watched us for a while, announced that we drilled so badly he was going to teach us the manual of arms, starting right from the beginning.

The rest of the morning we spent on the sun-drenched esplanade by the Tiber, facing and turning our behinds to the great dictator's marble obelisk, doing such elementary movements as standing at attention, saluting, sloping arms, till the sun stood almost directly overhead. Sweating, uncomfortable in my itchy uniform, giddy from the reflected glare, I began to see the scene superimposed on the dusty campus of the University of Georgia trampled by the sharp black riding boots of the State Militia, onto which in turn were superimposed the gentle meadows of Buckinghamshire and the heavy shoes and canvas leggings of the British OTC. Poor Major Howarth, I thought, if he could see me now!

How I survived I do not know, but at last they turned us loose, and I made for the latrines in the basement where I locked myself in and started to go through the small pile of messages Primo had brought the night before, and which I only now had the appropriate privacy to read—even Vito having to be kept in ignorance of their existence and my true identity as both Pietro and Roberto.

Finishing each message I burnt it with a match and dropped it into the hole of the Turkish latrine, a nauseating performance. The base had not answered. While I'd been trapped in the goddamn company, Coniglio had countered all my orders to Eugenio, intimidated him, tried to kidnap the radio, convinced Mario, the "messenger from the north," that "Roberto was an impostor," and thus wrecked our chance of getting into contact with the base. That he was up to something funny was now quite clear, for I had specified to everyone that if anyone were in doubt as to the authenticity and authority of Roberto he could establish it the minute we were in contact with the base, asking any queries he chose in order to satisfy his doubts.

Coming out of the latrine feeling mad enough to spit in Kesselring's eye I went straight to the *fureria* and asked to speak to the captain. Either the boldness of the approach, or the evident state of my temper, must have induced him to acceed to my request, for he came out into the hall, walked over to a corner by the staircase, and asked me what might be my troubles.

Under such circumstances there is only one recourse in Italy: family affairs. I must see the colonel immediately on a very urgent matter of a family nature.

I don't know what convinced the captain—whether my evident determination, the Italian's innate sense of family responsibility, or some psychic flash—but five minutes later I was ushered into the colonel's enormous office. He was a small, neat man, immaculately uniformed, his breast covered with braid and decorations, sitting behind a colossal desk at the furthest end of the room. Clicking my heels I performed an almost perfect Fascist salute, then stood at rigid attention.

Thinking me to be an Italian Air Force major hiding in his outfit, he assumed immediately the reason I was there. With only the two of us—*a quattr' occhi,* as the Italians say—he suggested that it might be best for all concerned if I were to revert immediately to civilian clothes and disappear into hiding, there being no way of knowing what the arrested lieutenant might choose to tell the Germans. If all went well, and the lieutenant was either shot or managed to avoid incriminating the rest of us (mark the irony!), in a week or two we could resume our identity as corporals in the company. Otherwise it was better to be deserters than be available for questioning.

Making another snappy salute I clicked my heels and went out as if walking on Aleatico. Almost immediately the captain received an order to demobilize us. So we turned in our strange variety of uniforms, guns and mattresses; but such was the attraction of good white bread that we postponed our departure till after chow in order to collect our ration.

This accomplished, we walked out into relative freedom. The last thing I saw as we slipped past the sentry was the seven-foot *brigadiere* eyeing the unshorn back of my head like a child forcibly relieved of a lollypop.

My main preoccupation now was getting a note to Eugenio to reassure him of my presence and authority, then arrange to see Coniglio personally so as to tell him in no uncertain terms to cooperate with my efforts or at least cease interfering. Primo was to take the message to Eugenio at his regularly established five-o'clock rendezvous by the lone pine in Piazza Pittagora; meanwhile Franco was to meet us at a small ambulant fair in Prati.

As we approached the fair I suddenly had to dodge behind a fat woman and scurry down a lane. I had spotted, of all people, the benny whom I had not seen in months. God knows what he was doing in that part of town, but I managed to avoid him.

Then, as Franco was late, and the fair boasted a shooting gallery, I could not resist the temptation. I don't know whether it was the euphoria engendered by being out of the barracks, or the good white wine Vito and I stopped to consume, but I hit almost everything I aimed at, much to the surprise of the pretty girl who ran the booth, whose eyes sparkled as she caught me staring at the firm round contours of her gypsy breasts.

Instead of Franco, Mario arrived. We embraced, as if we had not seen each other for years, then, bidding Vito adieu, piled into a passing *carrozza* and headed for Piazza Lovatelli.

The familiar feel of sun-warmed leather, the smell of horse, the noise of its hoofs on the cobbles as it clattered down the back lanes of Trastevere, caused a hundred associations to crowd my mind— Palermo, Sorrento, Crete, Algiers and the Azores. The same noise, the same swaying movement, the same exotic feeling of adventurous holiday in foreign lands.

Mario pumped me for details of our experience in the barracks, and, as I recounted them, already they seemed like a passing nightmare. Half an hour later I was once more sitting comfortably in a deep armchair in the big sunlit room at Palazzo Lovatelli, and, as Mario brought out a bottle of brandy, for the first time in a long time, I felt passably at peace.

PART FOUR

THE BEGIN- NING OF THE END

27 DOWN THE RABBIT HOLE

MY MEETING WITH CONIGLIO was to be arranged by Lele sometime the following day. As I did not wish Coniglio to know even what part of town I lived in, we decided it should be somewhere in Parioli, and that I wait at Baldo's for details of the time and place.

This constituted an excellent opportunity for one of Franco's alibis, and I did not need to be urged to phone L. to meet me at Baldo's in the afternoon.

To be with a well-dressed, beautifully perfumed creature after the barracks was like being transported to another planet, and I wondered what expression the *brigadiere* would have produced if he had seen us.

Then Lele phoned to say the contact with Coniglio could not be made till the following day at noon. This was an annoying contretemps, followed shortly by the appearance of Emanuele, who had come to collect some photos for a phony identity card, from which I gathered that during my absence he had been added to our band. This worried me as I considered him congenitally unqualified for any job that required security, but figured that if Franco had made the decision he must have had some reason.

As he vanished into the evening, and none of the others had appeared, L. overstayed so long she had to call her mother and say she was spending the night with her grandmother in Parioli, climbing out the back window two minutes before the curfew, leaving me with the aroma of her perfume and a lonely supper of ricotta with a vermouth-and-gin.

Sometime during the night, as I lay asleep on my familiar couch by the fire, I became aware that someone had entered the flat. Then I realized it must be the pregnant wife of the young Florentine actionist to whom Baldo had given a key to the back door so as to enter the building without being seen by the *portiere*.

The next thing I knew it was morning and L. was reappearing through the back window to stay with me till close to noon. But as

265

soon as she had gone Lele phoned to say that Coniglio had postponed the meeting till seven, which annoyed me, also because it meant I would have to spend another whole night alone at Baldo's.

Then, at the very last moment, Coniglio refused to come to an outside appointment, insisting I go to his building—where I had been on my first day in Rome.

I wasn't at all sure this wasn't a trap, but by now I had no choice. Franco offered to have an armed guard follow me. But there didn't seem much point risking any more people than necessary. If Coniglio planned to dispose of me he would certainly have taken an armed guard into consideration. So Lele agreed to wait for me at a safe distance, and, if I didn't come out within half an hour, advise Franco and the others.

It was a fifteen-minute walk to Coniglio's, which Lele and I did almost in silence, striding through a gray overcast atmosphere.

Leaving Lele some hundred yards from the apartment building I winked at him then proceeded to the door, gauging my arrival to the split second of the appointed hour. I had an unpleasant sensation that my back was uncovered, but before I had rationalized the sensation I found myself surrounded by a group of mean-looking characters. Two of them led me into the elevator. Though wary, I was numbed to the situation, prepared to accept whatever surprise might be in store.

As the elevator reached the fourth floor they motioned me out, then closed the door, leaving me alone on the landing. This, I thought to myself, is the trap. I could hear men on the floor above, and others on the floor below. Was Coniglio afraid that I had come to dispose of him with a silenced automatic? Was he preparing the same for me?

A door opened onto the landing and Coniglio appeared, squinting slightly behind the lenses of his glasses, a faint cynical smile on his lips as he stretched out his hand in an outward show of cordiality. Coming straight to the point I insisted that Mario the saboteur turn over the frequencies and plans the base had sent up to me; that once I had established contact he might file whatever he chose over the channel in any code he chose.

Instead of answering he went into a dissertation on Cervo and what had happened to him, adding all sorts of other "information" I already knew in detail. Cutting him short I tried to make him understand that

266

what I requested was an order, that I was an American citizen, a civil servant, an employee of the Office of Strategic Services, warning him that sooner or later he would have to answer to the OSS for his actions, that I had deposited a detailed account of all that had happened during the past three months so that it would reach both the American and British Ministers to the Holy See if anything were to happen to me.*

At first he complained that I had confused him with the Roberto-Pietro situation, then, pausing slightly, agreed to have the equipment turned over the following day.

But just as we got to the details of this transaction he began to hint that he was already in contact with the base.

"In that case," I said, "ask them for orders and see what you get for an answer."

From his reaction I realized he'd been bluffing; it made me wish to squeeze him like a pimple, but I controlled myself, being as polite as I could under the circumstances.

When there was nothing more for me to say, I indicated the interview was at an end. We shook hands, frigidly cordial, and I turned to go down the stairs. Reaching the first floor I felt sure someone with a silencer was following me, but managed to proceed slowly through the hall, out the building, then walk, not run, toward the corner. Lele was there and we rapidly left the area.

To be categorically sure that none of Coniglio's henchmen was following me I took four different trolleys to reach the Portici d'Ottavia.

Drinks and dinner were waiting at the Palazzo Lovatelli and I felt at home with Mario and his wife—a sweet, tranquil girl with a year-old baby. I described my interview to Mario and he too became excited at the prospect of resuming contact with the base; after dinner, we discussed the entire reorganization of the information service. A really imposing pile of material had accumulated, the processing of which would take me several days. Now that Ottorino was actually working

* Franco had arranged to have my diary smuggled into the Vatican, in segments, every week or ten days, where it was hidden in the room of an aging cardinal; neither Harold Tittman nor D'Arcy Osborne actually knew it was there, but if something were to happen to us, it would almost certainly find its way into their hands.

as a liaison officer to Kesselring's HQ in the vaults of Mount Soratte as well as in the Open City Command, we had access to the German daily intelligence digests. Through Marcello we had added a Party of Action chain to our sources; altogether we were in better shape than before we had lost our radio.

It was exhilarating to wake up the next morning with the prospect of real work to get my teeth into. But when Primo arrived at noon he brought bad news. The PAI lieutenant and two of his guards had apparently been shot by the SS. I could not help thinking of the poor man standing beside me on the trolley just one week earlier, and how I had been reassured by his presence. Little did I realize that of the two, he was in the greater danger.

Now we wondered how much, and if anything, the Germans had managed to squeeze from him first. Franco's life had become a nightmare during the last few days since the lieutenant's arrest, so much so that for the first time since I had known him he had lost his nerve. Not that he didn't continue to do everything with the same nonchalance as before, but we, who knew him intimately, could see it in the way he walked, in the way he tied and untied his handkerchief in knots while discussing some matter of importance.

Then Franco appeared in person to tell me the rumor that the lieutenant had been shot was false. According to Franco the colonel had turned cold on the poor man, doing his best to have the execution speeded up, phoning the SD at Via Tasso every two hours to see if it had happened.

I said I thought it fairly normal of the colonel, as his whole existence now depended on how much the Germans got out of the lieutenant, and that presumably, with what the SD already knew of the lieutenant's activities, they would be bound to shoot him sooner or later.

Franco disagreed, saying the colonel's behavior was unethical and dangerous; so far the lieutenant had not uttered a word and would presumably keep up his silence. However, if he were to find out that his own superior had abandoned him, he might, out of disgust and revenge, give them information.

Nor was that the only bad news Franco brought. Bruno Buozzi, the Socialist trade union leader, had been arrested, a blow to both the underground and the future of the Socialist party.

268

Sitting round the table we reviewed our situation. The Allies seemed to have no intention of being in Rome for at least another month or maybe more. For cover none of us was any longer in the good position we had planned, and our chance of survival, without such cover, was pared to the very quick.

Baldo, having failed to enter the Palatine Guard, had been obliged to accept the hospitality of a woman somewhat older than his normal choice into whose apartment he had moved, as it amused us to say, lock, stock and barrel; there he was fed like a prince, had his clothes washed and pressed, was given a hot bath twice a day, and could only complain about the overtime, which was inclined to be strenuous.

Lele and Emanuele, to dispel suspicion, were living in Baldo's place and indulging in parties with this or that set of girls in the fond hope of proving themselves so worthless that even if they had the bad luck of being taken to forced labor the Germans would turn them loose, as they normally did with homosexuals or playboy members of the Excelsior crowd.

Emanuele's present predilection, according to Franco, was for practical jokes; sending flowers or making phone calls to girls in such a manner as to arouse all sorts of jealous scenes. Though I was doubtful of this approach, Franco assured me it was probably the healthiest situation we could ask for; certainly no one would look for left-wing partisan agents among such wastrels!

Yet Lele went regularly to the hospital each morning; and he and Baldo carried messages to and from the most incredible people to keep the organization running.

All our hopes now rested on obtaining the promised material from Coniglio, making contact with the base, and tightening up our operations. However, if things did not rapidly improve, we concluded our only recourse would be to cross the lines and have a conference with the base.

The next day, April 19, I received a message from Eugenio that Coniglio had not appeared at the established rendezvous, but had later sent word he wanted a written order from Pietro before he would deliver the goods. Otherwise, said Eugenio, everything was ready: the radio was set up in a new apartment in an ideal position for transmitting. He had prepared two more houses for transmission and two others as safe refuges. Also, he had information about an airfield with 200 air force partisans, at which a plane from the Allied side might land and take out personnel and documents.

From Marcello—whose code name for the sake of simpler confusion we had changed to Alberto—I received a message confirming that to his certain knowledge Eugenio had kept the appointment but that neither Coniglio nor any of his men had appeared, and that it was now clear to him from his own sources that Coniglio was set on destroying our organization.

In a fury, but controlling myself, I sat down and wrote Coniglio a message saying that I had informed the base through the British agent that if they didn't hear from me within three days over Siria they could hold Coniglio responsible for sabotaging our activities.

Later in the day, to add to our troubles, Franco told me that Colonel Bonzani of the Open City, who had been responsible for Franco's nominal position in that organization, was getting cold feet and threatening to give up supporting Franco unless he could be provided with a written affidavit to the effect that he would be protected by the Allies for his efforts. I couldn't imagine what good it would do him *now*, especially if discovered by the Germans, or used by someone as blackmail, but I nevertheless wrote out a fancy document under the heading ALLIED FORCE HEADQUARTERS, etc., and signed it "OSS O.C. Rome Area," which document, such is the ingrained respect for documents on this planet, Franco later told me had so impressed the good colonel that he agreed to provide Franco with a police car complete with spare tire and two hundred liters of gas.

Franco, Mario, Lele and Baldo could now leave Rome to reconnoiter the possibilities of finding guides in the central Apennines, or a boat on the Adriatic, in order to get across the lines.

The next afternoon Franco was to take me to the house on Via San Teodoro where his uncle—then Counselor of the Knights of Malta to the Holy See—was living. I was to have tea with his debutante cousins Gloria and Franca.

This didn't seem like the *ne plus ultra* of security; on the other hand I must do something or go mad biting my fingers at Coniglio while our stacks of intelligence stagnated.

It was odd to think of going back to the house where I had lived till my departure for Greece in 1940, of seeing other people and

270

other servants living there, but a pleasant prospect after the stultifying routine of the Palazzo Lovatelli.

When Franco came to fetch me he had a worried expression; according to Ottorino someone had turned Franco's name in to the Italian police as that of a subversive element. The more we thought about it the more we realized it could not have been one of our own men who had talked or the police would have gone directly to the publisher's house on Via Veneto where Franco normally lived and worked. We now both suspected that after my note to Coniglio of the day before it must have been Coniglio who had turned Franco's name in to the police, for he did not know of Franco's home address.

It looked more and more as if our only hope of survival now lay in crossing the lines as soon as possible. All that was needed, now that we had the car and gasoline, was an official permit to drive it across the Apennines to the Adriatic, and there search for a boat.

But the water was rising fast. If the police were at all informed they would most certainly look for Franco at his only living relative's house, his uncle's, at Via San Teodoro.

But by now we were looking forward to the company of pretty young girls, the gin, and the excellent collection of records accumulated by Jack Creek (the Englishman to whom the house actually belonged, though it appeared officially as the property of Eddie Bismark). Besides, I had shaved and bathed, which would have been wasted on an afternoon locked up in the "hole."

Approaching the house in broad daylight, where any of a dozen former neighbors might see and recognize me, made me unpleasantly apprehensive, but it was nothing to the effect of actually going into the house, so filled with past associations.

Franco's cousins were gay and we danced and had a pleasant time. When tea was about to be served I was warned to step quickly into the adjoining room, as it was to be served by Santino, our old butler who had stayed on in the house.

Then the phone rang. It was Lele, who had at last got a pass for the car, authentic except for the fraudulent names of the bearers, which he had obtained from an underground pal who worked in the central licensing office (and who after the liberation became president of the Rome Automobile Club).

In fact Lele soon joined us with all the necessary papers. To celebrate the good news we finished off the bottle of gin. Lele, Emanuele, Primo and Mario were to leave immediately for the Adriatic with a couple of hundred thousand lire in cash to see if they could buy a boat from a man whose name Mario had obtained through the British agent.

Actually they did not get off that night because the car provided by the Open City immediately broke down (making me hope the same would happen with the document I had given Colonel Bonzani), and they were unable to obtain either the gas or the spare tire.

Then, back at the Palazzo Lovatelli, Primo brought me messages from both Coniglio and Eugenio. Coniglio's was as follows:

For P.—The crystals and the rest of the equipment are not in my possession. Mario only has that which has to do with Siria. If Eugenio had maintained contact with me he would have had everything by now. [Patently a lie!] Tomorrow morning I'm to see Mario [the saboteur] at noon and will give him orders [presumably to turn over the stuff to us]. I have advised the base that I decline all responsibility for the service in Rome. This was necessary because, as you well know, the whole organization depends from me as far as Italy is concerned, and, naturally, had you acted in accord with me and not tried to make me lose prestige the service would have been resumed long ago.—C.

Well, if nothing else, Coniglio had made himself clear. The service was not functioning because he considered it of subsidiary importance to his prestige! Furthermore, if, as appeared, he had a channel to the base, he was not only a cheat but a traitor, for he knew that I had information vital to the Allies.

Clearly there was nothing more for me to do but try to cross the lines and iron out the entire situation at the base.

28 BUT HOW DO WE CROSS THE LINES?

EVERYTHING SEEMED TO BE IN ORDER for the boys to leave, and the next day after lunch Lele, Emanuele, Mario and Primo set off by car. We had no idea if we would ever see them again; the chances seemed slim, but there was no alternative. Were they to be successful in establishing a means of escape we would all take the chance together.

I hated the idea of leaving while there was still a possibility of getting in touch with the base, but it was essential for me to accompany them lest the Allies, as was normal procedure, dispute their story, and the FSS or CIC slap them into some dungeon to rot for several weeks or the duration of the war.

Besides, the Coniglio business could no longer go unexplained and unsettled. I realized that when, and if, the whole thing blew over, there would be little sense in my trying to point out to the collected colonels that there was such a thing as OSS "prestige," and that *no* American OSS officer could be subordinated (let alone against his will) to a foreign agent. It was not a question of the *officer* losing standing, but the OSS, and the entire U. S. Army and government. Any explaining would have to be done now, in the heat of action.

Then Franco arrived to console me with a *case* of real authentic Old Tom gin. I don't know where he managed to dig it up, or how much it might have cost him, but I decided it might be wiser not even to inquire. Surely Lane Rehm, that superlative special funds officer, would take into consideration its very soothing effect on my most raveled nerves.

Sipping it straight we discussed the prospective opening of the "second front." Every day the BBC carried more threats and insinuations and sly warnings, but we had come to the conclusion there were still many weeks to go, if not months. We had no illusions about the brevity of the war or any slackening of the political struggle, comforting each other with the thought that if the Germans got us it would simply save us that many risks and unpleasant situations in the future.

273

Then Primo arrived to inform us that Eugenio had not turned up at his appointment. This sort of news was always a shock. If he too fell through, it would mean we would have no one left in Rome with whom to communicate, no setup to come back to, no one to get out the vital information we would need on the other side to organize future operations.

After they had gone, and Mario's wife had retired to bed, and I had gotten a little bleary-eyed from solitary drinking, I decided—in case the four horsemen of the apocalypse were to return that night with news that they had found some craft—to lie down on the couch outside the "hole," taking the precaution of placing a round in the barrel of my Beretta, which I carefully tucked beneath the pillow.

Roused by the sound of German voices in the passage leading to where I lay, too late to dive into the "hole," I instinctively took cover and removed the safety from the automatic.

I had left the light on at the end of the corridor just so it would shine on any interloper. To my amazement it fell onto Mario, followed shortly by the others, all apparently stuffed with brandy. My relief was greater than my anger, but they sobered up rapidly when they saw how close Emanuele's practical joke had come to exploding in their faces.

Their report was a mixture of good and bad.

The man whom they were supposed to have seen in the remote village had skipped the minute they arrived. Everyone else had trembled at the sight of their police car; soon they discovered that the person in whose name they had come was regarded with very little favor by the partisan populace. In chorus they cursed British intelligence for the types it hired. I felt like reminding them we weren't so hot ourselves, but remembered that Emanuele didn't know who I was.

Despite this bad news, they had some comforting tales to tell. To begin with, their false passes had worked like magic and every guard or cop or republican soldier had frozen to attention, kowtowing to the "Signor Tenente"—who was Mario!

They said that traveling was easy, except for the fact that the Allied air forces had a habit of laying waste the roads just at the time one wanted most to travel.

274

Though the trip had been a failure, Emanuele had developed the idea of going to visit an uncle who had a large estate near Osimo not far from Ancona (and the sea) where they might look for a craft with which to sail away at night.

By now it was close to 2 A.M. Deciding to discuss the matter more seriously and soberly in the morning they spread out on the various couches while I went back to bed.

By morning the problem seemed clear: someone would have to go ahead and find out if Emanuele's uncle's place was actually safe enough to use as a base, whether the old boy would let us stay there, whether there were in effect any boats available or a stretch of beach sufficiently unguarded to allow a PT boat to approach and take us off in a rubber dinghy. I still hoped that even if Coniglio refused, one of the saboteurs would eventually enable us to get a message out to the OSS; surely they must realize that to ruin an information service was one thing, but to jeopardize the life of an OSS officer by refusing to let him ask his base to send a boat was another.

Then, to my relief, I received a note from Eugenio—relief at the fact that he was all right and loyal. But I was not happy at the message: Mario the saboteur still hadn't turned over the equipment necessary to get in touch with the base. So I decided the time had come to see what I could do with a letter aimed directly at changing the saboteur's mind by revealing my true identity.

There was no question now that I must cross the lines, contact or no. Our next problem was to secure sufficient funds. If we were to have to buy a boat (there being no immediate way of returning one!) we would need a couple of thousand dollars. Coniglio, who had borrowed sizable sums from rich industrialists (to be repaid by the OSS) refused to part with any of it for me; and the money left by Cervo was exhausted. I did have 100 louis d'or of the original ones I had brought ashore, which had been recovered from Cervo's house, but these would have to be turned into lire, and the market was far from optimum.*
However, if we could get credit for a couple of million lire out of the Open City officials, when the Allies arrived we could pay it back in a currency that would do them far more good. I therefore wrote

---

* Eventually I did sell them at the peak of the market, netting the OSS a good two thousand dollars.

them out some fancy affidavits which I hoped would do the trick. The
big shots in the Open City Command were clearly scared of what the
Germans might do if it were discovered they were hedging. Our
situation was therefore not ideal: as in the case of the PAI lieutenant,
if anything went wrong, we would be the first to be thrown to the
wolves.

Our main worry was that Franco might be caught before we could
get going. It looked more and more as if Coniglio might have been the
one to denounce him, either out of pique, or because of the stand I
had taken with him, or merely out of fear that I would get to inform
the base of his attitude—assuming, no doubt, that by getting Franco
the Germans would eventually get me, and he would be rid of me
without its transpiring after the liberation that *he* had been responsible for my capture.

I was beginning to feel that if I managed to survive I'd take care
of the bird myself, though I knew perfectly well I was incapable of
losing my temper sufficiently to kill him or have anyone else kill him
for me. As I wrote in my diary that day:

This has worried me quite a bit; it seems to me there must be
times when it is really necessary. I suppose if it *really* were, I'd do it,
but when I think about it I cannot bring myself to do it; it means
taking an irrevocable decision, and I am still clinging to the theory
that I should try to keep an open mind and not go to extremes. Anyhow, I am fairly sure that as an individual, no matter how much it
may be necessary, one cannot ever take justice into one's own hands,
for justice must be an impersonal process carried out by legal representatives of the people who have nothing to do with the particular
case. Besides, when I think of Coniglio I sometimes think it may not be
his fault, that he is made that way. The great and unpardonable fault
lies with the man who recruited him and put the lives of so many
other people in his hands. . . . It is a dismal subject and best left alone.
Somehow it will resolve itself, and, pray God, be no more.

To handle our organization while we were away Franco and I
decided to put Alberto, Lele's doctor friend, in charge, tying him in
closely with Eugenio, who would handle both the radios and their
operators. Our own large network of informants would then head up
to Alberto who in turn would pass on the evaluated and condensed

information to Eugenio, who would also be making use of his own contacts and network.

The next morning I spent memorizing the ciphers I had worked out for Eugenio so as to have no incriminating evidence on me when crossing the lines.

After lunch, as I was sitting on the terrace sunbathing, Baldo suddenly arrived with a peculiar expression.

"What's the matter?" I asked, dreading another shock.

"They've caught the British colonel," he said, then went on to explain.

That morning when Baldo had made our usual daily liaison call to the British agent at 8:30 A.M. a strange voice had answered saying the *Ingeniere* was busy, but to come on around anyway, that he would be free in a while. Instantly Baldo realized that something was up; he knew the "colonel" was well aware that Baldo did not know his address. Simultaneously Baldo realized he had made a bad mistake. Strictly against our most stringent orders, he had got tired of getting up every morning and going round to the corner to a pay station (and who can blame him!) in order to make his call and had been negligent enough to do so from the bedside of his lady friend, while she was preparing his breakfast. He had therefore had to skip immediately, this time not because of any irate husband, but lest the SS had the phone controlled and promptly traced the call.

Later in the day both he and Lele called again from pay stations in different parts of town and each time a strange voice answered. They were sure it was a German for he had said the *Ingeniere* was "*molto occupatissimo*," a double superlative never used by Italians.

Baldo took off his shirt and despondently sat in the sun beside me. We both thought about the poor old "colonel" who had gone about his work so smoothly and so quietly for so long, passing for a white-haired Italian *Ingeniere*, and who had finally been caught. It was never pleasant to think of a colleague at Via Tasso.

To tease me, and ease the strain, Baldo started whistling "*Non e stato un sogno*," a record L. and I had played over and over. He told me she had come round to his house to collect it, thinking I was in Florence, in order to have it copied (it being out of print).

But at the back of our minds was the thought that the water had risen almost beyond endurance. Only Lele remained unburned, and his relations with Alberto (who had been the contact with Sorrentino) made him none too lily-white.

For the first time since I had come back to the Palazzo Lovatelli I didn't feel like crawling into the "hole" and doing some sort of work. I even felt like playing cards with Baldo, which I hadn't done in weeks. Then, remembering Baldo's bent for mathematics, I got out my new ciphers and decided to explain them to him; if we were both to cross the lines it would be better to have them fixed in his mind as well as mine, so that if anything happened, one of us, at least, might get them through.

Then Franco arrived with the good news that he'd got the Open City to relinquish a vehicle to us. But before they would produce any money I'd have to write them another guarantee.

On the bad side of the ledger, poor Peppino Craceva, the third member of the Socialist military underground triumvirate, saved once from the SS, had been recaptured in his cellar where he was recuperating from a bullet wound. Montezemolo's family had been told that he had definitely been shot in the Ardeatine Caves, after behaving nobly in the face of his captors. It made me realize it was more than three months since I had landed and he had been arrested. What hell the poor man must have suffered!

Then Franco produced a really startling piece of information. Emanuele had confided in him that, through a German agent in Rome, he had learned that his own mother, who had decided some time back to cross the lines to the Allied side, had, in fact done so as an agent for the Germans. I had long been confused by the De Seta-Pignatelli household, but now learned from Franco that Emanuele's mother had remarried a Pignatelli, who, as an adventurer, novelist and Fascist, had, after the defection of the greater part of Mussolini's Grand Council, decided to accept the unfillable position of Party Secretary in the Fascist Republic of Saló.

At first I thought the whole story another of Emanuele's practical jokes, the heat of his peculiar mind, but Franco assured me it was true. We were both a little worried by the news, but the more we thought about it, and the further we discussed it, the more it seemed likely that Emanuele might be, if we could trust him personally, an asset. So far Franco and the others had been very careful to disguise our intelligence

278

activities (the all-night parties had at last done their bit to give us a "proper" name!), pretending we were only anti-Fascist officers hiding from the Germans.

But looked at objectively, our situation was pretty peculiar. Here was an American agent living in the house of a German agent (the Palazzo Lovatelli apartment was the De Seta-Pignatelli home) whose children were actively but unwittingly aiding him in spying for the Allies! (Of the two, however, it was we who had more luck so far. We heard that Emanuele's mother was caught by the FSS crossing the lines and promptly jailed as a German spy.)

There was no question about its being time to decamp. Unfortunately, though Franco had arrived complete with new police car, it turned out to be no good. Among other defects it lacked a muffler— not exactly the ideal car for a bunch of conspirators wishing to approach a deserted beach in the stillness of night to get the hell out to sea and across the lines! What's more, the buzzards hadn't even given us the full amount of gas they had promised.

We decided therefore to try to get the permit for this useless vehicle transferred to Lele's own car, of identical make, but in far better condition, which he had secreted since the armistice. For this we would have to wait for the following day and the good offices of our friend in the licensing bureau, which offices turned out to be admirably successful. So in the afternoon, Franco, Lele, Emanuele and Baldo, all socially admissible to Emanuele's uncle's estate (being in their less subversive guises two barons, a count, and a doctor of medicine) were able to set off to see if they could find a boat or a spot to land an Allied PT boat.

However, no sooner did I think them safely on their way when the phone rang and Emanuele's voice, sounding very far away, asked me if I wanted to come to a cocktail party the following afternoon to meet a British PW. When I asked where the devil he was calling from he said he had decided not to go along with the others.

Controlling my temper and wondering how the devil the others were going to visit his uncle without him, and what deadly trouble he would succeed in getting me involved in during their absence, I quietly hung up the receiver.

29 IT'S ALWAYS DARKEST BEFORE THE DAWN

APRIL 29 WAS MY BIRTHDAY—I was now twenty-five. As no one knew it, the day would have passed like any other had I not decided to take the desperate step of meeting the saboteurs in person, to see if I could sway them with the weight of my own words in acting on our behalf.

What had prompted this decision was the receipt of a note from Mario the saboteur in answer to the strong one I had sent him revealing my true identity:

For Pietro: I never doubted that it was you. The situation is quite different from what you think. In order to comply with your orders I must know whether Coniglio is still in charge as I was informed by Captain A. at the time of our landing[!]. I must see you before some irreparable stupidity takes place. I trust I make myself clear. It is urgently necessary for me to explain to you certain things about Rome and further north. I must go north for a complexity of reasons which I cannot explain to Eugenio and cannot put on paper. I do not intend to disobey your orders, but I must make certain things clear.—Mario.

So! That was the genesis of all our troubles: Captain A.'s whispered instructions to Mario the saboteur the night we had landed telling Coniglio to disregard my authority! No wonder the base's cables had had no effect on Coniglio.

What it amounted to was a private conspiracy between a French Intelligence agent and an operator of the Italian Servizio Informazioni Militari to use OSS as a cover for their own operations, a conspiracy abetted by a gullible succession of American colonels, who, with no knowledge of the language, country or the mechanics of espionage, succeeded one another with head-spinning rapidity in command of the OSS in the Italian theater.

Waiting for the appointed hour, I typed in the "hole" or read the Enciclopedia Italiana to sooth my nerves, wondering if I would be running into an ambush—to round out this little life at an even twenty-five.

But what was the point of recrimination? The only way out was forward.

Toward six o'clock I got myself ready and discussed with Mario the advisability of taking a gun. Somehow I didn't expect them to stage a "snatch," or try to bump me off in broad daylight, yet I felt I would be safer with a gun. On the other hand if the SD or the Italian police should turn up in their stead, a gun would only make my cover story harder to maintain. In the end I decided against a gun, and so did Mario.

To avoid a trap I had done my best to arrange things carefully with Primo so that the saboteurs would not even know in what part of town they were to meet me till they were led to the rendezvous by him. Furthermore Primo had arranged for a route and methods of transportation best designed to prevent their being followed.

At twenty past six I put on my hat, coat and disguising glasses, and Mario and I started down the steps. Mario was to come with me to within the general area of the meeting place, then make a wide reconnaissance tour to see if we were being watched, guarded or followed.

The place I had chosen was in the small park, recently developed, which overlooks the Circus Maximus from the Aventine side. It was a spot open enough to be difficult to reach without being seen, and from which I trusted I could notice anyone approaching from no matter which direction. Yet the park itself had enough sparse trees and benches to afford an excuse for lingering, or sitting and discussing business.

Passing the Temple of Vesta I was reminded of my date with L., then saw that Mario was circling behind the building at the foot of Via San Teodoro. Starting up the hill toward the meeting place I had the distinct sensation of being watched, that my walk was too much like that of an American; yet the more I concentrated on amending my gait the more it seemed noticeable. Finally, to break the pattern, I stopped and lit a cigarette.

It was just time for the rendezvous, and I looked around apprehensively. Punctual as a Patek-Philippe, Primo appeared at the bottom of the hill, leading the two saboteurs. As I had presumed, they were, in fact, the two who had landed with me. I don't think they were yet

281

sure themselves, until they actually saw me, that it was I they were to meet; and they were obviously affected by my presence.

Their attitude was friendly; in fact, we had barely begun to talk when they told me they wanted to quit Coniglio and place themselves at my command, but that they needed a direct order from me to do so. Both of them insisted they could not trust Coniglio, that the whole gang he was with was but a group of former Fascists bent on seeing that the OSS accomplished nothing in the area.

When I asked for details they responded by saying that Coniglio had persistently refused to let them do any of the sabotage they had come across the lines to carry out, that he had held up quantities of excellent information collected by Sorrentino (of which they had a huge dossier), that he refused to give clear or specific orders, that he would not assume responsibility, that he lied continuously, that he was so tight with OSS funds that lots of poor agents could not eat or clothe themselves properly, and, finally, that he had antagonized virtually all the agents in the north, who now refused to have anything to do with him.

In a way this was cheering news, confirming what Eugenio and the others had maintained all along, giving further proof that Coniglio had been responsible for sabotaging Sorrentino as much as he was now trying to sabotage me—obviously so as to remain kingpin in Rome the day the Allies arrived. But all this did not help the present situation. Coniglio was, equally obviously, going to fight to the last agent to save his position. What I cared about was getting into communication with the base.

This, Mario, the elder saboteur, insisted could now be done only if he were to go to one of the agents in the north, say Florence or Milan, and get them to send a message to the base, maintaining that the base was no longer listening for Rome on the existing frequencies. To this I promptly agreed, wondering why it could not have been done before, as I had often requested, wary suddenly that the two saboteurs might still be acting as agents provocateurs for Coniglio.

The sun, about to go behind St. Peter's dome, was casting long shadows on the hilltop. Looking around to see if anyone suspicious were in the neighborhood, I took a few steps down the graveled path. Both saboteurs reacted immediately, and I saw that something important must still be on their minds. There was a slight pause, then they both asked if I would assume responsibility for all the agents in the north. Now I was really in a quandary. There was, obviously, nothing I would have preferred. With a quick trip through the north I could re-establish contact with the base, reorganize the whole network, get a PT boat to come to a safe place along the shore, go across the lines to report to the base, then come back in time for the eventual Allied offensive. But this I knew I could not do without explicit orders from the base. It was a horrible dilemma. To have taken the step on my own initiative, to have taken over agents in someone else's territory, no matter how bad the situation, without first asking the base, would have been unethical, and this I refused to do, for ethics was the only basis on which such an extralegal organization as the OSS could possibly be held together.

Yet the moment I regretfully refused, I sensed a sudden chilling in the atmosphere. Clearly the saboteurs believed that I was shirking the responsibility, just as they accused Coniglio of doing. What a nightmare to have to refuse that which I most wanted to accept, that which, had I done so two months earlier, would have given us a first-rate and effective organization all over the country! Instead I told the saboteurs that I would have to reach the base first, and, once the operation was approved, give them a password to that effect.

As for permission to break with Coniglio and go north, this I had no worries about giving them. I was in my own territory. Coniglio was totally out of line. I therefore gave them categoric authority to go north as soon as possible, with a message to send through to the base.

It had been an hour's conversation, but when I shook hands with them I had a feeling something might at last be accomplished.

Watching them go, making sure there was no indication of their being followed, I took a detour with Primo to reach a nearby meeting place for a scheduled talk with Eugenio.

I found him waiting for me by the river, and we set off under the plane trees along the Lungotevere. He was a slight young man with a limp, and a personality I would not normally have recruited, but I found him extremely conscientious and willing to work.

As he spoke I realized we were in for more trouble. One of Sorrentino's original recruits, whom I knew well from Naples (and re-

283

fused to employ) had now spilled the beans about the kind of work he was supposed to be doing, to a girl friend who turned out to be working for the SS.

This was all we needed! Luckily Eugenio had followed my repeated instructions to the letter so that neither his safe addresses nor the location of either of the radio operators was known to any of these other people. The danger spot, however, was Sorrentino. According to Eugenio, Sorrentino was up to his neck in debt, was personally sought by the SS, and in a hell of a mess generally as he had discredited himself with the underground by not being able to keep any of the grandiose promises he'd made to them (which, poor man, he had not been able to fulfill because Coniglio had blocked all his plans). Now he was apparently desperate and distraught because both Eugenio and the radio operators had left him to take orders from this man Roberto! But because of my experience in Naples with some of Sorrentino's neurotic tendencies, he was one person I had no intention of seeing. I therefore promised Eugenio I would procure as large a sum of money as possible, to be given to Sorrentino on condition he get out of town, once and for all, and lie low; the same to apply to his recruits.

Eugenio's morale seemed much improved by this decision and by our meeting in general. As I shook hands with him I had the feeling he would serve us and OSS as faithfully as anyone I knew.

Leaving the river I made a detour through the Ghetto, making sure once more that I wasn't being followed, then slipped back into the *portone* of the Palazzo Lovatelli.

Having mixed myself a good stiff drink and turned on Jerry's Front I thought to myself that if ever we got out of the mess we were in, all the big-shot colonels in the OSS would at least be forced to see the mistake they had made, how they had been bamboozled by a bunch of crooks who had prevented the OSS and the Allied armies from having a first-class intelligence service throughout Italy. But there was little consolation in the thought. Salerno, the Rapido, Anzio and Cassino were no longer recoverable mistakes.

The next morning at 6 A.M. there was a violent ringing of the doorbell. As this was the favorite hour of the SS for making calls I barricaded myself in the "hole," well armed, and began to put away

284

incriminating material, happy that there was little chance of their taking me alive.

A moment later I heard heavy footsteps in the corridor and a banging on the wall; but the banging was in the correct tattoo. Emerging, I found Lele and Franco, very much the worse for wear, but in good spirits. The Germans, or rather one measly German sergeant, had requisitioned Lele's car; but to compensate for this they had found and arranged for a system to get us across the lines through a series of guides high in the Apennines in the region of Sulmona.

When I asked what had happened to Baldo, who wasn't with them, they said that on a tour of the local fortifications (to keep his eye in practice) he had caught such a cold they had been obliged to bundle him up in bed in the local hotel till we all went back to cross the lines.

So the die was cast. All that afternoon and the next morning, while they worked on collecting the necessary equipment for a two-day hike across the snowy Apennines, I wrote out voluminous instructions to Alberto, Eugenio and Ottorino for the continuance of the service in our absence.

There was still no word from the two saboteurs, and the boys were now convinced they had been agents of Coniglio all along and pulled a double cross on me. I didn't want to believe it, but there was no telling, with such people, when one's instincts were right, or worse still, when, though right, circumstances could make them change their minds under the threat of outside pressure.

As a final precautionary measure it had been decided that we all see our respective females so as to give them some plausible story to cover our imminent absence; also, no doubt, because we wanted to.

Franco arrived in the new police car he had obtained from the Open City—the one in which we were to leave for the Apennines the following day—to take me up to Baldo's for my appointment with L. I still found it odd to drive through the streets of Rome in an official car, with semiofficial papers in my pocket and think of the surprise it would give the Germans, who kept passing us and looking at us as if we were representatives of law and order, were they to know who we really were.

L. arrived—completely feminine—wearing red Capri sandals, big dark tortoise-shell sunglasses, and smelling of fresh gardenias. Later in the evening she wanted me to go to a curfew party with her at Emanuele's, but I didn't like the idea of staying out all night with all that was ahead of us the following day, and figured that if Emanuele didn't find some way of landing himself, and all of us, in jail, there was really no sense to the police. Close to eight o'clock I said goodbye to her and waited for Franco to drive me back to what had come to feel like home—the Palazzo Lovatelli. And a good thing too! I found notes from Alberto, Eugenio, and—at long last—from Mario the saboteur; the latter as follows:

As per your orders I have delivered Siria material to Eugenio. I am now ready to leave to tie up the rest of the network: Florence, Viareggio, Milan. I propose to tie Florence in immediately in order to tell the base to call Siria. In Genova there is Stimolo, a close element of Coniglio's [three words illegible]. Enrico Sorrentino requests an interview with you. It would be opportune to concede it, as Sorrentino can do much in the field of information. I am keeping at your disposal all the work done by Sorrentino in the last four months as well as a report of his against Coniglio. Via Eugenio I will send you tomorrow a typewritten report on everything that has happened in these last four months, with particular emphasis on the most recent events. Camillo has spoken to Aldo, the man who drove you to Piazza di Spagna [my first morning in Rome]. Aldo is prepared to pass under your orders. Camillo will take care of details of travel. I await your orders. Your obedient, Mario.

P.S. For Florence, Viareggio, Milan let me have a password so that in future they may obey whosoever uses it.

So! Far from defecting, Mario had been working hard for our cause. Eugenio's letter confirmed the news.

The whole network now looked as if at last it might function smoothly. It was tantalizing not to be able to stay and make it buzz, but for everyone's security, it was time Franco, Lele and Baldo got to the Allied side; and, if the truth be known, I was by now looking forward like a schoolboy to being back in the mess at Caserta, among my own people, at least for a few days' break.

Ottorino, Alberto and Eugenio should be able to manage in our absence, and I had as much info in my head as they could file in thirty days.

To cinch the problem Franco brought news from Ottorino to the effect that the Germans were now looking specifically for the four key men who were working for the "American major." What's more, though they did not have all the names, the SD had pretty good physical descriptions of the whole quintet, and was concentrating its efforts on finding this basic link in the chain of our organization. It was time, *definitely*, to move.

30 A TRIP INTO THE MOUNTAINS

ALL DURING MY LAST AFTERNOON, while getting food and clothing for the trip, while carefully wrapping half a million lire worth of one-thousand-lira notes in an old newspaper parcel, while seeing to the countless last minute details of the information service, I kept thinking of what it would be like to be free again, of what I would say to the boys at the base, of what they would say to me. I thought of the expressions on their faces when I turned up, after so long; of all the various bennies; and of my friends. I pictured talking to the first Field Security character who would pick us up, the interrogation at the first CP, the ride to Naples or Bari, the gaiety of Lele, Baldo and Franco, a weekend even, in Capri, with M.T. and martinis in Eddie Bismarck's sunken bathtub.

But when it came time to leave the apartment in the Palazzo Lovatelli I felt sorry to abandon the familiar atmosphere, and more especially the good work that might still be done in it. But I knew it was essential that I reach the base to set the whole new machinery in action, as well as clear up the mess so that operations might be smoother in the future. And if all went well we might return to Rome in time to play a first-rate part in the eventual Allied offensive.

For the road I made a couple of good martinis, then we clogged downstairs in our heavy mountain boots. The doorman watched us curiously as we crowded into the four-door Fiat parked in the courtyard; then, as we pulled out into the piazzetta, doffed his hat, making me wonder when, if ever, I would see him again.

Unfortunately we could not leave town immediately, as we had to pick up a small bearded partisan from Aquila who was to be our guide (in his own small Fiat) on this first lap of our journey, and even when this was accomplished, we still had to pick up Lele at Baldo's house, where he had gone to wait for us after establishing the final contact with Alberto at the Polyclinic Hospital.

Lele appeared through the back window of Baldo's apartment, bashfully smiling, and it was apparent that Alberto had not been his very last contact!

"Afraid you might not get another chance?" said Franco, with a touch of envy.

Eventually, after one last stop for the collection of six bottles of brandy and two huge bars of black-market chocolate which, though heavy and expensive—about fifteen dollars a pound—we trusted would carry us across the mountains, we finally managed to set off toward Via Salaria in the early evening light.

I was a little apprehensive about passing the control point, never having recovered from my fear of roadblocks, but when both Germans and Italians saw the police plates on the Fiat they saluted and rushed us through with deference.

Once on the main road, after all those suffocating months, I felt more exhilarated than frightened, buoyed up by a sort of confidence in the small bearded partisan who was now behind us in his Topolino.

Skirting the railroad tracks—so often mentioned in our dispatches —I noted what an effective job of interdiction the air force had been doing: there was not a hundred yards of rail without a break for at least the first thirty kilometers, and even the twisted upturned shells of coaches were a pleasant sight.

A few German vehicles were on the road, traveling in both directions, but it was too early for them to be out in numbers, as they preferred the cover of night.

Turning off the road to Rieti we began to climb into the Abruzzi; the air, full of the smells and noises of a quiet spring night in the Italian countryside, evoked twenty years of holidays in Italy, to be capped by the sensation of stopping for a picnic.

At what should have been the halfway mark we pulled up along the roadside and set to eating hard-boiled eggs washed down with brandy, chatting with the bearded partisan about conditions in his territory.

Back in the car it amused me to take the wheel, press down the accelerator, hug the twisting road, as much to avoid the tedium of sitting idly as to be able to say, some day, that I had driven an army vehicle, in an official capacity, on both sides of the fighting lines. It was pleasant too to feel a car respond to my directions along the hazardous mountain road after so many months of enforced intellectual rather than physical action.

It was after midnight before the gray stone buildings of Aquila loomed up around us and we approached the county hospital where

Mario, Primo and I were to spend the night disguised as suffering inmates. But just as we pulled up in the courtyard a sidecar with two German policemen of the Feldgendarmerie drove up and parked beside us. At first I thought they had been following us, but they were delivering a woman to the emergency ward. Chatting with them about the weather and the latest army communiqué I wondered what excuse I could produce for our being in the hospital yard at almost one in the morning.

Then the doctor who was to provide us with beds came out and whispered that it was no longer safe in the hospital, that a detachment of SS had arrived in town that very day and were making specific investigations of all the hospital patients! As an alternative he suggested he drive us five miles higher into the mountains to a hamlet where he and his wife had moved when their own house had been bombed out by an Allied raid.

Luckily the Feldgendarmerie was called off on some other assignment, and Mario, Primo and I were able to squeeze into the doctor's Topolino, bid the others good night, and disappear once more into the darkness.

I was not at all pleased with the change in plans, or the thought that the SS were in town, and my fears were compounded—as we wound up a steep mountain lane—by the sight of a large truck just ahead, full of men in uniform. As we moved closer I saw that they were black-helmeted, heavily-armed Fascist militiamen.

There was no chance of turning back; it would be a clear indication of guilt.

The doctor said they were probably after deserters and Allied PWs hiding on the plateau above the village; so we accelerated, passing the truck, and, after much changing of gears and hairpin bends, reached a small hamlet perched atop a hill surrounded by peaks, with snow-caps in the distance.

The doctor was quartered in the stone schoolhouse, above the first-floor classrooms, and I had the distinct sensation of being a new boy at the beginning of winter term as I plodded up the dismal concrete steps.

Although it was almost 2 A.M. the table in the all-purpose room which served for living and dining was neatly laid for supper. Two

290

housemaids nodded politely, then scurried to douse the lights as they heard the truck whining up the mountain road.

With the doctor's wife we all stood by the blacked-out windows peering nervously at the Fascists. Twice they had come before, the doctor whispered, both times spending most of the night shooting in the barren hills, and most of the following day looting in the even more barren village.

Apprehensive lest they intended to search the house, we watched the truck draw abreast, slow down, grate its gears and slowly lumber on toward the steep central lane of the village.

As the small red tail light disappeared over the crest I had a twinge of regret that there was nothing we could do for the poor "rebels" and PWs who were hiding on the plateau at the top of the rough mountain track.

Early in the morning the doctor woke us to take Mario to the hospital for the final preparations for our journey. According to plan we were to leave that afternoon, be taken by a partisan as far as Sulmona —the largest town near the British Eighth Army front—where we would be put in touch with a mountaineering guide who was to escort us, the following dawn, on our rugged climb above the snowline to circumvent the fighting lines.

Left to ourselves, Primo and I breakfasted on fresh mountain milk and passable coffee, then sat around with the doctor's wife. To avoid her well-meaning but to us nerve-wracking small talk, I began to play on the phonograph, of all things, Bach's "Passion According to St. Matthew"! Strange music, powerful and somber, but crystalline like the mountain air and landscape all around us.

At length we had lunch—a nourishing and pleasant affair—throughout which our hostess entertained us with tales of the Allied PWs, mostly British, who roamed the area, of how they often came to the house for food or assistance, and of how, through that extraordinary machine, the political grapevine, they had learned that the doctor, though a city man, could be trusted and relied upon for help. For months, it seemed, the peasants and mountaineers had shared their almost nonexistent supplies with bedraggled British PWs, nursing them against all comers, often, sadly, at the cost of their own and their families' lives.

Gradually the PWs had come to rely on the doctor to climb up to their mountain hideouts when they needed medical attention, or to handle the more sensitive partisan operations. One PW, for instance, had escaped from a German train as it stopped in the Aquila station during a bombardment, thrown himself into a nearby stream to quench the flames that enveloped him, and there passed out, only to be brought to the hospital by a peasant, where he had been successfully kept until cured.

Suddenly there was a knock on the dining-room door. As in the case of Hauptmann Priebke, sensing I would be more in control of myself (and the situation) were I to handle it directly, I approached the door. Two silent men in peasant clothes stood before me. As rapidly as possible I tried to remember whom I was impersonating and attempted to act accordingly. Then one of them approached and whispered "Pane" in an even more nervous and apologetic voice than mine.

They were British prisoners.

I would have liked to burst into laughter, joke with them about the situation; instead I silently and controlledly waited for the hostess to usher them in, pour them a glass of wine and order the maid to prepare parcels of bread and meat.

Sitting on the edge of their chairs the two prisoners sipped their wine while I went to fetch them each two packs of cigarettes. I would have liked to give them the more cheering succor of a bottle of brandy, but forced myself not to, for fear that instead of saving it against cold and sickness, they polish it off in good Tommy fashion and start gaily shooting up the village.

Naturally I did not let on that I spoke English; so we chatted with them in pidgin "Eyety."

One of them turned out to be the prisoner who had escaped from the burning train. They were quiet and polite, occasionally whispering to each other, in what sounded like north-country dialect, that it was time for them to go.

When they did, I went onto the landing with them and stuck a thousand-lira note into each one's hand. They did not want to accept it. But, as I could hardly explain it was with the compliments of General Donovan and Uncle Sam, I had to turn and close the door on them, consoling myself with the compensating memory of the gruff expressions on the features of the kindly but austere English country gents who had tipped me "ten bob" or a "quid" when I had been a boy.

After that, with the excuse that we would get little or no sleep that coming night, Primo and I retired to our room for a nap. As I dozed I dreamed of walking all night through the mountains, of avoiding German patrols, of the snow and steep jagged rocks, of the relief of being safely on the other side.

When we finally roused ourselves it was almost 7 P.M. There was no sign of the bearded partisan who was to have collected us at four. Over a cup of tea we tried to listen to more of our hostess' conversation while I noted what a machine this clandestine living had made of me, a machine that concentrated on the noise of the wind in the rafters, which it magnified into the purring of an engine, the bleating of a distant sheep, confused with the sound of a horn.

Then the doctor's car was really there. Issuing from its cramped interior, Mario told us that we would not be able to leave that night, as our guide had not turned up. The trip would have to be postponed till the following afternoon. It was a nasty disappointment, only to be consoled by our usual standby, the ubiquitous bottle of brandy.

The next day, with the excuse that we wanted to try out some new nails in our boots (three-cornered affairs especially designed to give one a grip on icy terrain), Primo and I went out to walk by ourselves through the muddy lanes of the village and over the rock-filled fields from which the poor peasants somehow managed to squeeze a straggly crop of wheat and vegetables.

Returning to the house we were beginning to wonder what had happened to Mario when a car appeared on the road that wound up to the village. Instead of Mario, Lele issued from it. I was extremely pleased to see him, if for no other reason than because I was beginning to tire of the "genteel" atmosphere, and both Baldo and Lele could be counted on to avoid being bored by recourse to almost any subterfuge. But Lele brought far from pleasant news.

Two days earlier the SS had gone to the village in the mountains from which we were to set off with our guide, arrested dozens of villagers, and using one of their more fiendish but effective methods of stopping clandestine mountain-crossing, blown up the houses of the guides with families and possessions inside.

It seemed to be our fate that every new method of communication we discovered turned to ashes in our hands.

Still, there was hope. The little partisan with the beard thought he might get us into a monastery ten miles from the lines, further to the east, so that night he and Mario set off in the dark to see if they could arrange it with the Brother Superior.

Again there was nothing for us to do but spend another night—and uncork another bottle of brandy. Our host and hostess were remarkably kind, and to cheer us up the doctor prepared a huge and very special omelette much like the inflated affair produced by Gennaro at Capri's Marina Grande.

The next day being Sunday (May 7), Lele and the doctor left later than usual to go down into Aquila and find out what was happening. The rest of us—so tenacious is the spirit of the bourgeois Sunday—sat around on the front "lawn" under a beach umbrella, protected from a despondent sun.

By the time Baldo appeared, stepping in a distinguished manner from the doctor's car, I could not have been happier to see him, though the news he brought was worse than Lele's. The town of Aquila, he informed us, had just been overrun by German and Italian SS, specially detailed to clear the area of partisans. That morning Mario had spotted a double agent in the hotel, working for the Germans, who knew both him and Franco as partisans and had previously tried to offer them information. Luckily he had not seen Mario, and they had all cleared out of the hotel at top speed. Thereupon they had discovered that the Fascist militia was busy investigating the presence in town of Lele and Franco. The only thing that had so far saved them was the general belief in town that Baldo (who could easily pass for an Englishman and who we were terrified might be suspected as such) was actually suspected of being a Nazi agent disguised as a British prisoner to try to catch the local patriots. The sudden arrival in town of the SS had merely confirmed this opinion. Already four different men had warned our little partisan with the beard, as well as the good doctor, for heaven's sake to stay away from Baldo!

From Baldo I then heard a description of how he and Lele and Franco had spent their time in Aquila waiting for our contacts to materialize. Having captivated the hall porter with several goblets of brandy (which no one in the area had even smelled for months) they succeeded in having their meals (and God knows what else) served to them in their room. Having scoured the local bookshops for readable material they had come up with nothing better than a treatise on the Italian merchant navy and a set, in two volumes, of *The Theory and Practice of Marriage* by an unknown Calabrian doctor. This last had an extraordinary formula for enhancing virility, the precept that early morning was the only proper time for love-making, and the first plausible explanation for the southern Italian's custom of accosting women from what is normally considered an unorthodox direction.

Mario then described his trip to the monastery, which had ended up with his being politely towed back to town by none other than a German army wrecking truck, since he had succeeded, in his attempt to reach the monastery, in busting a hole a foot wide in our poor bearded partisan's crankcase.

We could now no longer go toward the lines; nor were there, in any case, any guides to guide us. We could not stay where we were, yet we did not relish the prospect of returning to Rome.

Suddenly one of the children shouted that a German vehicle was coming up the hill. Grabbing my coat and the newspaper parcel containing the half million lire, I stood by the window eyeing the sleek camouflaged vehicle with one eye and the drainpipe just outside the kitchen window with the other, until the vehicle drew up outside the house and a chauffeur appeared from within it. The chauffeur, it developed, though he worked for the Germans, didn't much like them, and was, in fact, more interested in the fatter of the doctor's two maids, visiting her every Sunday, presumably at the expense of the greater German Reich!

After that we went out and sat on the grass under a cherry tree and held a council of war.

There was one last hope that the little partisan with the beard might find us a guide to take us to the forest by the Maiella Mountain where we might try to slip past the Nazi patrols and reach the Allied lines, but this hope was pretty forlorn.

Then there was the possibility of Lele's going to Florence to get in touch with an agent there, but the address was too risky without the collaboration of Mario the saboteur who had given it to us.

We could not all six go back to Rome in the one car, for obvious reasons of dimension.

It was therefore decided that Lele, Baldo and Primo return to Rome, by whatever transport they could find, to see if contact had been established with the base, and failing any, have Lele proceed to Florence, while Franco, Mario and I went north to Emanuele's uncle's house near Osimo to see what the chances might be of finding a boat to buy, or a suitable beach from which to reach an Allied craft.

All this agreed upon, we scheduled our various departures, then went back and killed the brandy.

31 AN EXCURSION TO THE SEASIDE

THE NEXT AFTERNOON, after a last nourishing lunch, Franco, Mario and I bid our hosts and their assorted neighbors farewell and prepared to set off on our northward journey. The parting scene, as we stood round the car shaking hands, remarking politely on the weather, might have been the end of any middle-class weekend. To spoil this effect and a certain amount of our cover, a small red object fell off the car and lay on the ground face upwards. As everyone was clearly to note, including the conservative servants, it was a partisan "major's" insignia, boldly emblazoned with the hammer and sickle. I had no idea to whom it belonged or where it had come from, but any attempt at denial or excuse would merely have compounded the trouble. With a forced laugh—as if someone had inadvertently broken wind—I recovered the insignia while Franco jumped into the car and started the engine.

Turning onto a macadamed surface we sped away from Aquila with a feeling of relief. The Italian countryside on a sunny afternoon in May, buttercups sprouting and the smell of grass still beautifully fresh, was indeed a pleasure. Franco and I were in the best of moods, laughing over the discovery of the partisan badge, for we were now heading straight into territory thickly infested by partisans and were hopeful that it might save us from the very likely possibility of being either summarily shot, or, worse, having our means of transport removed from under us.

Mario, who sat in the back seat, we teased by letting no single "*borghese*" suggestion of his flourish without informing him, in as florid a language as we could invent, what he might do with it.

As we traveled I divided my time between admiring the buttercups and making mental notes of the insignia of passing German vehicles. We noticed quite a lot of Feldgendarmerie, and the sight of them did not please us particularly. At intervals we stopped to take notes on where and how the air force had hit or missed a bridge, an embankment or some specific military objective.

With a twinge of regret I thought of the backlog of information we had collected in Rome and not yet been able to file. Even as recently as the night before, on his trip to the monastery, Mario had put together a very neat description of the new German line of fortifications in that area—having stopped at various points to inspect it!

Eventually, in the late afternoon, we reached the town of Spoleto nestling on its hilltop—under different circumstances a picturesque medieval and Renaissance haven. Now it reminded me of Cobbett's "wen"—not so much because it had attracted all the rottenness around it, but because all the good had disappeared from it into the mountains, or been shot—and also of an illustrated first edition of the memoirs of the Marquis de Sade, which its titular duke (and uncrowned King of Croatia!) had once brought to dinner and left at our house.

At the gates of the town we were told that the main hotel was full to overflowing with German and Italian SS, about to organize an anti-partisan campaign.

As fast as the little car would run we quit Spoleto and headed northward again. Soon we began to pass German signposts warning: *Achtung! Tiefflieger!* It would be ironic, I reflected, to be polished off by one of our own *Tiefflieger,* but it was getting late and we saw no Allied dive bombers or low-strafing planes.

Then the signs took on another tone: *Achtung! Bandengebiet!* (guerrilla territory) and "Keep one round in the chamber!" We were now in partisan territory, which unfortunately meant that the villages were filled with Fascists, SD, SS, and the Feldgendarmerie, busy rounding up partisans and preparing large-scale operations in the mountains.

Passing quite near Visso I thought with sadness of our poor partisans who had had their hands cut off in the public square and then been shot because of the man Captain A. had recruited; and I thought also, not without a little bitterness, of the rotund, happy-go-lucky, devil-may-care young Republican businessmen who sported themselves in the OSS enjoying the thought of sending packages of arms, money, food, etc., by parachute, but who didn't really care if they got there during this or the next moon, while all the time poor devils in the mountains slaved at building fires in the snow, waiting, hoping, night after night, till the whole village, the whole mountain, the whole countryside, knew what was about to happen, and by the time the parachutes *did* drift to earth, some "bulgar" had betrayed the operation, and the Fascists and the Germans would be waiting on the spot ready to kill and maim the partisans who were doing their best to aid the Allied cause.

Sooner or later, I reflected, the partisans would find it hard to reconcile the BBC's exhortations to all patriots to fight the Germans, to risk their lives, to sabotage roads and rails, to organize rebel bands, only to discover, when the Allies finally did arrive, that it was the selfsame rebels who were put in jail while the Allies cuddled those who up till twenty minutes earlier had sold themselves, body and soul, to the Germans and the Fascists!

At Nocera we had decided to stop and get a bite to eat, but when we reached the main square we found it was still too early in the evening, and that we had best push on a little further.

A mile or so beyond the town we found the road blocked by an upturned German truck that littered the entire passage. Two dozen German soldiers were standing round shouting random orders; it looked as if we would be there for the duration, till a German corporal, spotting our police tags, came up and offered to get us through immediately if we would give him a ride as far as the next big town.

Moving over, I made room for him, being instantly reminded as I did so of a year earlier to the day, when, on the ninth of May, we had liberated Tunis and I had had my first close-up whiff of the strange and particular odor exuded by the German soldier's gray-green uniform, especially when damp. Franco offered the corporal a cigarette and started subtly to interrogate him in his polished German; there was no need, however, to urge the corporal, who seized on the opportunity to tell us two sad tales. Having spent two winters on the Russian front he had succeeded in getting himself transferred to *"Das Land wo die Zitronen blühen"* only to discover the winters in the Abruzzo were worse than Russia! And having selected the safest spot in Germany to place his family, a sparsely populated region where there were no industrial or military targets, he had now discovered it to be the area selected by the Luftwaffe, because of its uninhabited stretches, into which to lure or force heavy Allied bombers to engage them in combat and not risk destroying whole city blocks when the four-motored planes would crash, often with a large complement of bombs.

299

"They make a nasty hole," said the corporal pathetically, finally licking and lighting the cigarette that Franco had offered him.

Speeding through the evening light, looking out at the pleasant Masaccio landscape, I wondered about the efficacy of all those Psychological Warfare Section reports on the morale of the German soldier, till I was relieved of this tedious pastime by the appearance in the gloom of the town of Gualdo Tadino. There we deposited the corporal, obsequiously thankful, and Franco went off to look for rooms.

As might have been expected, there were none to be had in the main hotel, but with the aid of two packs of cigarettes Franco induced the local baker to produce for us two rooms in a *dépendance* as well as a cowbarn for the car.

Clogging across the cobbled piazza in our heavy shoes, with me clutching the half-million lire in its dirty newsprint to my bosom, we made a solemn entrance into the hotel restaurant in search of an evening meal.

"Guess who's in town?" whispered Franco as we urged the restaurant keeper to give us steak and a double ration of wine.

"Don't tell us," said Mario.

"That's right," said Franco.

Whereupon we were ushered upstairs to the special dining room reserved for the German "town major"—a captain in this case—who sat, surrounded by his stooges, both German and Italian, at one long table.

Selecting for ourselves a smaller and more private table at the other end of the room I embarked upon a series of shaggy dog stories freely translated from the English, so as to give the impression that we were a trio of carefree Fascists.

When the restaurateur's daughter arrived with a quarter of a liter apiece of good red wine, the totality of our ration, Franco went to work on her with a fetching smile and managed to get her to augment it by a half-liter dividend.

The food was good, but we dared not dawdle. The poor baker, terrified by all the police that had arrived in town (to clean up the rebels) had said that he would not show his face after curfew under any conditions. So after one last desperate attempt to wheedle an extra half-liter from the boss's daughter, we would have been ready to go, had it not been for a slightly embarrassing situation. Everyone who entered or left the upstairs private dining room invariably gave the Nazi captain at the end of the table a snappy Fascist salute. To me it seemed amusing to do so, just as it had been in the PAI. But for reasons of higher partisan ethics it stuck in the throats of Franco and Mario, who considered it undignified, and insisted that we walk past the captain's table and cut him dead, a performance, which, out of solidarity, I was unhappily obliged to emulate.

To me it was a foregone conclusion that the captain would take a poor view of this obvious insult and wish to discover the identity and purpose in Gualdo Tadino of three young men wearing what in that part of the country was the equivalent of a rebel's uniform: hobnailed boots and trench coats—not to mention a somewhat condescending attitude toward their German overlords. But Franco and Mario considered the gesture the least a free Italian could do for his country, and I was obliged to be content with bringing up the rear as rapidly as possible.

It took us some time to track down the baker, but when we did, all he would do was plead with us pitifully from the other side of a huge barn door that it was suicide to be out in the back lanes of the town after curfew when the Germans and Fascists shot on sight. But when Franco told him that people of our caliber were not in the habit of retiring with parched throats, he agreed to rouse the "waiter" of the *dépendance*, who appeared in a white coat with a liter of good wine, and three polished, tinkling glasses.

The *dépendance*, at the bottom of a cobbled lane, smelled strongly of animal urine, and appeared to be over a cowshed. But it was a refuge. God knows what purpose it had served before it was arbitrarily renamed; but our room, with its charcoal grate, had clearly been a kitchen.

Out of abnegation and comradeship for poor Mario (who complained he could not sleep in a bed with a fellow human being not of the opposite sex) and before he could discover that his single bed was in fact a coverted laundry basket, Franco and I had unceremoniously stretched out on the one double bed, each with a brimming glass of wine.

The next morning, looking from the window, we saw that we were perched on a hillside like the turret of a battlement. Chill wind blew through the valley, and distant clouds presaged rain. Deciding we should make as respectable an entry as possible when presenting our credentials to Emanuele's medieval uncle, we shaved meticulously in a communal bowl of ice water; then Franco, finding the toilet not up to his fastidious expectations, shocked us by proposing to make a special use of the third bureau drawer, convincing us only by his argument that the next incumbent of the room would almost certainly be, if not a German, at least an Italian SS.

Then a roadblock appeared and, instead of being waved through, we were stopped by a pair of Fascist militiamen who intended to scrutinize our papers. This looked bad, for either something unpleasant was happening in the area, or—and this was the worst of our doubts—they were looking for someone in a vehicle like ours, possibly ourselves! The discovery then ensued that the chassis number on the car did not coincide with the one on the sticker glued to the windshield. It was a tricky moment, and we began to suspect that Ottorino had made a mistake and stolen the wrong police vehicle, till Franco, rising to the occasion, barked out an order in such authoritarian tones that the militiamen were unbalanced, and promptly returned our carnet, waving us on.

Toward noon we found ourselves in the neighborhood of our destination. The country had changed considerably. The road, no longer macadam, was white and dusty, winding up and around a series of fertile green hillocks with villages perched on top that succeeded each other leisurely down to the sea. Then it struck me that if the count we were to visit lived in a decent house, as he presumably must, the chances were pretty certain it would be inhabited by Germans; I was about to offer Franco two-to-one odds on a thousand lire when he pulled up in front of the massive wrought-iron gates which closed off the park of the estate. Beneath the shady cedars a German unit was comfortably installed.

Franco being the only one of us presentably dressed, we sent him ahead, complete with coronetted visiting card—clearly the only means of admission to such an antiquated domain.

By this time we were no longer very hopeful of finding lodgings, a boat, or even any decent source of information, and when Franco came striding back, his eyes lowered, we could tell, even before he opened his mouth, that we were once more out of luck. Emanuele's count had gone to Bologna to attend—of all things at such a time—to his race horses; and his beautiful wife (the one Lele and Baldo had described so glowingly) would not even receive us—no doubt out of solid medieval respect for a jealous husband.

Our last hope now rested in a decrepit old gent who, thanks to Franco's uncle and his connections with the Knights of Malta, might be willing to receive us in his palace in the main town of Osimo about ten miles away.

Driving into the courtyard of the palace, or rather, hilltop fortress, surrounded by the town, we gathered from a scrutiny of innumerable coats of arms that the incumbent marquis must own the entire neighborhood, and figured that our chances of finding him a right sort of guy were likely to be slim. Certainly it would not be easy to go up to him and say: "I beg your pardon, sir, but do you happen to know where we can buy a boat to cross to the Allied side?"

When, eventually, he did receive us, one glance was enough to confirm our suspicions. Not only did he possess all the earmarks of a cantankerous and avaricious dotard, but was stone deaf to boot, which made the asking of almost any query, other than one about the weather, certain suicide.

Bowing our adieus, we headed for the local hostel and the consolation of a good unrationed meal, leaving the car, as a master stroke of cover and security, safely in the custody of the local Carabinieri police force. Who on earth would steal it there? And who but authentic representatives of law and order would be so bold as to park it there?

Walking into the Albergo Risorgimento I felt almost secure enough to eat our meal in the same room, if not at the same table, with the local German officers. But as we sat down at a military table the variety of spies and stooges that buzzed around this particular "town major"—a lieutenant—made me nervous by their mere inhuman exudation. There was a small crippled Italian, pretty certainly a pimp in civilian life (not that I am against pimps; it just depends which side they are on), who was fawning on a traveling-salesman-looking German lieutenant. More suspicious still was a tall shaven-headed, middle-aged German in tweeds whom the lieutenant jumped up to salute and who,

303

though possibly a senior Todt man, seemed very likely a dependent of Himmler.

The first part of the meal went very reasonably and we were just being restored by a carafe of good red wine and the unheard-of delicacy of real white bread and pasta, when I, spying a pretty girl across the room, inadvertently, or rather advertently, but foolishly, made eyes at her, only to discover that the German sergeant sitting next to her was eyeing me via a mirror I had not noticed, and doing so with evident disapproval. Rapidly, and most unchivalrously, I decided the girl didn't warrant my interest after all.

With lunch disposed of and while Franco and I checked with the manager to see about accommodations, Mario went off to see if there were any millers in town from whom we could buy a supply of flour.

There weren't; nor would there be any rooms till 5 P.M.; so we decided to take a drive to Ancona, twenty miles away, and survey the coast. Franco had a friend there, but as he was the most sought-after member of the local CNL, we figured it would be wiser not to try to find him without an exact address. Our main hope was in locating another friend of Franco's in a smaller town about ten miles up the coast, where we might establish a base of operations either to buy a boat, or have a PT come in for us if the boys had established contact with the base.

Ancona was something of a shambles, thanks to the air force; the station was almost unrecognizable. We noticed a few small craft in the harbor, flying the navy swastika, but it didn't look as if there were much in the way of maritime traffic.

It was pleasant to be near the sea again, even if it was the wrong side of the Adriatic (western and therefore sunless), and somewhat tantalizing to count the apparently abandoned pleasure sailboats. No one stopped us as we cruised up the coast road looking for a suitable place to launch a boat, but the water was very shallow and we realized it would be a hell of a job to try to land a rubber boat if the weather were at all rough.

The houses that lined the waterfront appeared entirely abandoned, like a summer resort in the middle of winter; and when we asked what seemed to be the only living inhabitant (who ran the local phone station) why the town was so deserted, he informed us that it had just been evacuated after the severest of Allied bombings. There were

304

bomb holes all right; but they didn't seem so bad. Our luck, however, was of the worst. As a result of the Allied raids, Franco's friend had left a few days earlier. What's more, his house would have been an ideal hideout pending the arrangements for a boat, situated, as it was, right on the waterfront! Now, without him, and in an empty village, we would be much too conspicuous to stay.

Sadly we turned the car and started back to reconnoiter the southern side of Ancona.

But Franco and Mario could not get out of their minds what an opportunity we had missed, and kept stopping every half mile to take another look at the beach. German vehicles kept passing, and I watched with growing anxiety as their occupants turned to stare at Franco and Mario who were unaffectedly gesticulating by the waves.

At last they gave up and we skirted Ancona to survey the terrain south of the port where the town sticks out into the Adriatic on a peninsular hill.

The main road ended and we found ourselves on a small country lane. I was beginning to wonder what explanation we could give for our presence, were anyone to ask, when, swinging round a corner, we ran straight into a patrol of Fascist militiamen with their ominous skull-and-crossbones insignia. They didn't seem at all convinced by Franco's explanation that we were simply going "thataway," but our police tags appeared authentic enough for them grudgingly to decide to let us proceed.

Then we started passing German sentinels and long barbed-wire fences and I began to feel more and more uncomfortable. Nor was my discomfort diminished by the sight of a car full of German officers in dark blue naval uniforms, followed, at irregular intervals, by the appearance of deep tunneling into the side of the hill that overlooked the sea from a height of several hundred yards. Reminded of a report we had filed some months earlier, it was suddenly clear to me what had happened. We had run smack into one of the most heavily fortified sea defenses on the Italian coast line. Nor, with the militiamen behind us, was there any means of retreat. Consoling ourselves with the thought that at least we were *behaving* like spies, we decided to pretend that that was what we had really wanted to do all along and proceeded to survey and note details of the vast fortified area.

Truthfully I thought that we were goners. Then, as suddenly as we had entered the area, we found ourselves back on the proper road. Ahead of us a small coastal village sparkled in the lowering sunlight, the beach this side of it, slightly wooded, an excellent spot for a date with a PT.

Turning inland we drove back to the hotel to see if the manager had succeeded in securing us a room, and if the hall porter had found us a source of black market flour.

Leaving Mario to cope with these details, Franco and I went up onto the battlements of the town, to what constituted its main piazza outside the gates of the castle. A small crowd had gathered and was standing by the railing overlooking the plain, scanning the apparently interminable rows of hillocks. Two Allied fighters were gliding gracefully in the evening sky. Suddenly they turned and dived. There was a rattle of cannon fire and a cloud of smoke from the curving road on the side of the opposite hill. They had got a German truck.

For several minutes we watched as they circled over the landscape occasionally diving on some poor prey. It looked like a pleasant sort of sport—especially with the lack of opposition—and we laughed to think that there, less than a quarter of a mile away, were two of *our* pilots, and that had they been there twenty minutes earlier they might have caught *us* and destroyed us without ever knowing or appreciating the irony of what they were doing.

Rejoining Mario we learned that we would have to wait another couple of hours before finding out about either the hotel room or the flour. Not wishing to parade around the town, tall (by Italian standards), and exotic-looking in our hobnailed boots, Franco and I decided to leave Mario in the car with a detective story while we sought shelter and camouflage in the local movie.

We felt a little foolish, walking in, in the middle of a war, to see a film about young women in prewar evening dresses and young men dashing about on skis, but, if nothing else, the atmosphere was a considerable improvement on the last time I had gone to the movies— the time I had thought Cervo's father was following me.

Franco's wisecracks about the Hungarian talent in the film were pleasantly shocking to the provincial audience, and I too would have enjoyed them had I not been worried by his accent. Brought up in France most of his life, Franco spoke Italian with a slightly foreign (or aristocratic) accent—depending on which way the listener chose to parse it—and on many occasions I had forcibly to interrupt and speak for him, despite the fact that *he* was Italian and I a foreigner.

At length the film came to a scratchy end, its sound track wheezing through the faulty amplifier, and we went out in search of Mario, only to discover I had lost the parcel with the half-million lire. Luckily it was still lying on the floor beneath my seat, and I managed to recover it, only to discover, as I came out, that Mario had disappeared, car and all.

Knowing Mario's punctiliousness I found this too a shock, but to avoid showing panic Franco and I decided to go into the hotel and see if we could buy some wine, preferably in bulk.

Crossing the hall I spotted a beautiful female in a clinging white summer dress. Franco, who had been feeling feverish up till then, revived almost instantly. While he ordered the wine I moved around to get a different angle on the apparition, only to spot the shaven-headed man in tweeds spying on me from behind a pile of dinner plates. He did not realize that I had him covered in a mirror, and I felt I had the situation reasonably in hand till two Fascist militiamen, armed to the nostrils, came in from different directions and began to stare at me with disconcerting intensity. As I could see no sign of Franco, and felt the sensation creeping over me that something was wrong, I headed for the men's room.

The toilet, such was the antiquity of the hotel, was on the third floor and in a very bad position to escape from. Nevertheless, I stolidly started up the stairs. Safely inside the malodorous closet, with the door well locked, I had the eerie and unpleasant sensation of seeing the handle being turned from outside by someone whose footsteps I had not heard. Holding my breath I peered out the window trying to decide whether to rely on the drainpipe or my phony documents. Settling for the latter, I slowly pushed open the door to find myself face to face with Franco! Behind him I could see the pretty girl coming up the stairs. Had he succeeded in so short a time, I wondered in awe? Looking straight at me the creature smiled a smile so ravishing I was on the point of addressing her when I noticed a German officer of field grade stalking behind her. Discreetly (and feeling like a cad) I pulled myself to one side and let them pass. To add his insult to my cowardice, just as he came abreast of me, the officer looked me straight in the eye and saluted curtly.

A moment later Franco joined me in the hall and we both advanced on Mario as he appeared through the main entrance, telling him in chorus that despite his excellent efforts at producing us a room we were leaving that night . . . in fact immediately.

Our insistence on leaving without even waiting to collect the flour he had gone to such trouble to procure infuriated Mario, and it wasn't till we were speeding along a country lane—thanks to twenty-five liters of black market gasoline also produced by Mario—that Franco and I regained enough of our composure to explain to Mario that we had left entirely on instinct. Poor Mario, being a Neapolitan, was obliged to accept this. In truth, as we were later to discover, our departure saved our skins.

Meanwhile we were left with a serious problem.

Our excuse to the maid, to Mario's parents, to the *portiere* at the Palazzo Lovatelli, to friendly officials in the Open City, to everyone in fact, had been that we were going north on a bona fide black market jaunt to obtain some badly needed flour and staples, and that if we succeeded we would be happy to cut them in. Now we could not healthily return empty-handed. Buying black market flour after sunset, when it is a capital offense to sell it even in daylight, did not prove to be an easy venture.

The first mill we stopped at, a friendly fat miller came out rubbing his hands, but his eyes betrayed horror when he saw the car. Though we tried for three-quarters of an hour to convince him we were harmless, the police plates had him paralyzed and he would not give up an ounce. We knew he had it; but the poor man, or so he explained, had been held up first by the Germans, then by the Fascist militia, then by the "rebels," and finally by a bunch of "honest" crooks, and wild rhinoceri would not get him to admit he had so much as a half-loaf worth of unbaked flour. We tried passing brandy bottles under his nose, but it had no effect. His five children began to scream, and it was only with the aid of a pack of cigarettes—the likes of which he had not seen in over six weeks—that we were able to get one loaf of bread with which to assuage our hunger later in the evening.

Only as we pulled away did his expression soften. "It breaks my heart," he said, "not to be able to help you boys, but I've been held up and cleaned out so many times I don't even trust myself any more. It's a hell of a world. God bless you!"

It was dark by then, and we wound on round the hillside wondering how many years it would take to restore law and order and some sort of reasonable economy to Italy.

The next village we came to we stopped and asked if there were any place to get a meal. It was close to the curfew hour; there was much shaking of heads, but finally someone directed us to the town's solitary one-room "hotel."

There we were greeted by a fat innkeeper's wife and the information that she had nothing for us to eat, that no one had spent the night in the "hotel" for several years, but that, by the laws of hospitality, she would be glad to give us her children's room if we insisted on spending the night. As for food, if we hurried, there were three general stores in the village, though they seldom had anything to sell.

While Franco and Mario got the local Carabinieri to put the car up in their barracks, I managed to collect nine eggs, a small piece of lard, and a handsome pinch of salt. With the miller's bread, and a bottle of wine, we would have a meal.

Back at the "hotel" Franco informed me that the Carabinieri were very upset by our arrival—not, however, for the usual reasons. The village, it appeared, was in the middle of partisan territory and the Carabinieri had already been disarmed three times during night raids by the "rebels." They did not like the idea of harboring such an obvious target as a functioning police car, but, succumbing to Franco's authoritative manner and his Open City title they finally agreed, warning him, however, to stay indoors from the very first to the very last minute of the curfew as it was their custom to shoot at any shadow without challenge, it being mathematically certain that no villager would venture out of his door after 9 P.M. and that any shadow could only be a "rebel."

Seated in the family dining room we consumed our nine-egg omelette, washed down with several bottles of good local wine, both red and white, while the innkeeper, a thin, frail man with a beard and delicate eyes, ventured in and sat beside us. It didn't take more than a few minutes' random conversation to sense that he was more in sympathy with the "rebels" than the Fascists, and Franco, through many subtleties of conversation, managed to convey the idea that we too weren't really as terrible as we looked or pretended. Finally, exhausted by the day's adventures, we found ourselves in the children's immaculate room, all three stretched out in a gargantuan double bed between rough homespun country sheets.

310

32 BACK IN THE BREACH— LIKE IT OR NOT

SUNLIGHT, STREAMING IN THROUGH THE STARCHED CURTAINS, woke us in the morning.

No rebels had raided.

We breakfasted on vermouth and sweet cookies, recovered our car from the Carabinieri, who were very happy to wave us goodbye, and set off in search of victuals before undertaking the drive back to Rome.

On this search we had expected to spend an hour, at the most a couple.

By the time we got back to the main road it was midafternoon. Both the car and ourselves were unrecognizable, and we were so sick of the sight of food we were close to retching. It had taken wheedling and threats, sometimes almost love-making, and many bribes; but after scouring the countryside, narrowly escaping being arrested, lynched or run out of town on a rail, we had got what we wanted. Every available nook in the car was crammed with a corpse—chickens, ducks, pigeons, rabbits—interspersed with cheeses, bacons, two sacks, weighing a quintal apiece, of flour and of cornmeal, and, in every unused space the size of an egg—an egg. Strapped to the roof was a two-hundred-pound bleeding, throat-cut, uncleaned pig, stuffed into a sack padded with straw.

This last item almost caused a riot. Bought live, against all the rules and regulations, we had taken it off to a deserted spot to be slaughtered.

Now, several hours later, blood still dripping from the back of the Fiat, the brute's screams reverberating in my overheated brain, our dusty, perspiring bodies squeezed into the foul, gamy-smelling interior of the Fiat, we were once more on the road to Rome, a somber circle of peasants waving halfheartedly in the background.

Whoever chose to stop us, whether German, Fascist or partisan, would certainly remove the pig. But would they, we wondered, let us go, as a sort of payment for the pig, or put us in jail for having killed it!

Our considered estimate of the possible variants was that the Ger-

311

mans might take the pig and dispatch us on our way, the Fascists, staggered by such conspicuous black-marketing would consider us Fascists of a higher order and bow us on, but the partisans, having taken the pig, the entire contents of the car, the car itself, and the shorts off our bottoms, would then shoot us as impostors. Who, they could justifiably claim, had ever heard of such a type of anti-Fascist!

The first patrol that stopped us was made up of Fascists. Our prognostications came close to being true: they were so busy shooting at the car ahead of us, which had not stopped for their signal, and shouting at us that it was a damned "Vatican" vehicle, they did not bother to notice our load. Assuring them that as police officers of the Open City we would immediately overtake and arrest the culprits, we were allowed to speed on our way, though "speeding" is hardly the appropriate word.

Italian cars suffer easily from overloading; ours was no exception. At each corner the centrifugal effect of the animal on the roof came close to landing us upside down in the ditch.

Just outside Spoleto we were again flagged to a stop by the muzzle of a Fascist militiaman's tommy gun. As we swayed to a standstill in a cloud of dust, the militiaman wrinkled his nose in disgust. The pig, not having been cleaned, and it being the middle of May, was beginning to exude an unpleasant odor of carrion. Luckily, just as the militiaman prodded him, a German truck came up behind, honking frenetically, and there was nothing for the militiaman to do, in obedience to his Nordic masters, but to wave us on.

Staggering ahead, I began to wonder what would happen at the roadblock outside Rome, it being strictly forbidden to take meat into the city.

The mere thought of Rome was depressing; and the only way I could think of cheering the atmosphere was to expound on my hunch that a big attack would be launched by the Allies between the fifth and fifteenth of May and that it might have been our saving that we had not been able to attempt a suicidal crossing of the lines.

This, they knew, as I did, was nothing but an effort on my part to keep up morale. We were all perfectly aware that our chances of survival in Rome for more than a few days would be extremely thin. If Eugenio had made contact, our best hope would be to make the earliest possible date for a PT boat or submarine to fetch us out. If, on the other hand, there was still no contact, Franco insisted our only alternative would be to go to Turin and take a crack at crossing the Alps into Switzerland. We had enough gold so as not to be interned, and, once there, could arrange for the others to follow.

By the time we got to Terni it was almost dark, and we were pretty well out of gas. When we asked a militiaman how we could get some, he informed us there was none to be had in the town except in the German army depot, for which application had to be made directly to the German command. This, for obvious reasons, we did not wish to do, except as a last resort, deciding instead to make use of our usual method of simply asking people at random till someone came up with an alternate answer. Sure enough, in about fifteen minutes we had collected thirty liters—by the simple expedient of paying three dollars a gallon for it, and the even simpler expedient of stealing some from a German garage.

We also decided that instead of going through the ordeal of eating in a German mess we would open a can of sardines and drink a swig of brandy; it was getting so late we would otherwise not reach Rome till early in the morning.

By the time we left Terni it was already dark and German traffic, taking advantage of the obscurity to avoid Allied strafing, was getting pretty heavy. As the road began to climb across the piedmont of the Apennines we began to be held up more and more by long convoys of trucks moving at a snail's pace up the winding road. It was slow and sometimes tense progress, for we were obliged to dart ahead of or in between trucks, lights blacked out (the Allies had started interdicting by night as well as by day), and it was some hours before we eventually came out into the plain and headed for the last fifteen-mile stretch into Rome. Then it happened! A flat! Changing the tire was neither easy nor pleasant, but our worst fear was that now that we had no spare some fiend of a partisan would catch us with *our own* three-cornered nails! In which case we would be immobilized till the following day, the pig would start to disintegrate, and so would we. For one thing, we would never be able to pass a roadblock by daylight, let alone circulate in Rome with such a dripping cornucopia of supplies. But, obstinately, having gotten them, the one thought none of us would express was the possibility of jettisoning them.

Then the reddish light of the police post came into sight and a

German and a Fascist guard, one from each side, came up to the car. Would they squabble, like Fafner and Farsolt, over the loot, or split it amicably?

But one look at the Open City police tags on the windshield was enough for them and they motioned us on without a word, leaving us with the unspoken thought that truly there must have been some fancy black marketing going on in the higher echelons of the Roman police, carried in official vehicles!

At any rate we were back in Rome, speeding down the Corso, and I was on the point of reviewing in my mind the horrors of the journey when, at the intersection of the Tritone and Piazza Colonna, we ran straight into a roadblock. This time, despite the police tags, we were peremptorily ordered to produce our documents, while several ugly-looking policemen circled the car. Again I felt it was the end, and was preparing to meet it when some angel or genie came to the rescue in the form of a small collision across the piazza and the police, attracted by this newer form of police bait, ordered us on.

My last fears were now that the *portone* would be double-bolted and that we would have to wake the *portiere* with a sort of Macbethian scene—"here you may roast your goose!"—and with him half the neighborhood, or, worse still, that we would get another flat tire before reaching home.

From the depths of Mussolini's empty square the great white sepulcher of the Unknown Soldier rose before us and we darted from it with the gait, or so it seemed to me, of a surfeited, pregnant rat into the "Street of the Shadowy Shops." By the time we reached our own piazzetta and prepared to make a stealthy entrance it was 1 A.M.

The *portone* was *not* double-bolted, for which we all whispered a rapid prayer, but as Franco parked the car beneath the loggia in the courtyard and I climbed out stiffly, I saw, and pointed out to Mario, that the left front tire was absolutely flat!

The worst, however, was ahead of us. When we finally managed to rouse poor Mario's wife and convince her to let us in, she greeted us, sleepy-eyed and in a wan and frightened voice, with the news that the house was no longer safe, that Baldo had made a hectic appearance a few hours earlier to clear out everything incriminating. We were to phone him the minute we arrived, no matter how late, because a whole lot of our men had been caught while we were away.

314

And where could we go, so late after the curfew, with two flat tires! Too worn out and disconsolate to conjure up any idea, and aware that Baldo could explain nothing over the phone, we decided to stay where we were. But before we could even do this we were obliged to make several trips, padding back and forth to the courtyard in our stocking feet (so as not to rouse the Rossi sisters and any German lover who might be with them), in order to bring up the loot, which had suddenly lost its glamor, dragging the pig up the marble stairs with a drip-drip of blood behind it.

At last, worn out and frightened, while Mario and his wife retired to their connubial bed, Franco and I fell asleep by the fireplace.

At dawn, even before the comfort of a cup of tea, I was obliged to drive bits of heavy wire through the pig's trotters, string it up to a beam in the kitchen, and, by the pale light of dawn, split it down the middle, thereafter proceeding with one of the most nauseating ordeals I have ever had to indulge in. Never would I have imagined a brute so difficult to clean! Nor ever have I smelled such a stench! Now I was convinced our hideout would be blown, not because of any lack of security, but by the smell of carrion for blocks around. Nor would the bloodstains on the staircase—in an even more luridly Macbethian manner—admit of being cleansed!

Eventually Lele and Baldo turned up and gave us the bad news in detail. The very morning after we had left, Eugenio—poor stalwart Eugenio who had tried so hard and done so well—had been caught and taken to Via Tasso. The thought of him there, locked up in a cell awaiting torture, was all we needed. Nor was the manner of his taking out of line with everything that had happened recently. Eugenio, beseeched by Sorrentino for a meeting (just as I had been the previous week), had finally agreed to see him and give him enough money to leave town. Promptly and at the correct time and place, Sorrentino had appeared—followed by plain-clothes agents of the SS. For some time, it now developed, the SD had been using Sorrentino to walk around the streets as bait with which to catch us. How close, I thought with a shudder, had I come myself to falling for the trap? Nor was this all the bad news.

When Eugenio had failed to turn up at his later appointments with the Siria and Iris radio operators, instead of clearing all the stuff out of Eugenio's house, and saving the radio and crystals (we had fought

315

so hard to get), they had done nothing. Two days later, and just one day too late, Alberto had decided to send his wife and another man to the flat to see if they could save the equipment, only to walk into a second trap. The SS were waiting for them, and now they too were at Via Tasso.

Though none of the agents knew our real names, or even our real "false" names and addresses, it was going to be unhealthy to hang around the city, and somewhat pointless if there were no more useful work we could do without either operators, plans or crystals.

The more we thought about it the more Franco and I decided that Switzerland was our only hope, unless, of course, we could get in touch with some other agent in some other city and through him get into contact with the base.

Then Mario arrived and produced another blow.

He had just come from seeing our expert on travel orders and permits for the car, and brought the information that during our absence the SS had got wind of a police car such as ours being used by what they presumed to be Badoglio officers, and had sent out an alarm throughout the country to have it traced. With a twitch we thought of how we had been riding around while the SS were sending signals to have just such a car as ours picked up. Reluctantly we turned in the police plates.

There was still a chance we might get civilian permits for the car, but how then would we be able to negotiate the roadblocks and patrols! It looked as if we were once more trapped, and the prospect was bleak and depressing.

The date: May 12.

After lunch, sitting alone with Mario, while his wife took care of the baby, I poured myself a glass of wine and turned on the radio to keep my mind from the horrors that beset us. As if in a dream I heard the announcement: "Forces of the Eighth and Fifth Armies under General Alexander have launched an offensive along the entire southern front. The strongest fighting is taking place between the Apennines and the Tyrrhenian sea. . . ."

Jumping up, I danced around with Mario, who, until I explained, couldn't understand what had hit me. I felt like running out into the streets to shout the news, but reflecting on it a little more calmly realized that it would not necessarily mean instant relief for us personally. In all probability the most nerve-racking days (if not weeks), would still be ahead, during which we would have to hold out against being captured while the Allies battled toward Rome. Yet this realization was tempered by the enormous boost to our morale of at last having an objective, having something concrete to work for. Somehow, if it meant going up in smoke, I must get into contact with the base and resume what could now be a vital service to the Allies.

But the more I studied the problem the more I saw that the only immediate means of getting into contact would be for me to go on the air with the remains of the Vittoria and Trieste crystals and operate the radio myself, lousy as was my touch.

As a place to transmit, and then quickly disappear, I chose the benny's top-floor apartment on Viale Aventino, a block from the monstrous unfinished mausoleum known as the Ministry for Africa (many years later to become the seat of FAO). Going there, setting up the antenna, tapping out the call letters on a frequency known to the Germans, listening for the base and not hearing them answer, was as frightening and frustrating an undertaking as I had yet attempted. But it had to be done.

Faithfully, and true to his own peculiar form, the benny stood waiting for me in the doorway to the building and took me straight to his top-floor apartment. This turned out to be typical of the area: cold boxlike rooms with flowered wall paper, shiny sideboard and aspidistra. The benny insisted on standing at attention and calling me "Commandante," a title which sounded odd in my ears, since I hadn't been thus referred to for so many months. But the benny seemed so very pleased to see me and have me there that it made up for the rigors of the sad performance.

The next day the benny reported through channels that, by pure chance, he had run into Oliviero, the second Vittoria operator who had been with Enzo up till a minute before his capture, but of whom we had heard nothing since. The immediate question in both our minds was whether he had actually escaped and was in hiding, or whether he was, in effect, being used by the Germans (like Sorrentino) to track us down. With a stroke of good sense the benny pretended that he too had been abandoned after the arrest of Cervo and did not know what had happened to the rest of us, insinuating that I (Pietro) had left town. As a result of this information I told the benny to keep an eye on Oliviero and slowly sound him out. If he were to turn out to be in good faith we might be able to use him as an operator.

In the meantime, back at Palazzo Lovatelli I stayed glued to the radio, listening to all the belligerent's communiqués, following the progress of the Allied offensive, or, when I could no longer stand the strain, trying to lose myself in such incongruous reading as *Tortilla Flat, Xmas Holiday, Kitty Foyle* and other light books kindly provided me by Franco's cousins, the sisters Malfatti.

The days passed, the offensive progressed but slowly, our intelligence mounted, but the base gave no signs of life.

Then, on May 19, just one week after Alexander's stirring communiqué, Mario came in and told me that the Germans had arrested the colonel in command of the PAI. After his behavior at the time of the arrest of the PAI lieutenant, we had no idea now if he could keep silent, or blurt out everything he knew, especially about Franco.

After lunch, bathed and shaved, and reasonably confident that the SS would almost certainly arrive during the course of the afternoon, Franco and I went over to Via San Teodoro, complete with a bottle of Old Tom gin, to visit his cousins and distract ourselves from the atmosphere of suspense and impending doom.

Sneaking down the sunny lanes that skirt the Capitoline Hill, shading my eyes against the resplendent marble in the Forum, I managed to slip into the Via dei Foraggi doorway without being spotted by any of the fifty neighbors who might have recognized me—or so, at least, I hoped.

It was in any case a relief to find myself back in the cool, tiled, well-appointed rooms I had known so well for so many years.

The girls were gay, chatted easily in a mixture of English, French, German and Italian, and we danced and made martinis. Their brother, a young man in his late teens (who had the good fortune through his father to be enrolled and dressed as a soldier of the Sovereign Military Order of the Knights of Malta) was there, and I asked him, still to maintain my cover as an escaped PW, whether he would consider trading, there and then, his private's uniform for the promise of a major's uniform in the U. S. Army after the liberation; but he laughed

318

and shook his head, pointing out that in both situations he would be getting the dirty end of the stick.

Occasionally I would have to skip quickly into the next room, as Santino, our old butler, brought in canapés, fresh ice or drinks. When the gin had gone we switched to brandy, and so managed to forget about the war, the SS and all our complicated problems, until, as I was dancing with Gloria, the elder of the sisters, in walked Santino. The expression on his face was truly that of a man seeing a ghost. As everyone in the room stood frozen, a smile slowly spread across his face. Taking him out into the hall I shook his hand.

"You're a prisoner, no?" he asked. Then, with a frown, realizing how many people in the neighborhood might have seen me: "You must be very careful!"

I smiled and reassured him, told him all was well, but for heaven's sake not to mention it to the Barone, who should not be bothered with such a silly situation.

This little episode successfully negotiated, I was informed by the others that there was to be a party that night at Emanuele's apartment on Via Paisiello, and that my presence was earnestly requested, if for no other reason than because Lele had not been able to forswear any longer letting his girl Anna Maria know that he was back in town, and this news was bound to be conveyed to L.

I don't know what gave me the nerve to go—or perhaps it was that I no longer had the nerve to sit around the Palazzo Lovatelli waiting for the SS or the base to pay attention to me—but I undertook to walk right up the middle of town, right up the Tritone, up Capolecase, through the park, and to Emanuele's place in the late afternoon when all of Rome was on the streets taking its constitutional before the curfew, and anyone in the world could have seen me. The mixture of gin and brandy, I supposed, helped a bit.

In any case I arrived, tired and hot, to find the party in progress. Making myself a long cool drink I took off my coat and was about to search for L.'s favorite record when she appeared in the door. The effect on her was amusing to watch. As the sun went down we went out onto the terrace, propped ourselves against the balustrade and gazed up at the slowly appearing stars in the warm spring night, music pulsing in the distance, the tinkle of ice in our glasses.

319

The atmosphere was so dense and peaceful it seemed impossible to believe we weren't still in the thirties and that the war had never existed.

People came out in relays bringing platters of spaghetti and more and more wine, till we finally climbed up the emergency ladder onto the roof, almost, it seemed, within reach of the stars, and found refuge in the seclusion of the water tower.

At odd intervals during the night I found myself downstairs dancing with one or the other of the four or five women who were left and at one point I remembered a tile and pillow fight during which a cantankerous neighbor complained to the police; but nothing came of it. Another part of the night I spent arguing with a Fascist militia-man who arrived as the escort to some girl who joined us after the curfew and who kept boasting in a hoarse whisper that he worked for the German Secret Service, while I, for the sake of security, and the general amusement of those in the know, attacked him violently, ac-cusing him of being an imposter, a filthy partisan in disguise, a saboteur, if not a damnable British PW.

In the morning, when I woke up, with something of a hangover and a sudden lowering of morale, most of the guests had gone, though some were still draped over couches or nestling in corners. L. and I had breakfast in the sunlight on the terrace of iced wine and vermouth, discussing the problems that are usual in the circumstances, then set off to make the longest possible detour back to my part of the world. As the Germans had taken seriously to halting trolleys at regular intervals, removing all men to forced labor, that method of transport was no longer advisable, so we decided to take the long walk through the park. As we passed the zoo I would have liked to wander through it with L., but was anxious to be home by noon in time to get a report from the benny via Primo, on his progress with Oliviero.

As I passed a flower stand my attention was taken up with a plant of flowering gardenias so that when my eyes fell on Mario walking toward me flanked by two unknown men, the shock was considerable. My first reaction was that he had been arrested and was being used like Sorrentino, but this changed when I saw his barely disguised smile. Each of us to avoid running into anyone we might know had taken the most circuitous route! The result gave me pause for thought, and I decided immediately to cross the river, which we did, much to L.'s distaste, right in front of the Regina Coeli jail. How many poor partisans, I wondered, were languishing in its sinister "Sixth Arm." There were about fifteen guards lolling about the main entrance all armed with submachine guns, and I thought how easy it would be to catch them in a death trap formed by the well-like embankment and the narrow street, with the use of one well-placed German grenade, at virtually no risk of fragments to the thrower. But this was no time for such plots.

Further on we recrossed the Tiber on the narrow foot bridge, then stopped at a coconut stand for a drink of cooling synthetic lemon. L. had no idea where I lived, other than the general area, so I bid her goodbye. As soon as I was sure that she was out of sight, I slipped through the Portici d'Ottavia and made my way home.

When Mario returned he told me that one of Giuliano Vassalli's cousins who had been caught working for the Badogliano information service, had apparently given eleven of his colleagues to the SS, along with details of our organization, openly admitting that Giuliano Vassalli had been engaged in espionage. Though he had apparently informed on Franco's position in our organization, Franco had been careful enough to be known to him only under a phony surname. It was depressing, though, especially because the Germans were bound to shoot him anyway.

That night, to cheer us up, the BBC announced the capture after bitter fighting of Terracina. The Allies were obviously advancing, but we were now very doubtful that they would reach us in time. I wished that I could be down there fighting with them, and it made me sick to think of the wasted information we had in hand. Ottorino, who had really close tabs on what was happening, was now turning over our material to a Badogliano contact who claimed to be in contact with Brindisi; so the information might not be totally wasted. But I distrusted their judgment after seeing the fantastic items they had formerly put out.

Then, May 22, the benny told me that Oliviero seemed on the level and was anxious to operate the radio on a regular schedule.

So I arranged to have him meet me at the benny's that afternoon. It was risky, but it would have to be done if we were to get a contact. Besides, I had come to the conclusion that the Germans weren't as smart as they seemed, and most probably didn't have the time or the men with which to watch places over a long span of time, relying more on the haphazard method of catching what people they could and then torturing them to get what they wanted.

When Oliviero arrived I explained to him the mechanics of the radio. Thereafter he tried the set for half an hour but couldn't get the crystals to resonate. As I had a second date with Lele, who was going to try to send a message to the base via an air force contact of his to indicate which of our frequencies was most suitable, the situation was tricky. Finally, I had arbitrarily to choose the frequency I thought most likely, and leave Oliviero to his devices.

After meeting Lele I went back home and sat on the terrace. I was beginning to notice that I had become terribly superstitious since the beginning of the Allied offensive. I kept saying to myself: "If that ant walks all the way along that piece of wood without turning off, everything will be all right." Or: "What time is it? *Araignée du matin, chagrin; araignée du soir, espoir!* Damn that spider!"

I was also worried about what Coniglio might be plotting. We had discovered that while he had been subsidizing parties of the CNL with one hand (and great sums of OSS money) in order to obtain their favor, with the other he had been busy building up anti-CNL elements in the city. His main accomplishment, however, with all this petty political intriguing in the name of General Clark, had been so to ruin the prestige of the Fifth Army that almost everyone was sick and tired of hearing of Fifth Army "representatives," and no longer wanted anything to do with them.

As things stood, the Badogliani groups, with their backs to the wall, were soliciting royalist support by promising safety to all and any Fascists who wished to remain in the city (issuing them phony documents which attested to their having played a part in the resistance— for the reasonable sum of 1000 lire) on condition they help the royalists prevent the CNL from taking the situation in hand.

The curious part of it was that the CNL, as best I could gather, knowing it now had a majority in the southern government of Badoglio, and thus certainly in any Roman or northern one, had no desire to take things in hand by force. Everything had changed since January, when there was still no representative government in the south. One thing the CNL would not stand for, however, was the Badogliani

322

buying Fascists and trying to stage a coup. The CNL was interested in two basic points: seeing that a couple of hundred war criminals were arrested and tried—among them the more brutal of the Fascist torturers; and preventing men who had sent partisans to their deaths a few weeks earlier from buying their freedom by supporting royalists and quick-change artists of whatever species.

For my own part I was satisfied that I could carry out the various OSS jobs that would be required (even without getting into contact with the base)—the neutralizing of mines, the protection of utilities, the impounding of German secret documents, the methodical tracking down of men left behind by the Germans to carry out espionage and sabotage. And if there were anything in particular any branch of the OSS might want, I could always get more men. However, if *no one* were to be in direct contact with the Allies to receive instructions before and during the liberation, it looked as if they might be faced with the one situation I presumed they would most like to avoid: chaos.*

For the next twenty-four hours while Oliviero attempted to make contact there was nothing I could do, so I decided to avoid the tantalizing torture of waiting, by resorting, at Lele's suggestion, to the only means of keeping our nerves in trim: a small party *a quattre* in Baldo's apartment.

The next day, May 24, when I got back to the Palazzo Lovatelli, I found a note from the operator saying he had managed to tune the set with three of the crystals, but that the one the base should have been listening for didn't work! It seemed almost too much that we should have such lousy luck, and I decided that if nothing happened soon, I would eventually begin sending in clear, and to hell with the risk involved.

On the twenty-fifth, news of Allied progress was cheering. Franco came to tell me he was reorganizing all his men for the last moment. As far as could be made out his group was now the biggest and the best equipped. When the moment came for action he was to put several squads of men at my disposal for specific OSS jobs. There were, of course, no longer the exciting plans for taking and holding the city as we had planned back in January! Now the situation was totally dif-

---

* Though we were inclined to discount it, there was a rumor that the Germans might try to do with Rome what they had done with Cassino: contest it street by street and house by house with the advancing Allies.

ferent, merely a matter of organizing the transition from German to Allied rule, gaining all possible advantage and avoiding all possible damage.

Having gone over our plans I asked Franco to see if he could get the various men in the various groups to keep a running account of what was happening in their territory, to be forwarded to me by courier, so that, if we were in contact with the Allies, we could give them an over-all picture; and if, by ill luck, we weren't we'd at least have an accurate picture ourselves of what was going on, both for our own guidance and for the record.

The next day, May 26, we heard that the Germans had shot twelve more hostages from Via Tasso, but could not learn the names. I wondered if Giuliano was among them, or Eugenio or Sorrentino.

Franco had given me an account of Giuliano's interrogation, which had come back to us through the grapevine. When he had been taken to Via Tasso and subjected to continuous interrogations he had merely answered: "I'm a Socialist. I fight Germans because they have invaded Italy; I fight Fascists because they have corrupted Italy. Do with me as you wish, but remember—I will always fight you. I have nothing more to say."

The Germans had apparently been impressed, more so at any rate than they had been with his cousin, who, when they had squeezed out of him eleven names of his colleagues, they had proceeded to shoot.

Now the Pope was intervening directly for Giuliano, but we had little hope of saving him from the firing squad. His cousin's accusations of espionage had made the case more difficult.

Each day I spent hours glued to the radio catching every last bulletin and looking forward anxiously to the next morning to hear the latest communiqué, or a sign from the base. As I noted in my diary: "To risk one's neck and go through continual nervous tension and be absolutely of no use to anyone is the most demoralizing position in the world!"

Then on May 27 I received an urgent message from Alberto:

An agent has arrived in Rome from the base. You probably know him. In any case I can only tell you by voice who he is. He has brought frequencies and plans. I have an appointment with him tomorrow at 1300.

324

Please let me know with the utmost urgency how I am to handle myself; on what conditions to deal, etc. This may prove very interesting to us, but I think it essential I speak with you first in order to arrange matters rapidly one way or the other. Best regards.—Alberto.

For one brief second I wondered whether the agent could be my good friend Raimondo Craveri, with whom I had recruited and organized the network of Party of Action agents to cover northern Italy, in which case our problems would be over and we would immediately be in contact with the base; but I realized almost as quickly that the agent, unfortunately, must be Raimondo Lanza di Trabia, a youth for whom I had no use whatsoever, known as a dope fiend, Fascist, playboy, gambler, and ex-lover of Edda Ciano. Just the sort of agent our friend Captain A. would be likely to recruit!

Sadly I was right. What's more, Lanza turned out to be in close contact with Coniglio. As soon as Alberto had had his meeting with them he informed me that Lanza and Coniglio wanted me to turn over my radio to them and would then find a house for it from which transmissions would have to take place *in the presence of us all!*

This idea, quite naturally, was preposterous. To begin with, there were altogether too many indications that Coniglio might be the one responsible for the capture of so many of our men by the SS. Secondly, the scheme of risking so many key people at a transmitter when we knew the Germans had DF-ing equipment in the city was ridiculously insecure. Thirdly, there was the fear that Coniglio's agents might have been "turned."*

Apart from this it was still an obvious matter of prestige that I could not take orders from an Italian agent. I had made it clear to all concerned, including the base, that if I was to be in Rome it could only be with the requisite authority. Once they had clearly assigned me as chief in Rome, and until such orders were countermanded by them, it would be impossible for me to accept orders from an agent, no matter if he were Victor Emmanuel himself. Furthermore, there was

---

* According to an item in Ottorino's concentrated daily information bulletin (which kept us abreast of developments in both Kesselring's HQ and the various offices of the Open City Command) six clandestine radio stations of the Fifth Army in Italy were at present being used by German counterespionage, who, in possession of the proper signal plans, were in regular contact with the Allies, feeding them false information.

so much information to be filed I intended to make quite sure I controlled my own radio and that no nonsense went out over it. I therefore sent Lanza the following message by courier:

Please turn over plans and crystals to the bearer of this note. If you need a radio, I will give you one in return for signal plan and crystals. If you have only *one* plan, give it to me, and as soon as I have established contact I will make a new plan for you. I do not intend to operate jointly. You use your set and I will use mine. If you wish to send messages via me, even if they are already coded, simply send them to me. I believe I have been clear and explicit.

And I signed the message with my own name, which I knew Lanza knew perfectly well.

When my courier returned he reported that he had been screamed at and thrown out by Lanza, who had said he intended to have his radio and wasn't going to take orders from anyone, that he'd be damned if he'd turn over any plans or crystals, that he had already risked too much *even having a meeting with anyone from the OSS.*

This last phrase surprised me, and I had it carefully verified. I had almost decided that as he appeared to have crystals and plans I might as well turn over my radio to him so that someone at least would be in contact with the base; though sad for me, this was better for the Allies, no matter who was on the other end of it. But the more I thought about it, the more I wondered why, if the OSS had sent him on a mission to Rome, knowing I was in the city, they would send someone up with plans and crystals, and nothing for me, not even a word. Something was clearly wrong. That Lanza might have been a double agent all along was far from impossible. Yet if he were, he should easily have been able to get a radio with which to transmit. Certainly he would not need mine. Unless it was to control or "turn" it too. The problem was more complex. He must have come from the OSS, but via Captain A. Hence the rub. Still, I might as well give him a set that was useless to me, and then take it out on the OSS when they finally arrived.

But just as I had come to this decision Mario came in with a small scrap of paper from Oliviero the operator. He had heard the base, got a QRK2 out of them, and had therefore been heard by them! This did not mean the certainty of a contact, but it was the biggest step forward yet. I decided not to give the set to Lanza, but wait till I had established proper contact and got some sense and directives from the base.

It was awful to have an inside seat on German strategy (and their understanding of Allied strategy) and not be able to communicate it, and even more infuriating to know it was not because of any bad luck or deficiency, but because of a purposeful conspiracy between a French agent and a Fascist dope fiend. Forty-eight hours had been wasted on the Lanza development! But that was enough.*

From now on my diary and notes give a play-by-play report of developments.

* After the war Lanza was arrested trying to smuggle a large amount of heroin into Switzerland; eventually he killed himself in a racing-car accident.

33 AS THE FASCISTS ONCE CRIED, "ROME OR DEATH!"

MAY 29.   It is evening now, and the air is full of twittering swallows. Occasionally planes pass overhead, and the sound of cannon is continuous. I am listening to the Fifth Army radio on the beachhead. They have just finished a pep talk in Italian to the inhabitants of Rome, but their only order was to wait.

The city, from all I hear, is pretty calm. The Germans have apparently given orders to stop raking in men. In Trastevere there was some shooting this morning. Eggs have risen to twenty-five lire apiece (about a dollar an egg by prewar standards).

While we lay in the sun on the terrace Mario cut up three kilos of *zucchini* into slices then put them on a board to dry. He says it saves oil that way, when you fry them. They may be the last green vegetables we will see for a while. As I watched him perform this meticulous task I assured him that if you cut a cucumber from the wrong end it tastes bitter. I wonder if it's true, and if so, why. He simply looked at me and remarked that *all* Americans are crazy.

I have the last bottle of Old Tom gin by me now, and the roof tops have turned from red to purple. I suppose we will eat again at half past ten tonight. In a way the routine of this life is not unpleasant—if only I could get that contact with the base it would be wonderful. We continue to plan for the last moments, but do not think about it too closely, as we know anything may happen to us before the end. I was thinking this morning that if we do last out, it probably won't be at all exciting being liberated. We'll have so many things to do and so many problems will arise that we won't even think about it. The thought of a party with all the prettiest girls and being able to be who one really is, is appealing; but God knows if I will feel like it at the time. There is so much work to do, there are so few people who can do it properly, and the boys at the base, though they may mean well, do nothing but screw things up by using such people as RAI.

Don't they know that the only possible hope of making this war worthwhile is by doing things cleanly ourselves, and that a secret service, though essential in wartime, can justify its existence only if its members play straight with each other and do not do what the Fascists do? Still, as most of them do not know what Fascists are, and, if they did, would probably agree with them, there isn't much one can do, except try to develop a sense of humor—or become a Fascist oneself, or a Communist! But, as in the dentist's chair, when nitrous oxide brings home a conscious understanding of infinity, I'm afraid there is always something between the two no matter how tiny or how wide the spiral—it can always be tinier or wider! So I guess the only thing to do, is to do that which you are sure is right, and go on to the next problem.

IT IS MAY 30, and I don't think I've ever been so depressed. The offensive has bogged down, the whisper of a contact has vanished, and there is no sign of the base. God knows there is something rotten somewhere!

Mario says that Lele's contact keeps querying the other side by radio for an answer, but that the other side has finally sent him just two words: "Not interested."

Was the contact a phony? A German plant? How could the base not believe the messages were from me when I gave them the number of my passport which is firmly locked up in their own safe?

What with this and the time the British colonel [who was later captured] told Baldo that the British in Bari ordered him not to accept my messages, it looks very much as if there is something rotten somewhere, yet I can't make out what it is.

Further reports on Alberto's lunch with RAI and Coniglio are that the latter insisted I was nothing but a militarized civilian, and had been sent up to Rome to requisition houses for the OSS! [Shades of Captain A. with his knife in my back!] Coniglio then boasted he had been thirteen years in the SIM [the Fascist Military Secret Service], a great recommendation if ever I heard one, and was going to have me beaten up (in true *squadrista* fashion) as soon as he could lay hands on me. Luckily he thinks I'm hiding in the Vatican!

And all the while Franco and I are planning what could be an incredibly good counterespionage service, if only we get a chance to put it into effect.

God, but it's all depressing!

From our inside source we learned today that the Germans are all concentrated in the Valmontone-Frascati area and shoot out wherever the Allied pressure is strongest. But from this, and the BBC, I cannot understand what the hell is happening between Carroceto and the sea. *Vox populi* has it (a) that two German divisions were seen going down the Ostia road, and (b) that there isn't a single German in the whole coastal area!

I presume that the riddle is that the Allies are naturally more interested in trying to cut off and wipe out Kesselring's forces and do not yet intend to point on Rome—even if the road is clear. I also suspect that the Allied admonitions over the Fifth Army radio that the people of Rome should "not come out into the streets yet" is to try and prevent a left-wing rising by not telling them until it is too late, and the City of Rome is occupied.

But such things no longer bother me. I think I have perfected the mechanism for catching and wiping out all the hundreds of German and Fascist spies that will be left behind; and if those dumb mugs at the base do not let me carry it out the way it should be done, I may have to do it without their knowledge. It would be silly, after almost five months of hiding from the Germans in this city, and waiting and praying for my own side to arrive, to have to hide from them too in order to do what I think, even though it may sound pompous, it is my duty to do with the taxpayers' money.

Anyhow, no matter what those guys say or do—they will never take away those long, juicy messages that went out for six little weeks, and which, if they had not been so stupid, would have been going out ever since.

[My notes for June 1 were lost.]

JUNE 2.   The Allies are a little more than ten miles away, but even though they are attacking hard, and seem to have brought up reinforcements, it doesn't look as if they will be here before another week; at least that is the opinion of the German High Command. (As Ottorino put it: "All German reinforcements have been assigned to

330

XIVth Army, whose job is to prevent an Allied encircling movement. The German High Command has ordered all-out resistance in the Alban Hills until Xth Army has managed to withdraw [from the Southern Front]; thereafter both armies will fall back to the Viterbo line [north of Rome]. . . .)

I am now listening to the Fifth Army radio station, to a band of GIs on the beachhead! It never struck me they could be calmly playing swing music in the open air at the beach and broadcasting it; however, it's pleasant.

I wish to God, though, they would quit broadcasting the names of Italian spies for the Germans. We have hundreds and hundreds of them listed, with names and addresses and telephone numbers, and have our men ready and waiting, not to catch them, but to shadow them and that way get at the real spies, not just the small fry. Now, every time a name is mentioned over the Fifth Army radio the SS drive up to the guy's house, pick him up (whether he wants it or not) and send him off to northern Italy. So I wish to God they'd shut up broadcasting the names!

At lunch Franco suddenly said: "Oh, by the way, I think you'll be interested to hear that an old friend of yours has gone over to the Germans. I heard on the radio that Lemaigre Dubreuil has skipped over to Spain and turned himself over to the Vichy authorities!"

Many times I had gone over with Franco the political mess we had gotten into in North Africa at the time of the Darlan deal, telling him I believed we had been made fools of by agents such as Lemaigre Dubreuil and had in fact compromised our whole heritage and good name in return for a specious political deal based on the sophistical grounds of "military necessity." At the same time Franco had confirmed to me, what I had strongly suspected and vociferously pointed out at the time, that while we were involved in this nauseating political chicanery, its purport had in no way been lost on aware political minds in territory such as Italy and France yet to be "liberated" by us.

Now I felt a great wave of relief at the news of Lemaigre's defection, taking it as an indication that perhaps our work would not be in vain.

It is just a pity that we are always a year or so behind. My only depressing thought is that the OSS, or somebody, may have sent him over as a "double agent." They seldom seem to realize that our "double agents" are usually German "triple agents."

And to top things off in Rome, what do you suppose those Badoglio characters have managed to put over this time! Not only has that idiot General Oddone, whom they put as number two to Bencivenga to head up the "United" Partisan Forces, decided he wants to *review* his men at six-thirty in the morning at Piazza del Popolo! He actually does so, and gets himself caught! Quite naturally they caught most of his men in a roundup before they could be warned. The scene as described was typical: a Fascist patrol approached Oddone on a street corner, two of his bodyguards opened fire, wounding two of the Fascists, but in turn being killed. Oddone was then transported to Via Tasso where he was reportedly shot within two hours.

Now we hear he wasn't shot.

At any rate—and this is the *pièce de résistance*—the Germans found his plans for occupying the city (as the Germans leave) and the names of the leaders of the various resistance groups! Nice people! And their qualifications for the job are having been Fascists for twenty years, having fought *against* the Allies throughout the war, and thus having greater experience than the poor partisans, who merely fight for a cause!

JUNE 3.   There was nothing new on the Italian one o'clock news. The Germans say the line from Valmontone to the sea is still holding. It wasn't till the five o'clock BBC that we heard the Fifth Army had cut through east of Velletri. At five-thirty Ottorino came in and said he figured the Germans would clear out tonight, after the blackout. Via Tasso no longer exists. Somehow forty of the "worst" prisoners seem to have been liberated, but we don't know yet who they are. There is no news of the prisoners at Regina Coeli. Franco has been trying to get the Germans to let them out in return for guaranteeing the German wounded in local hospitals—variously estimated at between fifteen and thirty thousand—but nothing has come of it so far.

At about 6 P.M. I noticed the phone had stopped working.* Later

* General Maeltzer had ordered it cut so as to interfere with the clandestine plans of the CNL—only to have to reinstate it because it had confused the Germans more!

Mario came in and said there was a continuous stream of German trucks, tanks and even long-range guns pouring along Via del Impero, going north.

The eight o'clock Fifth Army radio in Italian said to stand by for imminent instructions, but said little more. It continued to give names of spies for the Germans, which annoyed us all, as they will now be taken north.

At half past eight I heard a car drive into the courtyard and sent Olga, Mario's wife, down to see what it was. It turned out to be a German; so I put on my coat and got out my automatic. However, he seemed to be going to the Rossi sisters beneath us.

Early in the morning I had heard one of the sisters say to the other that her German boy friend was back from the front, that all the Germans who had used to come to see her had been killed in action; I can't say, somehow, I was terribly sorry.

The nine o'clock BBC gave General Alexander's special communiqué that the Fifth Army had broken through all along the line from Valmontone to the sea and that the Colli Laziali were entirely in our hands.

It looks as if the Allies may be here in the morning—for all we know. I looked over our emergency supplies and they are pretty satisfactory. There is no ice left, naturally, and only two bottles of wine, which we shall drink tonight. It's funny, I've been saying for some months now that the day the Allies arrived I'd get so drunk I couldn't walk. Now I don't feel the least like a drink. At nine-thirty I filled both bathtubs to the brim, as an emergency reserve of water. At nine-forty-five the water was cut!

After dinner, which we didn't have till about ten-thirty, I went to bed, but couldn't sleep. The excitement of thinking that within a matter of hours the Allies would finally be in Rome was something of a strain. I wondered too if after all these months we were going to be able to get away with it right to the end, or whether, at the last minute, we'd get caught, or shot, through some trifling bit of fate.

JUNE 4.   At 8 A.M. Ottorino arrived with the latest dope on what's going on in town.

The Germans are still pouring through Rome. He says the latest rumor is that Kesselring has ordered Maeltzer to stay and turn over the city intact to the Allies and thus "maintain order"; that this accord was reached through the Vatican and that Osborne and Tittman guaranteed a safe conduct for Maeltzer if he would stay and maintain order till the end.

So I sent Ottorino up to Maeltzer's headquarters and the Command of the Open City to find out who was, or was not, in charge of the city, and to see if anyone were trying to take over for the Badogliani or the CNL.

I then began to make our big sitting room into a workroom, as during the course of the day some three dozen of Franco's men were expected. When I was through arranging the place it looked something between the editorial room of a newspaper and the OPS room of an Army headquarters.

Franco had arranged that everyone possible, no matter what his regular assignment, report anything and everything that happened in his district to the district leader, who, in turn, would send the information straight to us by messenger. I hoped that way to have a running commentary on the events of the day, no matter what happened to normal communications.

At ten o'clock Ottorino came back and said he had just been up to German headquarters only to find Maeltzer stinking drunk, speaking in lamentable French, the place in complete confusion. So far no Badoglio, CNL, or Allied authority had taken any initiative. Clearly the time had come for me to act. So I wrote out official orders to General Presti, head of the police forces in Rome, and to General Chirieleison, head of the Open City, to take charge of public order, telling them immediately to employ all their forces (a) to prevent sabotage to all possible buildings and public utilities; (b) to arrest and intern German and Republican deserters; (c) to prevent civilians from leaving the city.

These orders were written out in official military form on paper headed "United States Office of Strategic Services." I then signed them OSS O.C. Rome Area, by which title I was already known to them, and affixed the special OSS rubber stamp I had had prepared for just such an occasion.

The orders were then taken to their destination by Ottorino, and both Presti and Chirieleison professed themselves anxious to carry them out to the best of their ability.

I had no idea whether any other authority was around to issue orders, but I figured it was the only thing to do in such a case.

Throughout the morning reports kept coming in that the Germans were still streaming through Rome, pushing carts, trying to steal cars, marching on foot, and that the population was out in the streets, everywhere, watching them as if it were a parade. The cafés were open and doing big business—also because it was hotter than hell.

About twelve-thirty we heard the report from a German soldier that there had been an armistice to allow the Germans to get thirty kilometers beyond Rome, but so far there was no confirmation of it.

[From then on I jotted brief notes:]

The light has gone, so no radio news till Vito turns up with a battery.

At noon two different sources reported seeing hordes of ill-clad ruffians wandering around starry-eyed. They were the political prisoners from Regina Coeli who had apparently escaped. I guess the Italian police let them out the minute the Germans had scrammed.

About one-thirty, Mario, in nothing but his shorts, went down to the kitchen, brewed up an enormous cauldon of spaghetti, then got out the emergency biscuits we'd saved for the occasion. The place was full of odd young men who came and went bringing the latest dope, but principally busy about their various jobs of liaison and countersabotage. There was obviously not going to be much fighting with the Germans. The partisans all understood Alexander's orders, which I had repeated to everyone in detail and which by now had even been dropped on the city in leaflets, and they seemed to have decided to comply with them exactly. I gathered, though, that they intended to get rid of some of the top-ranking Fascists and pro-Germans on the main black lists, judging them summarily before a people's court. I didn't like the idea, but there wasn't anything I could do about it, and, in a way, I suppose you can't blame them, for the bastards will otherwise get off and the Allies will leave them peacefully at home or give them the best jobs!

My main desire was to let them live and then shadow them from the very beginning without molesting them, and thus find out who their friends are. It's a cinch that whatever German espionage and sabotage units have been left behind, apart from the ones we already know about, are bound to be recruited among the worse Fascists and ex-German stooges, and if we follow them—using all the tricks the Germans weren't smart enough to use against us—sooner or later we'll catch up with them. It is really nothing but a problem of personnel. If I could get a chance to organize a CE bureau and employ about two or three hundred ex-partisans, for about six weeks, I'd guarantee to turn over every enemy agent, mathematically, one by one. Actually, I don't think they are going to get a chance here to shoot many Fascists, and even if they do, it won't hurt our CE operations, as our lists run into several hundreds.

The first problem, as soon as the Germans are out, is getting vehicles, then gas and batteries, then requisitioning villas, so that we, and the OSS, when they turn up, can start right in operating without running around like chickens with their heads off looking for cars and real estate and getting into arguments with other agencies, the way we have always done everywhere else we have occupied.

Right now squads of men are ready with a list of the 700-odd cars with permits to circulate issued by the SS (and therefore patently suspect), as well as a nice list of German and Fascist-occupied apartments.

Two-fifteen: The PAI have taken off their "MMs" (Mussolini Militia insignia) and put back the army *stellette*, or five-cornered stars, and the population is kidding them about it, asking where they put the "MMs"!

Two-twenty: Some bastard just strafed the hell out of us from about a hundred yards away. I can't imagine what is going on!

The light came back at two-twenty-five, just in time to hear the BBC and Alexander's order to save the city. If Presti and Chirieleison do their stuff, we many have it in the bag.

Two-thirty: Franco says the shooting outside was the PAI preventing looting, just around the corner. (An indication that our orders, via Presti, are being carried out.)

At four o'clock I took the following random notes from Matteotti's son, who had just come in.

336

Ponte Cavour and Ponte Margherita were mined by the Germans this morning. At ten the gates of Regina Coeli were opened by Austrians under orders from the Germans; all, including Jews, and ordinary criminals, were let loose. From six-thirty this morning all bridges were being guarded by Germans with tanks and machine guns. The Caserma Mussolini in Prati, evacuated by the Battaglione [Battalion] M, was sacked by women and children. At ten the Germans distributed food at the Macao Barracks. Two mines blew up and wounded some women. The Quadraro has been evacuated and the Germans have put artillery in it. 155's have been placed in the Forte Trionfale, and I believe the Forte Boccea, to hit the Cassia north of Rome. Between seven and eight, in front of Rubinati on Via Flaminia, the Germans were distributing food. Battaglione M passed in trucks and shot into the crowd, killing three women. At the Ist Infantry Barracks women are reported to have fired rifles. This morning three Communists occupied a depot of food at Via P. Valle, but abandoned the place without a fight upon the arrival of the PAI. At Ponte Milvio, early this morning, the Germans collected about a hundred young men who were milling around and marched them off, covering them with automatic weapons.

[At five o'clock I resumed my own notes:]

The police are now going from house to house saying the curfew is for six o'clock (there being no other way of advising the populace). They speak of a "state of emergency," whatever that may mean, but seem to be carrying out our orders pretty well. An hour ago a man, stripped naked, was shot by the Germans publicly in front of the Quirinal Palace. Four others are reported to have been summarily executed, but it's not known where or for what.

Five-fifteen: I have just learned that Coniglio lost contact with the CNL after the Oddone affair and is now "commanding" his so-called "Dissident Forces." What he's doing isn't clear, but at least I know where he is.

Five-twenty: This morning the Germans were selling typewriters on Via Veneto at 1000 lire apiece! Yesterday they appear to have sold cars at from 25,000 to 40,000 lire, in order to collect enough money to buy civilian clothes with which to hide out or desert.

At seven o'clock I decided everything was going so smoothly that nothing more could be gained by sitting at a focal point for intelligence and that I might as well go out and take a walk round Piazza Venezia to see for myself what was happening.

The Germans, I noted, are leaving in a pathetic state, some are trying to get away with cars that no longer have tires, driving on the rims. One motorcyclist had a flat tire but went right on. Some were on bicycles, but the most pathetic were the ones on foot who had been walking so long they could hardly stand. The PAI has occupied the Insurance Building opposite the Palazzo Venezia.

While we sat on a grassy island by the Palazzo Venezia watching the remnants of a German army go by, three men from the PAI came up and told us to go home. Afraid they might turn out to be old comrades from my own "company," and to save any complex explanations of why I was no longer with them, I decided to comply with the order promptly. It amused me, however, to think that it was really *my* order; that I, who had been the lowest corporal in the force, was now virtually their chief, having issued explicit orders to their commanding general.

Though I had not yet received news from him, Ottorino had in fact succeeded admirably with Chirieleison and Presti, whose police forces were now distributed throughout the city carrying out my orders to the T. Early in the afternoon there had been a moment of panic which had delayed the whole operation as the rumor spread that the Hermann Goering division, falling back from the advancing Allies, intended to move through the city, and both Presti and Chirieleison decided to make themselves scarce, neither general showing the least inclination to tangle with so redoubtable an opponent. The Hermann Goering, however, did not materialize, and during the rest of the afternoon police forces were posted at all important buildings, including the Campidoglio, remaining in charge of the situation except for a few minor clashes with the Germans, preventing looting by the civilian population, and, in most cases, peacefully dispersing the crowd.

As we wandered slowly back to our own little piazza we wondered if the Germans would try to hold out anywhere in the city itself and if they'd succeed in blowing any of the bridges.

Then, as we were about to enter our *portone,* I noticed the children in one of the contiguous lanes seemed to be excited about something. I could hear shouting from the far end of the lane. Figuring the Germans or the PAI must be up to something with the local population, we decided to keep out of the way. An old man came jogging up the lane and I asked what it was all about, but he didn't seem to know. Then a young girl came tearing across the piazza.

"They're at San Paolo!" she kept shouting.

"How do you know?" we asked her.

"Because one of them gave a man a can of meat and beans!"

To the others this sounded like a rumor, or a trick to get the partisans to come out into the open, but I knew damned well it was the truth. If they had said tanks and guns and American uniforms, I might have doubted it, but not *meat and beans*. Only a GI could be dishing out those goddamn "C" rations to the populace!

Running up the stairs four at a time with Franco, Baldo and Lele I felt more excited than I've ever felt in my life. Telling the others the news, we each grabbed a gun and came tearing down the stairs again, setting off toward the river—just the four of us—to see what we could see. Though excited, we were also a little wary. It would be silly to get mowed down by a burst of machine gun fire from either retiring Germans or advancing Allies.

It was getting on for eight o'clock, but despite the seven-thirty curfew there were still groups of civilians standing at corners. Down by the river we came across a reassuring sight. The bridges were now unguarded and undamaged. An Italian soldier who passed us said there had only been scattered German patrols in the neighborhood and that in Trastevere they were trying to desert.

Moving away from the river we approached the Capitoline Hill only to find it entirely surrounded by Public Security guards with tommy guns. We tried to climb the hill but they waved their guns threateningly, so we decided once more to avoid complicated explanations and go over toward Via San Teodoro. We couldn't decide in our minds whether the Allies would be coming in first on Via dell'Impero or along Via del Mare; so I suggested we climb to the top of the Palatine Hill, overlooking the Forum, from where we could see them no matter which way they came.

There was almost continuous firing throughout the neighborhood, both small arms and artillery, though we couldn't see where it was coming from, or whom it was directed at.

As we passed through the popular quarter behind Via San Teodoro, the populace looked at us angrily from their windows till Franco and Lele pulled out their tricolored partisan arm bands and the onlookers began to gesticulate and a great cheer went up cursing the Germans and crying "Long live the Allies!" It was moving.

Then we ducked through the gate where a path leads up to the top of the Palatine Hill, and I thought of the last time I'd been there with L.

Suddenly, as we approached the top, a burst of machine gun fire went over our heads, causing us to fall on our faces. Two more bursts succeeded one another; though we couldn't figure where they were coming from, or who would want to be shooting at us, there was no doubt they were intended for us.

Crawling on our stomachs, we managed to take cover and creep back down to the comparative safety of the streets.

Not till later, when they were eventually captured, did we discover that forty German paratroopers had entrenched themselves on top of the hill to make an all-out desperate stand against the Allies!

In the streets there were now bursts of shell fire, sounding like mortars; to take cover from shrapnel Lele and I got separated from Franco and Baldo. Then someone started shooting in our direction from the top of a nearby house and we were forced to duck into a sort of air-raid cave dug deep into the foot of the Capitoline Hill. It was full of odd refugees, half starved and covered with vermin, who had been sleeping there for months for fear of the Allied raids in the poorer quarters of the periphery.

To avoid this congestion of humanity but also avoid getting shot, we tried to enter a small side cave from which we could get a better view of the general terrain, but three bedraggled bums explained, politely but firmly, that the cave was for members only, a sort of private club!

Again there was a burst of machine gun fire aimed at the mouth of the bigger cave. Women and children in the catacombs below began to scream and wail and intone religious chants. It was a horrible sight and sound.

The men by the entrance to the cave cursed whoever was shooting, pulled a great iron gate across the entrance and said no one could leave.

By this time Lele and I were anxious to get back to our headquarters so as to join Ottorino and formally turn over the city to the Allies, but the populace around us had begun to grumble at our presence. They could see by our clothes we weren't refugees, and we were afraid that any minute they might take us for Fascists and tear us to pieces, yet we could not display our partisan arm bands, as whoever was shooting was believed to be a partisan. Later he was discovered to be an ambushed Fascist, but that didn't do us any good at the time.

Standing against the dank stinking wall with the grumbling and wailing of the people all around me I suddenly had a good idea what happens in revolutions, and decided, if possible, they were to be avoided. It wasn't so much that I was scared of being killed; it was the exasperation of being in utter chaos where it wasn't the right people who got killed, but just anyone at random.

Though there was still sporadic shooting Lele and I decided we were damned if we were going to sit in a dank cave full of howling women while the Allies entered Rome, even if we risked being shot. Taking advantage of a quiet moment we slipped out and ran across the piazza bent almost double. A headlight shone at the far end of the road, and we ducked for cover, figuring that if it were a German he'd mow us down, and if it weren't a German we wouldn't know it anyhow.

Actually it turned out to be one of our own teams just back from requisitioning a couple of good cars from an "ex"-Fascist. So we climbed in while a couple of partisans shifted onto the running board waving their submachine guns and we headed for our headquarters at Piazza Lovatelli. Unfortunately Ottorino had just been there looking desperately for me to go with him to Presti, officially to turn over the city to the Allies. Not knowing where or how to find him I decided to head for Piazza Venezia on foot, picking my way along the winding back lanes which, thanks to a complete interruption in the power supply, were absolutely black.

As I hit the Via del Plebiscito I could see and hear people milling around. Then at Piazza Venezia in the faint light reflected from the monument to the unknown soldier, neatly arranged in a wide semi-circle from underneath Mussolini's balcony, almost all the way round to the Corso, stood a row of GI halftracks with an occasional jeep fore or aft.

The Fifth Army had entered Rome.

The GIs, still stony-eyed from action, dusty and tired, not altogether conscious of the historic fact they were the first Allied soldiers to occupy an enemy capital, lay in their blankets on the hoods of the halftracks, or gazed in a friendly way at the excited "*paesanos*."

I knew they would not understand if I went up and addressed them in English, or told them who I was. They were combat troops fresh from killing. But I could not resist saying just "hello" to one of them.

A young lieutenant jostled past me in the crowd. I caught the glimmer of his silver bar in the sticky darkness.

"Hello, lieutenant," I stammered; and he turned suddenly on his heel.

"Could I . . . could I bum a cigarette. I haven't had an American cigarette in almost five months."

Automatically the lieutenant reached for the pack in his shirt pocket and offered me a Lucky Strike; then as he reached for his .45 I disappeared into the crowd.

Dragging deeply on the cigarette I blew smoke into the warm Roman night. It was strong and perfumed and made me a little giddy. It was odd to think that after all those months, when the Fifth Army had finally arrived, I had to hide from them too; but I knew it would only be for a little while. In a matter of hours my own people would arrive.

Back at headquarters in the Palazzo Lovatelli I picked up the phone to call L. and tell her, at last, the truth. As I dialed the number there was an explosion, the phone went dead, and there was a ringing in my ears. Slowly I realized what had happened. From across the room a partisan lowered his rifle and apologized: it had gone off, he said, accidentally, and the bullet had sliced the wire of the phone in my hand.

For a second we both sat palely looking at each other, then burst into laughter. It would have been a silly way to die!

But the tension was ended. Franco came over, bringing a candle in one hand and a bottle of brandy in the other. Technically we should have been out turning over the city to some Allied general, but we were suddenly bored with the idea of band-wagon climbers. For one whole day we had been absolute commanders of Rome. That day was over, but not the war.

Leaning back we surveyed the chaos left by the bunch of anxious partisans. It had been a long hard pull, but somehow we had survived. There would be plenty of time to resume operations the following day. In the meanwhile Franco stretched out his arm, winked, and poured us each a good big swig of brandy.

34 THE PANGS OF LIBERATION

JUNE 5.   A bright sun sparkled on liberated Rome.

Though it was barely eight o'clock the streets were full of parading, shouting, flag-waving Romans.

Selecting a large black Lancia from the pool of Nazi-Fascist vehicles our boys had collected during the night I had myself driven up to the Hotel Excelsior where I ordered a room for me and one for Franco as uptown overt offices. It was an exquisite sensation.

To locate my OSS colleagues I then went searching for what I knew, from past experience, would be a conglomerate spearhead of special types known as S-Force: soon enough I found them among the pines and laurels atop the Pincio.

There were some familiar GI faces, then I spotted an OSS Captain, who, though Italo-American, was not of the bootlegger or Mafia type. With amazement he greeted me: "Everyone at the base thought you were dead!"

Breakfasting together on Valadier's terrace overlooking Rome he told me that of the OSS outfit I had left in Caserta, virtually nothing remained. Since I had crossed the lines six successive U.S. colonels had come to command the outfit, none of whom spoke a word of Italian, or knew a thing about espionage. My good friends, including John Roller, had all moved to England to prepare for the invasion of France.

"But there are a million things to be done," I said. "And now. All sorts of spies and saboteurs to catch."

"In that case," said he, "your man is Major Berding."

An ex-newspaperman, now in uniform, Andy Berding had in fact arrived to handle counterespionage—an innovation in the field since I had left Caserta. Delighted to see him, I immediately turned over to him several squads of Franco's men, complete with lists of names, addresses, covers and suspected plans, while he, amazed at my appearance (still in grubby civilians) wrote me out a pass to the effect that I was to be allowed to circulate anywhere at any time and that no one was to interfere with what I did—and such is man's awe of documents this crazy piece of paper was never questioned by a single person, except once: almost immediately!

Crossing Via Veneto I found my car being picketed by some of Badoglio's Carabinieri, and my partisans, gesticulating, under arrest. Unable to explain the situation to these numskulls fresh from Bari, my temper rising, I whipped out Berding's piece of paper only to see the southerners' eyebrows lift, their jaws set firmly and their carbines lower to a menacing angle. Perplexed, I leaned forward: it was my pass as a Fascist republican officer. Whipping it back I exclaimed: "Oh, no!"

But to get us out of jail it took a former IBM representative in Italy, now a lieutenant colonel in the OSS, who, once I was released, wanted nothing better than to show me off to his crony general officers.

Evidently, if I was to get any work done on the Allied side, I had best go back underground—which I did, with results that might have made old Molière chuckle.

In the Excelsior bar, where I was to meet Giuliano Vassalli, miraculously escaped from Via Tasso, I was greeted with effusion by Dino the barman (whom I had known since we were kids) and a fellow drinker—the German collaborator who had been our host the night of the meeting with Hauptmann Priebke—already being befriended by a U.S. general's aide whose single word of Italian seemed to be *Martini*.

Then Giuliano made his entrance and I cut him dead, not recognizing him; after twenty-eight days on the floor of a cell with his arms behind his back, and constant beatings and interrogations, he was reduced almost to a skeleton.

Franco joined us and told us of the latest happenings in the city. Bencivenga, out of hiding from his convent in San Giovanni, had installed himself on the Campidoglio to issue high-sounding orders, and ceremoniously submit the city to the senior Allied political officers, my old friend Sam Reber and my old enemy Harold Caccia, staunch supporters of Badoglio and the king!

But the political battle had been won—by the CNL. With the liberation of Rome, Victor Emmanuel was obliged to abdicate, and Badoglio to resign. Bonomi was to become Prime Minister and soon my true friends from the south, such as Croce and Sforza, were to be installed as cabinet ministers. Eventually Nenni was to become Minister of the Interior with Peppino Craceva, bullet hole mended, as his *chef de cabinet*.

But our wounds were still fresh. As I came out of the Excelsior, Oliviero rushed up to tell me that a few miles out of Rome the SS had killed fourteen of the prisoners from Via Tasso. They had laid out the bodies in a small country schoolhouse. Along with Bruno Buozzi, the Socialist leader, they found Enzo the Vittoria radio operator, Sorrentino, whom the SD had been using as bait with which to catch us, poor Topolino (whose real name was Di Pillo), the man who had come to fetch me at Via Giulia my first day in Rome, and, last, poor faithful Eugenio. Later, on the wall of Eugenio's cell at Via Tasso, we found the drawing of a rabbit and the warning to beware!

But how was I to explain all this to these Johnny-come-latelys to the OSS? The commander of the unit in Rome was a bewildered but pleasant West Point colonel, seconded by a humane but politically hopeless Italo-American lieutenant colonel.

To add to the confusion, a unit of the OSS attached to AFHQ Algiers had inserted itself in the Fifth Army picture, and, with several of the Italo-American *Mafiosi*, were squabbling with each other beyond belief.

The general, on a whirlwind tour through town, patted me on the back, asked about two Roman principessas, then went off to a much more interesting front.

To investigate the Coniglio episode a board was empaneled and in charge of it was placed: Captain A.!

When I threw up my hands they complained I was suffering from overtaxed nerves. Do you wonder?

Jealous of our intelligence, someone had failed to pass on to AFHQ, let alone to Q Building in Washington, copies of what we had filed over Radio Vittoria—presumably so that there be no record with which to make invidious comparisons. (They had not counted on the medieval cellar at the Palazzo Lovatelli!)

Worse, to discredit my efforts some jealous character accused me of having embezzled $2000 worth of special funds while still in Naples. When I had them locate my safe from Via Crispi and the signed receipts for $1998 of the money, I never heard another word about my use of special funds. Except that in Washington members of the SI Italian Desk were happy to inform anyone who cared to listen that my intelligence could not have amounted to much as I'd spent so little money, and this to members of the rival X-2 (or counterespionage) desk, which maintained my contacts were so good I must have been working for the Germans! At a cocktail party, years later, an ex-member of the Italian Desk came up to me and said: "Ah yes. I've heard of you. You're the man we sent to Rome to requisition houses!"

C'est la guerre!

With the invasion of France I realized I'd best move on to greener fields. Nor were my new colleagues, or the military brass, loath to offer me thirty days' leave in the States before going on the landings in the south of France.

And so it would have been had I not run into John Roller in Washington, who, with his pal Ken Mann, was then in charge of a desk called Morale Operations. Together we cooked up a scheme for me to parachute from France into northern Italy and then fall back into Hitler's redoubt. A fascinating scheme; it might have been my last. As it was, Hitler failed to carry out his part of the plan and I found myself instead with the advance guard of the OSS in Berlin, where, well inside the Soviet Zone, with a Russian major and a bottle of vodka, I realized, sadly, that our enemies had changed.

The only constant in this crazy world would appear to be one's friends.

ABOUT THE AUTHOR

Peter Tompkins was born in the United States and educated in Italy, Switzerland, France, England and this country. He was an under-graduate at Harvard, and studied at the Sorbonne and Columbia, before leaving to become a war correspondent.

From 1939 to 1941 he covered the war in Europe and Africa for a number of British and American newspapers and American radio networks. From 1941 to 1942 he worked as a news editor with AFHQ in North Africa.

He then joined the OSS and served in Italy, France and Germany until the end of the war.

Mr. Tompkins now lives in Washington, D. C., with his wife and two children. He has published two other books: To a Young Actress, *an annotated collection of letters from George Bernard Shaw to Molly Tompkins, and* Shaw and Molly Tompkins, *a biography.*

3/15/62